OCCUPATION

OCCUPATION

The policies and practices of military conquerors

Eric Carlton

London

First published in 1992
by Routledge
11 New Fetter Lane, London EC4P 4EE

Typeset in 10/12pt Palatino by
Falcon Typographic Art Ltd, Edinburgh & London
Printed in Great Britain by
T. J. Press (Padstow) Ltd, Padstow, Cornwall

British Library Cataloguing in Publication Data
Carlton, Eric
Occupation.
1. Military governments
I. Title
322.5

ISBN 0-415-05846-5

Contents

Foreword

In this text we are going to examine in historical and comparative terms some aspects of the relationship between civilian populations and military authority; and particularly the ways in which ideology conditions the exercise of power and facilitates control by forces of occupation. The range of possibilities which is open to occupying powers in their dealings with conquered peoples is limited. Some set of policies and practices *has* to be adopted; whatever combination is chosen will involve different attitudes to, and applications of, some form of relevant ideology. But ideology tends to be conditioned by practicalities. It does not exist in a vacuum. It is influenced by all manner of social exigencies, not least of all the level of culture or type of culture of the conquered themselves. So where, for instance, the level of culture is regarded as 'low', which is how the Europeans regarded the Indians of the Americas, the whole question of assimilation and re-education may be 'shelved' until the indefinite future. Similarly, where the level of culture is seen as equal or, at least, comparable to that of the conquered, as with the Japanese and their subjects in South East Asia, there may be still no clear move towards social integration, particularly if the conquered people are regarded as ripe for exploitation. And where the conquered fall into the category of a 'high' culture, as in the case of the Macedonians and the Persians, there may be special difficulties as the conquerors will continue to see their subjects as potential rivals.

All occupying powers, then, must employ mechanisms which will ensure control in some form or another, and these will be affected by the circumstances existing in any one place at any one time, and by the respective ideologies of the powers themselves. This begs the question as to whether ideologies condition policy, or whether conditions determine the nature of the ideologies. And if so, how and in what ways? This is a chicken-and-egg issue which we cannot answer, but we can at least elucidate. To try to do this, we are going to look first at the phenomenon of power itself and the ways in which it is exercised (chapter 1). Then in order to demonstrate the range of possible policies and treatments that have been used, a spectrum of 'solutions' to the problem of control is introduced as a series of case studies. The material used is largely historical, in the hope that this will add colour, variety and interest to the discussion, especially where the societies concerned are perhaps relatively unfamiliar to the reader. But some of the material is roughly contemporary, especially the studies relating to the Second World War. This includes some analysis of the Nazi occupation policies in the East and West which is followed by a special discussion on the Holocaust. Finally, there is some recapitulation of the themes with a relevant treatment of the whole question of control and the extent and limits of its applications in subject states. As we shall see, there is a finite number of 'answers' to the control problem. Modern technology has added little to the possible range of strategies that can be adopted – it has merely facilitated their implementation.

Introduction: Ideology and control

Successful conquerors, imperialists and sundry would-be expansionists face a common problem: they take what they can get – but how do they keep what they take? Having wrested lands and possessions from others, how do they contrive to retain them? More particularly, how do they organize and govern territories which are inhospitable and often actively hostile?

This is the central concern of this entire discussion. We have to examine certain critical factors in the relationship between military authorities and civilian populations, and, more specifically, we must look at the manner in which ideology conditions the nature of that relationship. For convenience, ideology can be defined as a set of beliefs in a preferred social order which enables adherents to interpret their past, explain their present, and develop a vision of the future. So what really concerns us here is the exercise of power – whether coercive or merely persuasive – and the way in which this facilitates control in conquered, subject and client states, where necessary by forces of occupation. (A conquered state may not necessarily become a subject state; a client state may be neither, but simply have a favoured status relationship with the dominant power.)

Control is usually achieved by a combination of force which induces compliance, and persuasion and/or indoctrination which generates a sense of commitment. In other words, control is either attained by compulsion which, in the end, is frequently counter-productive, or by some kind of value-consensus which is often very difficult to effect, but which can pay handsome dividends in the long term.

Social control is about rules, and all societies have rules which govern behaviour both within and between groups. These rules may not be codified as, for example, in simple, pre-literate societies. But they have a binding force for the members of those societies in so far as they help to ensure uniformity, regularity and – to some extent – predictability of conduct. Even where the rules are broken, this too can take an institutionalized form. This can be seen in certain

1

pre-literate societies (e.g. the Nupe of Nigeria), where there were times when festive licence was allowed, but when it was over, conventional norms prevailed. This implicit recognition of social infringements is quite apparent in our own society in all kinds of leisure activities and even commercial dealings, and is so accepted that it has all but become normal conduct.

Social control denotes processes which ensure conformity to the norms of a society or group. In the social sciences, it is said to refer to the vast system of expectations and restraints through which deviant behaviour – either of individuals or whole populations – is either prevented or restrained. It therefore has both positive and negative aspects. It can include active processes such as the deliberate inculcation of ideas and values, and it can imply passive processes whereby these same ideas and values are subtly internalized by those concerned. In short, social control is facilitated by socialization, the transmission of ideas and values from one group to another, thus ensuring the continuity of the system. It is through socialization that basic ideological beliefs are implanted and perpetuated. This may occur at the pre-school primary stage or more commonly at the more advanced secondary and tertiary stages through such agencies as the educational institutions, peer groups and the media. In these ways, attitudes are formed and values are refined.

Socialization, then, is important as an agent of social control – but here a cautionary word is necessary. Social scientists often refer to socialization as though it were an explanation. When trying to account for, say, extreme prejudice and even the persecution of one group by another – a not uncommon experience under occupying forces – it is quite usual to hear it attributed to faulty socialization. This is a perennial kind of conceptual confusion. Socialization is *not* an explanation, it is a *description*. To say that something is all due to socialization really tells us nothing. It simply describes a *process*; it certainly does not account for the origination of the values which are transmitted, nor can it determine the social forms these values take, nor why – at the psychological level – some are accepted and others rejected by particular individuals.

There are obviously many kinds of control. It may be achieved – as we shall see – through laws, legal codes of conduct, or it may be exercised through customs which are uncodified but which are nevertheless highly institutionalized such as those governing, say, the exaction of revenge. Convention is a very broad category and can cover almost anything from kinship obligation to the finer points of social etiquette. Closely allied to both law and custom are moral precepts which are presumably prescribed to promote personal and social harmony, or perhaps because they enshrine some believed intrinsic

2

good such as happiness or freedom. And, lastly, there are religious precepts which are held to be interpretations of the will of the gods. These may enjoin ritual, ethical and general behavioural obligations upon believers. Usually these are attended by supernatural sanctions which, of course, have to be accepted and acceptable to be effective. These may be this-wordly sanctions, a belief in 'fate' or fulfilment now or in the very near future. Or they may be other-wordly – a belief in the postponement of punishments and rewards until some other life. Historically, these have been very influential in the conduct of war and in the determination of occupational policies. One has only to consider the current resurgence of certain religious movements and their moral demands upon believers – for example, the obligation of *jihad* (holy war) for Muslim fundamentalists – to see how important religion still is.

Underlying the entire question of control there is the essential problem of the 'real' nature of society. For Marx the key element in trying to understand the whole historical process was that of conflict. Society and experience proceeded by successive resolutions of conflict. Life was all about conflict whether at the individual or the social level. Marx's preoccupation with the conflict between classes is but one aspect of his overall philosophy of history. For some theorists, notably the sociologist Talcott Parsons, the real issue is not conflict but consensus. For Parsons, social *order* was a problem. In effect, he asked how it is that society is possible in the first place. How does it cohere? Why isn't there chaos? Why doesn't everyone pursue his or her own selfish interests? And how is order actually achieved? Parsons acknowledged the importance of conflict in any understanding of history, but – essentially – his position was that the social forces making for consensus and order must be more influential than those making for disorder, otherwise there would be a total breakdown of society.

Really this whole problem of conflict versus order derives from what might be termed the nature-of-man issue. Are humans naturally good and law-abiding or are they inherently self-interested and mutually contentious? There are dichotomous traditions about this which are diametrically opposed. On the one hand there is the optimistic view which maintains that humans are basically 'good', and that it is society which is the corrupting agency. Left to themselves without the insidious influences of economic inequality and the resultant class antagonisms, they would create a conflict-free society. On the other hand, there is the opposing argument which we may call the pessimistic (realistic?) view of man. This argument insists that humans are congenitally egocentric and incapable of existing in anything better than a state of uneasy equilibrium. There may not be permanent conflict, but social harmony is only achieved at a price. Peace is always extremely precarious. This view does not regard society as the villain of the piece. Indeed, it is society that is seen as the restraining influence. Man needs society to round off nature's rough edges. Society is the civilizing agency. The very existence of society forces people into the necessary measures of conformity and co-operation. Thus control mechanisms are required to resolve conflicts of interest and ensure some degree of – albeit sometimes enforced – unity.

In relating general social-control problems to the main theme of our discussion – occupational control – we have to bear in mind a number of very important factors. The first concerns the fundamental policies of control. What is the overall purpose of the occupation? Mere pacification, economic exploitation, political incorporation, or what? Second, there is the actual implementation of control which necessarily involves not only the *mode* of control, but also the point and intensity of implementation of the control to be achieved. For example, when occupying forces are faced with sabotage and other forms of resistance activity, they obviously not only have to decide what steps to take, say, infiltration of the resistance networks, they also have to determine what sanctions to employ. Should they, for instance, take hostages? And if they should decide to do so, at what point should these mechanisms be introduced, and with what degree and intensity should they be used? Too little, and the whole operation may look ineffectual – even farcical – too much, and the entire exercise may be counter-productive.

Much will depend on dimensional factors, that is, the *scale* of the problem and the *size* of the population concerned. Also important are what we might call focus factors, that is to say the *direction* of the deviant acts themselves. What specifically is being attacked, and is the avowed target the actual target? If we take a simple example from traditional society: the Zulu of the Transvaal in the early nineteenth century did not find it too difficult to deal with their subject peoples. Their impi made short shrift of would-be recalcitrants. But when the European colonialists became the dominant force in South Africa, the whole nature and focus of Zulu aggression had to change.

Control may be exercised in more subtle ways. Occupying forces can shrewdly utilize already existing systems of checks and balances, and exploit the subject populations' social norms and practices. Again in traditional society this was often effected not just through sheer force but by manipulating the ideological dimension. Not all conquerors were like Cortés who destroyed – perhaps rightly – the blood-smeared idols of the Aztecs. The Romans, for instance, often incorporated the gods of subject peoples into their own Pantheon. Similarly, the Persians and the Macedonians, as we shall see, would sometimes make use of affinities of religious belief to maintain a quiescent subject population.

The recognition of a common set of religious ideas might serve to appease recalcitrants and malcontents. Shared value-systems had their advantages – as the Nazis found when they 'shared' their distinctive ideology with those of their subject peoples who were prepared to join in the common cause, for example, by foreign recruitment to the SS.

Control is almost always the primary objective of the conqueror, but it is rarely achieved without some measure of physical or cultural repression. In these circumstances, ideology can work either for or against a successful occupation. Most conquerors are not in the game of proselytization – they are aiming for higher and more lucrative stakes.

1

Analyses of power

The policies and practices of occupation control are merely one aspect of the problem of social control generally. So here we are not just concerned with theories of control – important as these are – but also with the actualizations of control, and this really means examining the ways in which control is practically *implemented*. But before we see how this operates in particular societies, we must ask just how this implementation of control is possible. How can it be achieved? The short – and obvious – answer is that occupying forces must have the *capacity* to implement their policies. Theoretical political plans can only be operationalized through the medium of *power*. So it is therefore the nature and exercise of power that require some analysis.

The term power is variously defined. Theories and interpretations of power are more or less useful in their particular ways. So it might be helpful if we looked briefly at these to see how they can be related to the societies under discussion. The word 'power' is really an abstract noun with many 'concrete' applications. It used to be said that 'the Greeks had a word for it', and seeing as so many of our political ideas derive from the Greeks, it is worth noting that they had at least two words for power. The term *exousia* which is loosely translated as authority, and the more arresting term *dunamis* (from which is, of course, derived the word dynamite) which denotes the ability to change something – by force, if necessary. This is well exemplified by Mao Tse-tung who suggested that the most effective command grows out of the barrel of a gun. Perhaps, therefore, it would add definitional clarity to the discussion if we distinguished the terms and regarded authority as *legitimized* power.

Power has a variety of associations, from the might of armies to the energies driving machines to more intangible influences such as, say, modern advertising. We regard – perhaps with legitimate fear – the terrible potentialities inherent in the power of modern science, but so many of these fears can only be actualized by the state. It is states that set up institutionalized methods of utilization and control. *They* apply and exercise power. As far as we know there is no cosmic nemesis awaiting mankind; no Damoclean sword waiting to descend of its own volition. Barring unintended nuclear disaster, the sword will only fall when somebody deliberately wants it to. Power, therefore, for our present purposes is not an abstract commodity, it is rather the capacity to impose policies and practices, usually by institutionalized means. Power can be exercised as persuasion or manipulation, but essentially it implies the ability to change things – by force, or the threat of force, if necessary.

Among many sociologists and political theorists, a distinction is made between 'constant-sum' and 'variable-sum' approaches to power. 'Constant-sum' theories are normally associated with marxists who maintain that power is held by a particular section of society whose members try to ensure that it stays in their hands. This dominant group use their power to the detriment of others. Thus power is not primarily about agency or intentionality but about class relations. In this sense it is seen as 'illegitimate' as it derives not from social consensus but from the ownership of land and capital. This power is 'explained' by ideology – a distorted set of beliefs about the historical process and the social situation – and is mediated through education, the media, and other agencies of political socialization. Thus it is insidious yet acceptable, and is rarely seriously questioned by the majority of the population. The continued inequalities of capitalism are therefore seen to be perpetuated by the subtle promotion of the view that it is really in the interests of the proletariat to support the status quo, which means the power structure as it currently exists.

These arguments have a certain cogency. They are rather reminiscent of Mosca's contention (1939) that the history of mankind can be seen as a perpetual conflict between the tendency of certain traditional groups ('the old forces') to monopolize power, and the attempts of others ('the insurgent new forces') to dislocate the status quo and replace it with a new system. This really results in what the sociologist Pareto (1966) termed the circulation of elites. A political merry-go-round in which the more things change, the more they remain the same.

The 'variable-sum' or consensualist view of power maintains that there is no invariable concentration of power in the hands of the few – at least, not in the long term. Of course, coercive capacities are necessary and must be exercised from time to time as an important back-up in certain difficult social situations. But this power is merely increased and decreased in order to further desired goals; it can be varied in accordance with public commitments as in, say, the case

7

of war. But it is admitted that the actual exercise of this power may lie with those who justify their actions in terms of birth (the *aristoi* ∞ the best people), or merit, or simply the strength that comes from military superiority.

One of the main difficulties with the sociological approach to power is that it can lead to forms of theoretical reductionism. Every relationship, from sex relationships and familial relationships (especially of parents *vis-à-vis* their children) to teacher–pupil relationships and on to class and political relationships are seen in terms of power. Any careful analysis will show that in most, if not all these instances this kind of reductionism is a dangerous half-truth. On the other hand, this approach does have certain merits. There are undoubtedly situations where the power dimension is not fully recognized. For example, the current problems in South Africa which are usually attributed to racial factors are almost certainly much more to do with power and which factions are to hold it or maybe share it. Similarly in Northern Ireland; this ostensibly religious conflict is really about power, and it would be naïve to assume that if the British troops were ever to leave the province that the IRA would consider their work done. Who is going to rule is what it's really all about.

Another kind of approach is that associated with Kenneth Galbraith, in which he identifies three different kinds of power: (i) condign power, i.e. straightforward coercive power (ii) compensatory power i.e. inducive or persuasive power, the power to get others to do what you want them to do, and (iii) conditioned power i.e. manipulative power, a more blatant form of (ii) in which power is exerted in such a way as to make disapproval or refusal difficult. In effect, Galbraith is not really saying anything very new here. It is an exercise in nomenclature rather than analysis. The key issues and the main divisions are pretty much the same (Galbraith 1984).

The particular dimension of power that has perhaps not been suitably emphasized in this discussion so far is that of *legitimacy*. For the sociologist Max Weber, for example, the capacity for coercion is at the root of all power relations. This gives political – and certainly military – action its operational effectiveness, and this, in turn, is facilitated by belief in the legitimacy of the system. This can, of course, be called into question in particular cases. There are recognized instances where the system flourishes while its *acts* are expressly – if confidentially – deplored. For example, in the upper echelons of the German hierarchy during the Second World War, there was often less than fulsome support for the behind-the-line atrocities of the SS. Ulrich von Hassell, one-time German ambassador to Rome (1932–8) who was eventually executed in September 1944 after the abortive plot to assassinate Hitler, noted in his diary in August 1942,

> very strained relations in the occupied territories, thanks to the evil Party administration ... particularly ... the bloody reign of terror [in places in Bohemia] where all the men are shot, the women deported and the children taken off to be compulsorily trained ... the same thing has now happened in Norway. In France too ... draconian measures are constantly taken. In Poland, terrible things continue; it is like a nightmare and makes one red with shame.
>
> (Ulrich von Hassell 1948)

Perhaps one of the most generally useful models for the analysis of power has been put forward by Almond and Powell (1966). They direct their attention to the *capacities* of political systems to ensure that certain functions are fulfilled – a point which can be particularly well illustrated from the Nazi period in Germany, especially in relation to their occupational policies from 1938 to 1945.

First of all, they suggested that a state or system must have EXTRACTIVE capacities. The emphasis here is essentially quantitative. A system – the state or military authority – must be able to mobilize resources, recruit manpower and accumulate funds – whether voluntarily as taxes or involuntarily as tribute – and there may be a very fine line between the two. So much here depends upon the compliance of the subjects themselves and the willingness of subordinates through whom the policies are mediated. For instance, during the Second World War when the Nazis tried to induce their allies the Italians to co-operate in their anti-Jewish policies there was a marked reluctance to do so. All sorts of temporizing and prevarication took place which successfully denied the SS their full complement of victims. So no state or system can be completely immune to the needs and aspirations of *all* its subjects.

Second, the state or system must have REGULATIVE capacities. This is obvious and self-evident. No system can survive without stability, and stability requires controls which maintain order. This may be achieved by either formal (legal) or informal mechanisms which in their own ways ensure political and social coherence. The use of sanctions is the key element here. What kinds of sanctions? How are they used? When are they used? And with what frequency and intensity are they used? In Nazi Germany, this was facilitated by a leaven of Party members at every level of state organization, and by the ubiquitous presence of the SS – the state within a state – whose ideology was most notoriously expressed (as we shall see) in its racial purity programmes in the occupied territories from 1938 onwards.

Third, it is suggested that a state or system must have DISTRIBUTIVE capacities. This has marked economic implications, and concerns not only the distribution of goods and services, but also defines the allocation of statuses and rewards within the state or system. Thus again in Nazi Germany, as in so many autocratic systems, rewards and particularly statuses were predictably linked to one's position within the Party hierarchy, or related to ownership of those industries such as Krupps and I. G. Farben whose products were most closely linked with the interests of German expansionism.

Fourth – and, in some ways, most insidiously – a state or system must have SYMBOLIC capacities. Here we are thinking of something qualitative rather than quantitative in nature. Every system has to explain itself to itself, especially the – as yet – unconvinced or those who are still free to doubt at the margins. Just as important is its need to assure the world outside of its good intentions. On rare occasions even Nazi concentration camps were cosmeticized for pre-arranged visits by the Red Cross. In the early days of the regime it was important to create the right impression; it was regarded as essential that neutral observers should remain neutral.

Symbolic capabilities may be credible and persuasive, or they may appear as trivial and faintly ludicrous – as with some of the traditional rituals surrounding monarchies. On the other hand, particularly in more repressive systems, they are not without a hint of menace. Where power is monopolized in this way, it is usually found necessary to control the 'symbolic flow' from rulers to people. This may be accepted on the basis of believed autocratic charisma, connoting as it does impressions of infallibility and inspiration. And this, in turn, may be rationalized or justified in terms of certain absolutes, in the case of Nazi Germany the myth of racial superiority, and the special mission of both ruler and people. As Mosca (1939) once indicated, those who rule do not have to justify their power by its exclusive possession but try to find a moral and legal basis for it and represent it as a logical and necessary consequence of their doctrines and beliefs. In their own way, symbolic mechanisms validate the system and provide unanswerable legitimations for its policies and practices.

Lastly, a state or system should possess RESPONSIVE capacities, that is, the capability for eliciting enthusiastic support for the current regime. In Nazi Germany this was reinforced by social and military rituals such as the Nuremberg rallies which served to generate national-istic fervour and anaesthetize critical judgement.

The discussion until now has concentrated on the uses of power in autocratic/totalitarian systems, and it may therefore have been supposed that there is something essentially different in the way power is exercised in totalitarian/autocratic systems from the way in which it is exercised in a democracy. This is quite a natural inference which sometimes serves to reinforce chauvinistic attitudes. But we must be careful here. The 'truth' in so far as we can ascertain it is much more complex than this – as some of our case studies will show.

Before that, however, some preliminary discussion is called for. As types, the autocracy (the rule of the one) and the oligarchy (the rule of the few) are both forms of elitist systems, and are usually contrasted with democracies (the rule of the people) which for convenience can be designated People's systems. Elitist systems can be equated with what has been called 'the role of the conscious part' in that society is likened to an organism – in this case, the body – comprising limbs, trunk and head. Thus the brain is the 'conscious part' – the thinking, deliberative part of our being, and which, by analogy, represents the elite, those who alone are fit to command. All other members of society are required to endorse that command and conduce to its requirements. As the political philosopher Thomas Hobbes once suggested that by surrendering our rights to rule ourselves to this man or that assembly, the multitude becomes a single person (Hobbes 1963). If, of course, this surrender is to an autocrat or an oligarchy, it means that they are entrusted with a right of command that can have – though rarely does have – no limits. Individual rights are given over to others in whom is vested the collective right. It is a view born of despair of the masses to make intelligent decisions for themselves.

This has interesting implications for modern Western societies in particular where they pride themselves on their political sophistica-tion, and their ability to take a detached, educated view of the situation. Political activity implies the ability to make considered choices, but it is worth noting that where education is both intensively and exten-sively developed it does not necessarily lead to more enlightenment and therefore the capacity for more knowledgeable decision-making. Education is a two-edged sword, and can be an agent of reform and also a tool of repression.

Elitist systems are said to ensure greater social stability even if there are curbs on various kinds of political freedom. Hobbes conceded that the state of subjects who are exposed to the irregular passions of the man or men who own such unlimited authority may be one of great misery. The ruled not only have to endure the arbitrary potentialities endemic to such systems, they are also often faced with the actualities of unacceptable political repression. How can they ensure that those who rule will not only serve their own interests but also those of the ruled? And what guarantees can be given that this arbitrary power will not be transmitted to others – possibly heirs – without any due reference to those who must obey, or endure, the dictates of the rulers? This was the abiding problem with tyrannies. It is worth noting that in ancient Greece, tyrants, who were to be found in many city-states, were often men who seized power unconstitutionally, and were seldom able to perpetuate that authority through their sons. They were often rather charismatic figures who ruled by some degree of popular consent, but their sons were rarely able to command such respect, and therefore had to resort to repressive measures to secure the same degree of conformity. Needless to say, this was their undoing. As with the sons of the tyrant Pisistratus of Athens (sixth century BC); they were either ousted or assassinated. Greek tyrannies rarely lasted more than two generations.

Two advantages of an elitist system are, first, that when it is eventually overthrown or suspended, the late ruling elite can always be blamed for the ills that have befallen the society. Taking the Nazi situation once again: in the post-war period, it was common to find the 'evil days' blamed on the Nazi hierarchy alone – and especially on the SS. The ordinary people often disclaimed responsibility for the support and conduct of the war, and sometimes denied all knowledge of its worst excesses. Second, the disgrace of the late ruling elite can be used to *justify* the take-over of the new ruling elite, as happened in post-war East Germany. People hope that life is going to be different under the new regime, but in so many cases this is little more than a delusion.

Elitism, then – particularly in its more moderate forms – can be defended in special kinds of circumstances. Elites are frequently faced with the debris of failed democracies – a common factor in the ancient Greek states. They often set out with the very best intentions but their particular brands of political rationalization tend to ignore circumstantial complexities in favour of quick and radical solutions. Not uncommonly, therefore, they turn out to be little better than the systems they replace. Religious elitism too – especially in its institutionalized quasi-political guise – has often proved to be a considerable disappointment to those idealists whose designs are rarely matched by their actual programmes. One has only to glance at Cromwell's Long Parliament or, more recently, Iran's theocracy to see how contentious and fragile such systems can be. When metaphysical edicts have to be operationalized by mere mortals they are shown to be no real improvement on secular systems.

Whether some kind of cultural-cum-philosophical elitism would ever work is open to debate. This was Plato's solution – that philosophers should become kings, or kings philosophers. In a sense we may now be witnessing the realization of such ideas in the growing dominance of the scientific community. This is a new kind of cultural elite and not quite the thing Plato envisaged, but an elite nevertheless, and one whose ascendancy is unprecedented and generally accepted. Even the back-to-nature advocates do not normally disparage science *per se*, only – as they see it – the wrongful applications of science.

Respect has increased with the scientific facility for improving the general lot of the ordinary citizen. It is, of course, vitiated by all sorts of disturbing anomalies (how we can put men on the moon and still not eradicate the common cold, let alone cancer, etc.), but whatever the reservations about science, it either does deliver the goods or is believed to be capable of delivering them in the not too distant future. How this new cultural elite will exercise its burgeoning power is anybody's guess. It could be an exciting yet frightening prospect; the past has shown that so-called disinterested scientists are not always noted for their keen moral sensibilities.

So much, then, for elitism. How, by comparison, have societies fared under People's systems? What has been their experience when subjected to the not too tender mercies of the General Will? Jean-Jacques Rousseau (d. 1778), said by some to be the father of revolutionary philosophy in France, argued that the General Will was righteous and tends always to the public advantage. Needless to say, in time he modified his opinion on this and probably would have abandoned it altogether had he lived to witness the excesses of the French Revolution.

There is no doubt that the 'will of the people' is a potent and persuasive idea, but does it work in practice? What happens when the Popular (General) Will takes over? As the historian Edward Gibbon once suggested, from enthusiasm to imposture, the step is uncertain and perilous.

The writer Bertrand de Jouvenel has made a particularly cogent attack on the idea that People's systems are in any way inherently superior to other forms of political organization (De Jouvenel 1948). He points out that it is People's systems, *par excellence*, that are most susceptible to demagogic influences. The applauded virtue of free speech is exploited by gifted but unscrupulous orators for their own advantage. In the right conditions, such as political or military crises, free speech can give way to common rabble-rousing. Demagogues of almost any political persuasion can use their 'platforms' as mere echo-chambers for the furtherance of questionable political programmes. If anyone should doubt this, they should read the 'Melian Controversy' in Thucydides' *History of the Peloponnesian War*, in which the Athenian democratic Ecclesia (Assembly) is persuaded to condemn the whole population of an island state to execution and slavery simply because they wanted to secede from their alliance with the Athenians.

It is also particularly significant for our discussion about the occupational policies of military expansionists that there is some correlation between the evolution of People's systems and the extension and magnitude of war. De Jouvenel contends that this has come about primarily because in earlier autocracies two essential controls were lacking, namely, the power of conscription and the ability to impose taxes.

13

This does not seem to be a particularly strong argument, especially in view of the fact that many earlier autocracies were small scale and tightly controlled – certainly at given periods in their development – and were often more than adept at raising the necessary revenues to wage war. New Kingdom Egypt and Inca Peru would be just two cases in question.

A much more important and more obvious issue is that of the increasing scale of society; sheer demographic factors have made war more terrible and even more likely. Population pressure is probably the most critical issue in the modern world, and is at the root of so many of our most intractable problems. It has also been a critical factor in historical development. The growth of population and increasing economic anxieties generated a greater need to guard against the encroachment of others. This then led to the establishment of local militia supplemented by a small professional bodyguard for the rulers. Later these levies developed into citizen armies. The situation in the classical Greek city-states (*poleis*) is a typical example of this process. In very many states, the citizens took over the major military role of heavily armed infantry (*hoplites*). This understandably led to an increasing democratization of the social system. After all, those who fought for the state wanted a greater say in political affairs. And those who had a stake in the political process were honour-bound to further that process by military means, if necessary. Thus there evolved a direct correlation between the People's system and military activity.

There is little doubt, as we have seen in the case of Athenian democracy, that when the people were in charge their degree of control – indeed, their demands – were as great as those of any autocrat. And this could be exemplified from numerous other societies, especially those in revolutionary situations. When the people take power, they are often worse – even to their own kind – than those they have overthrown. The French revolution, for instance, freed the peasantry from many previous feudal burdens, but it forced them to bear arms, and eventually involved them in a ruinous war with much of Europe. It proclaimed Liberty, Equality and Justice, but denied these not only to members of the largely discredited aristocracy, but – in its paranoia – to the more unorthodox in its own ranks and untold numbers of innocents as well. There can be no better example of the revolution that swallows its own children. The Russian revolution too made way for an authority structure unprecedented in Russian history. Its depredations, especially under Stalin, were both more intensive and extensive than under any Tsar. Of course, it could rightly be argued that here we are not talking of a true People's system – this was something of a fiction – but it was a revolutionary system, and its policies and practices were carried out in the name of the people.

Similarly, in modern China, where the regime admitted that it had 'purged' some two million people, or in North Vietnam where the official figure was 50,000, or – perhaps most incomprehensibly – in Cambodia where it really was a question of the people versus the people, to the tune of at least a million lives. Wasn't it Marx's *alter ego*, Friedrich Engels, who once suggested that any state is an instrument of oppression – no less so in a democracy than in a monarchy? Indeed, some marxists claim that democracies are worse in that they persuade the people to cut their own throats.

The People's system is a very attractive idea – replete with heady notions of freedom and self-expression. But it may just mean freedom to slaughter and to starve. One suspects that in some instances, the idea of the General Will has been merely a device which rulers have used to convince the masses that their tyranny is acceptable – as in, say, Stalinist Russia. But there can be a 'tyranny from below'; a tyranny of the proletariat. The people are not always right just by virtue of being 'the people'. Like autocrats, they can be wrong both morally and prudentially.

The exercise of power is usually either buttressed or camouflaged by some rationalized system of beliefs that we commonly designate 'ideology'. The term ideology is often used perjoratively to suggest some kind of conscious deception. In cruder types of marxism particularly, the term has come to mean the medium through which a distorted view of social life is conveyed to the masses. It is thus a contrivance of the dominant classes to facilitate their continued political and economic superiority, an interest-based artifice to ensure the willing subserviance of the people. So many marxists have very little that is good to say about ideology. But ideology can be rather more than this. It can act as the precipitating factor in political action, not least of all in its religious guise. Where men believed that every act, particularly military conquest, had to be sanctioned by the gods, religion was a critical element in political thought – indeed, the two were often inseparable. Sometimes war was thought to be actively commanded by the gods, as in, say, ancient Assyria. In other societies, it might be more customary to find military action justified and sanctified in religious terms.

By extension this also applied to policies of occupation. Subjugated peoples were treated not just in accordance with economic require-ments or political necessity, but in relation to their ideological status. Thus in certain earlier societies, notably Carthage and pre-conquest Meso-America, captives might actually be dedicated to the gods as sacrifices. Prisoners who could have been better employed as slaves on state projects were killed off for no other reason than that the gods required it. Of course, it remains to ask whether religion was the cause or the victim. Do men really believe that the gods command these things, or do they use religion to serve interests that are determined elsewhere? Frustratingly, the evidence points both ways.

Ideology can be politically inflexible, and will not always seem to accommodate the ever-changing needs of society. But this too is open to debate. It is interesting to see how ideology operates in actual cases. For example, in modern Islamic society, contradictory forces are at work. Some Muslim societies are obviously attracted by the West and its wealth of scientific know-how and therefore wish to maintain close contacts with it. Others of a more fundamentalist persuasion see the West as decadent and its values depraved – but are still not disposed to decline its military technology. Perhaps all ideologies are never really adopted in their pristine forms, but are always *adapted*. This applies whether the ideology is secular, as with marxism, or religious as with, say, Christianity and Islam. All are selectively interpreted to meet the needs of the societies in question. So, to concentrate on Islam, if the needs are primarily economic development – as in modern Egypt, Islamic law will be liberally interpreted to accommodate Western assistance. If, on the other hand, the overriding need is a powerful form of nationalism, a more inflexible fundamentalism may be called for. But whether the adaptation is conscious and deliberate is questionable. It may not be a simple matter of 'the context determining the pretext'. Instead it may simply be – as our case studies show – that particular circumstances generate certain 'solutions'.

2

Assimilation: The expedient policies of the Roman Empire

Roman power was so dominant for so long in the ancient world that some outline of the key phases in the empire's development is necessary to appreciate the full significance of her imperialist practices. Assimilation will be seen to be not so much a product of political magnanimity as a policy of political expediency.

Although there is no firm evidence to support it, the traditional date for the founding of Rome is thought to have been about 750 BC. For many years, the Romans were just one of many Latin peoples struggling to survive amid the warring tribes in Italy. They were pressed from the north by the powerful Etruscans, and found themselves in fratricidal competition on their home ground with various tribal coalitions who threatened their very existence. Rome's first expedient moves were to come to terms with other Latin peoples in order to neutralize Etruscan power, and to crush the Apennine hill tribes – especially the Sabines – who had long been an obstacle to Latin tribal development. Eventually, by stealth and tenacity, Rome gradually assumed hegemonic overlordship of the Latin League, and slowly began the conquest of the rest of Italy.

It was hardly all plain-sailing. At about the same time that Rome was plundering the important Etruscan city of Veii and killing or enslaving its people (396 BC), successive waves of Gauls (Celtic tribes from France) began to pour into northern Italy. They overran much of the country, further weakening Etruscan civilization, and using its territory as a base from which to menace the Latin cities of south and central Italy. They finally sacked Rome and beseiged the Capitol for seven months. The defenders, unaided by their erstwhile Latin allies, were starved into submission, and survived only by buying off the barbarian invaders.

Rome learnt some valuable lessons from all this, and thoroughly reorganized her army. More attention was paid to personal protection and weaponry, and greater scope was given to the light-armed infantry. By c. 350 BC, Rome had become the dominant power in central Italy, and then embarked on a policy of expansion which took on the whole of the southern peninsula. She launched a series of successful campaigns against both the hardy Samnite peoples who inhabited the mountains adjacent to the Campanian plain, and the Greek colonies on the southern coast who were aided by Pyrrhus (of Epirus in north-west Greece) and his almost triumphant army of mercenaries.

It took Rome another seventy-five years to subjugate all her enemies on the mainland. But this was not enough. Her appetite for conquest had merely been stimulated. By accident and opportunism, she became enmeshed in wars in North Africa with her former allies, the Carthaginians. This involved a titanic struggle which lasted over a hundred years. Late in the third century BC she was nearly beaten by the ingenuity of the Carthaginian general, Hannibal, who actually had the temerity to invade the Roman heartland and might have taken Rome itself, had he had more support from the Carthaginian Senate. These Punic Wars ended with the total destruction of Carthage in 146 BC, the same year in which other Roman armies also destroyed Corinth, thus neutralizing the power of Greece. These campaigns netted the Romans a tremendous amount of booty, including thousands of slaves. The result was that this once-disciplined, almost austere people now tasted the fruits of previously unimagined wealth. But being the dominant power in the Eastern Mediterranean had its disadvantages – their troubles had only just begun.

The Romans were now caught on an expansionistic roller-coaster. Having embarked on a policy of conquest, they could not afford to stop. There was no standing still; they had to go on or go down. After Greece, there was the Near East and the Middle East. Roman armies never seemed to stay still, and never seemed to get any smaller. Recruits were mobilized from conquered territories to swell the ranks of the Legions. There was more reorganization, more conscription and more training. All this in addition to such innovations as the construction of impressive strategic roads, garrisoned outposts, and the introduction of regular military procedures, including the building of highly fortified camps which often saved the troops from disaster. The Romans were no more courageous or determined than their enemies, but they did have a disciplined and totally rational approach to military conquest.

The efforts that Rome made to hang on to what she had won, and the temptation to take even more facilitated the rise of a series of military dictators – commanders who not only set up new colonies and client kingdoms, but also became a threat to the Republic itself. The first of these, Gaius Marius made his reputation in campaigns in Africa and against the barbarian hordes of Teutons and Gauls who ravaged Italy's northern borders. Marius was technically not a Roman, but an Italian, and he pressed for increased rights for the Italians who were demanding the franchise in recognition of their services to the state. Indirectly this led to civil strife in Rome, and the advent of a more conservative – and ruthless – dictator, Cornelius Sulla, who, after victories in the East, was unwilling to disband his legions – something strictly forbidden in Roman law – before marching on the city itself. This was followed by the proscription of political opponents, and many thousands died in the witch-hunt which followed. It didn't pay to be on the wrong side in Roman politics.

Sulla ruled Rome from 81 until his death in 79 BC, and was succeeded by Gnaeus Pompeius (Pompey) who took his victorious armies to Pontus, Bithynia and Cilicia (modern Turkey) and to Israel and Syria. He returned to Rome in 62 BC, having settled Rome's Eastern frontiers for generations to come. Meanwhile, a new star was in the ascendant. Julius Caesar, who at first formed an alliance with Pompey but later became his rival, had conducted successful campaigns in northern Europe, notably against the Gauls and the Germans, and – at the punitive level – against the Britons. It became virtually certain that these two would-be military dynasts would come into conflict eventually; their respective political ambitions made civil war inevitable. Caesar emerged victorious from this conflict in 48 BC having defeated Pompey's legions in the crucial battle of Pharsalia in Greece. Pompey fled to Egypt where he was assassinated by those trying to curry favour with Caesar as the new force in Mediterranean affairs. They need not have bothered. Caesar had them executed for their pains – Pompey may have been a rival but he was also a Roman who deserved better treatment from subjects of a client kingdom.

After an inordinately prolonged dalliance with Cleopatra, the young Egyptian queen, and incidentally sorting out the untidy state of Egyptian affairs, Caesar returned to Rome, only to be assassinated himself (44 BC) by those who suspected – probably rightly – that he was seeking to make himself emperor. His successor, the youthful Octavianus, out-manoeuvred and out-proscribed his rivals – especially Marcus Antonius (Mark Antony) – and became, as Augustus, master of the Roman world. The Republic was now effectively at an end; and although this was followed by a gradual evolution of governmental forms, what is classified as the 'Empire' began. From now on Rome was ruled by a motley series of emperors. Some were extremely able, such as Augustus himself (d. AD 14) who evolved from being a pale assassin to a respected elder statesman, and Trajan (d. AD 17), under whom Rome probably reached its greatest pre-eminence. But the list also includes such pathological rulers as Caligula, Nero and Commodus who – if they lived today – may well have been regarded as insane, and who epitomize much that is questionable about unchecked autocracy.

The main features of the republican system had been government by *two* consuls, each of whom was elected for one year only, with each having the power of veto over the other. Each was invested with the 'Imperium', supreme authority by the wish of the people and the endorsement of the gods. Their power was theoretically checked by the Council of Elders, the Senate, which at times in the history of Rome became the real instrument of government, and by other appointed legal and religious officials. It was in times of war that the consuls were able to exercise their greatest authority, nominally with the approval of the Senate. They were primarily military leaders, and in the field, there was no one to question their discretion.

In the early days of the Republic, all these administrative arrangements were the preserve of the aristocracy, the patricians. But as time passed war became so extensive that it could no longer be a privilege of the upper classes. More and more of the lower classes – the plebeians – wanted a share in the fortunes of the state for which they were providing military support. Gradually the patricians relaxed their hold on governmental control, and plebeians were allowed their own assembly, and were permitted to elect members of their own class, the 'tribunes of the people', to high office in the state. By 350 BC there had been a partly effective merging of the classes, and it became accepted that one consul had to be a plebeian. But republicanism, as a form of governmental organization – with all its overtones of egalitarianism – should not be equated with non-aggression or any kind of unwillingness to pursue imperialist policies.

As Roman armies met with success after success, and Rome extended her interests throughout the Mediterranean world and beyond, she faced the unavoidable yet intractable problem of retaining what she had won. What had begun as a bid for political autonomy had become a policy of expansionism. She used every method in the book to maintain her empire; diplomacy, intrigue, and certainly coercion. Such ambitious imperialism paid high dividends, especially for the aristocratic families who were able to secure lucrative posts in the newly won provinces.

These offices were often coveted for their opportunities for peculation and exploitation. Perhaps not entirely untypical was the case of Verres, the propraetor of Sicily (73–71 BC), who was eventually indicted and prosecuted by the famous aristocratic lawyer, Cicero, in 70 BC. Provincial governors were known to have got away with a great deal in the past, and Verres, who was accused of having milked the system of money and valuables worth 40 million sesterces – a huge sum – saw no reason to think he would be an exception. He openly boasted that he had made enough for himself and his patrons and friends, and had plenty to spare to pay the jurors. It was the representatives of the exploited Sicilian cities who retained Cicero to press their case for restitution. He spent 50 of the 110 days allowed him gathering evidence in Sicily itself, while the defence tried every conceivable device to prevent the case coming to trial at all. Before the hearings were concluded Verres went into exile, and was condemned in his absence.

When we come to the empire period and the reign of Augustus, the 'Roman Peace' had been established. The state was recovering from the civil strife of the past fifty years or so, and Augustus set about consolidating his authority as the princeps of the empire. He shrewdly surrendered the extraordinary powers that he had enjoyed during the recent struggle with the forces of Mark Antony and Cleopatra and in 27 BC became the 'first citizen' of Rome. He was granted by both Senate and Assembly the imperium of the provinces of Spain, Gaul and Syria. In effect, this made him commander of the imperial army, and emperor in all but name.

The traditional structure of society did not change with the evolution from republic to empire: the highest order, the senators, was open to those who had served the state in any of a number of important official capacities, military tribunes, magistrates or quaestors (treasury officials). From this a man might go on to higher offices and be appointed to a provincial command. Normally, these were the preserve of previous senators' sons who were groomed for office, and who had property qualifications of a million sesterces. Augustus purged the senatorial ranks so that the Senate consisted of 600 members which was informally divided into a number of factions. Political advancement became really a matter of imperial patronage. Below the senatorial order was the equestrian order, open to males from the age of 18 who had a property qualification of 400,000 sesterces. Admission to the order was controlled by the princeps, and gave eligibility to both civil and military appointments. Unlike the senators, this class was periodically enlarged, and might even include select members of the lower classes and – exceptionally – freedmen. The Assemblies of the citizens remained elective bodies, but had only nominal legislative powers. The higher magistracies effectively controlled them by vetting all laws submitted for their consideration.

During this period, the army was also reorganized. At the end of the civil war, Augustus may have had as many as half a million men under arms. Over half of these were released either to go to their native municipalities or to the colonies. The army itself retained its customary division between praetorians, legionaries and auxiliary troops, but severe restrictions were placed on those of the lower orders rising from the ranks to become members of the officer class. Such promotions had been easier during times of national emergency, but now that there was to be a settled professional army, strict preference was given to those who were being prepared for higher office, equestrians and budding senators.

The Praetorian guard, which numbered 9,000, was drawn exclusively from Romans and enjoyed shorter service and higher pay than other troops. Legionaries were also recruited from Roman citizens living either in Italy or in the provinces. Each legion comprised nominally 6,000 men of whom 120 were cavalry, but often they were not kept at full strength. From AD 6 their period of service was extended to twenty years after which they were given a bonus on retirement. Auxiliaries were normally recruited from either allies or subject peoples in the empire. Their numbers were about the same as those of the legionaries, and they were organized in units of mixed infantry and cavalry, either 480 or 960 strong under Roman officers. They were usually on fixed-term engagements (from AD 6 normally twenty-five years) and when their period of service had expired, they and their families were granted Roman citizenship. Rome also maintained a regular navy, but it did not attract the same esteem as the army, being serviced mainly by provincials and even freedmen.

The time of Augustus is regarded by some as the golden age of Rome but it was a golden age that was not without its difficulties. Not least, it was faced with an acute population problem. The city itself may have housed as many as a million people, many of whom were recipients of free grain, a kind of dole that the state made to its poorer members. Ironically, this was largely the produce of slaves on the extensive slave estates (*latifundia*) in Italy and Sicily, who undercut the cost of free labour and generated a degree of agricultural unemployment. This, in turn, led to the migration of landless labourers to the towns to swell the ranks of the urban proletariat. Economically, it was a vicious circle. Slaves produced food for the poor that they themselves had unwittingly helped to create.

What was the answer to all this? First of all, employment had to be found for the surplus labour in the city. Augustus reorganized the security and police systems, and also initiated a number of public works schemes, especially buildings for public celebrations. He tried to reawaken a sense of the old Roman virtues, so state cults were revitalized, and the priestly colleges re-established. Temples and shrines which had fallen into disrepair were refurbished and restored for public worship. Second, Augustus sponsored two laws which restricted the number of slaves that could be owned by any one man, and also limited the number of slaves that any master could liberate during his lifetime, thus reducing a potential increase in the numbers of free urban poor.

Third, there were the public festivals. The Roman mob was reputed to be lazy, fickle and excitable. Not only were they dependent on state largesse, but they also craved entertainment. Greek plots and plays – particularly tragedy – had been largely abandoned; instead the public preferred pageants, comedies, and especially gladiatorial games. These public spectacles which included chariot racing, wild beast shows (first introduced in 186 BC) as well as gladiatorial combats (reputedly introduced as funeral games in 264 BC) could be brutal in the extreme. Sometimes animals and hunters were chained together, the beasts having been starved and goaded beforehand. The empire was scoured for suitable animals – bears, panthers, tigers, etc. – at tremendous expense, and sometimes several hundred were killed in one day. And this was often only an *hors-d'oeuvre* to the main attraction, the gladiatorial contests themselves. The gladiators, often slaves or war captives, were organized in schools. Their training was harsh, but the rewards could be considerable providing they lived long enough; a skilled gladiator might survive for as long as three years, but few lived beyond the age of 30. Evidence suggests that the average was about seven contests each. The wastage in human life was enormous. Augustus, for example, produced 625 pairs of gladiators at the average spectacle, and Trajan (98–117 AD) – one of the more 'enlightened' emperors – celebrated his successful completion of the Dacian (Balkan) wars in AD 107 with 126 days of games involving 10,000 contestants, many of them unskilled prisoners. Pitting trained men against the unskilled and even unarmed was not that uncommon. Caligula (AD 37–41) sometimes forced ordinary citizens into the arena, and Titus, an army commander and later emperor (AD 79–81) after the sack of Jerusalem in AD 70, had 2,500 Jews slaughtered to celebrate his brother's birthday.

Lastly – and most importantly for the present discussion – emigration was encouraged, and many thousands of citizens, especially veterans, were re-settled in the colonies. This, of course, was not always to the liking of the indigenes. It was bad enough to be one of a subject people, but to have members of the dominant culture foisted on you without your permission, and thus to be made doubly conscious of your inferior status, was hardly welcomed. And to have to defray the costs of civil and military administration added insult to injury. To be fair to the Roman overlords, laws were passed to protect the rights of the indigenes in order to prevent, or at least reduce, exploitation, but inevitably injustices still occurred.

Broadly speaking, there were two types of provinces, imperial and senatorial. In general, the former were garrisoned by troops and the latter were not. This was subject to change and variation depending on the exigencies of the time. Certainly all the new provinces in territories conquered by Augustus' generals remained directly under his control. Outside these two classes of provinces were the client kingdoms

whose rulers acknowledged Roman overlordship. These had internal
autonomy and were not subject to taxation by Rome, but their foreign
relations were controlled by Rome, and they were bound to contribute
military aid when it was required, usually when a campaign was being
launched in their area.

Governors of senatorial provinces were called pro-consuls, and
each was assisted by a quaestor and three legati approved by the
princeps. Imperial governors were either legati or procurators, men of
equestrian rank who were usually in charge of lesser military districts
garrisoned by auxiliaries. The exception was Egypt which was ruled
almost as though it was the personal province of the emperor himself.
Egypt occupied a unique place in imperial affections as it supplied
something like a third of the grain consumed in Rome. Its special
administrative status did not change until the reign of Septimius
Severus in AD 200.

Governors of provinces usually held office for one year, but this
varied with the type of appointment. Imperial officials might continue
in office for as long as the princeps required, and the payment of
regular salaries helped to reduce the temptation of officials to resort to
extortion. But these men had considerable power within their areas of
administration, and it was therefore impossible to eliminate all abuses
of authority.

It is often assumed that Augustus' main aim was to secure a peaceful
state behind well-defended frontiers. This is debatable. As the great
'creator' of the empire, no one had added more territory to Rome
than he, and – to all intents and purposes – he wanted to keep it
that way. He had been an aggressive expansionist in his earlier years;
unscrupulous to his enemies, and not that kind to his friends. He had
personally conducted campaigns in Spain (26 BC) in order to subjugate
completely its unruly inhabitants, and, in the same year, his generals
moved against the Alpine peoples, and those that were not massacred
were sold into slavery. As the years passed and his rather unsavoury
reputation for ruthlessness transmuted into one of respectability, he
appears to have tried to relax in the quiet acknowledgement that he
was the 'father of his country'. But events would not allow it; the
frontiers were ever restive.

Rome had made lots of bad friends during her most active expansionist phase in the late Republic. Now it was a question of trying to
defend her frontiers, and this could only be done by yet more aggressive
and never-ending campaigns against the native tribes on the borders.
Gaul had been largely pacified and was divided into sixty-four separate
entities (*civitates*); no attempt was made to latinize them, and they were
left largely in the control of the native nobility. Their rich lands were a
valuable source of revenue, and it was also a useful recruiting ground

for auxiliary troops. Germany, on the other hand, was another matter. It was divided into a number of separate tribes, often warring with each other, but they were also a continual menace to Gaul. Augustus planned an all-out campaign against Germany, but it never really materialized, although there was a successful pacification of the tribes between the Elbe and the Rhine between 12 and 9 BC, by Augustus' eventual successor, Tiberius.

It was during this same period that the Roman military experienced one of its greatest setbacks. In AD 9, a new commander, Quinctilius Varus, convinced that the Germanic tribes needed stricter control, provoked some of them to rebellion. Ironically, this was led by Arminius, a man who had been both trained as a member of the Roman auxilia and had actually been promoted to the rank of equestrian. Varus and his three legions were ambushed in the Teutoburg Forest and completely annihilated. Fortunately for Rome, the Germans did not follow up their success, but it caused Rome to pause, and settle for a frontier on the Rhine instead of the limitless expansion once contemplated in Central Europe.

On their Eastern frontier, and particularly between Asia Minor (western Turkey) and the upper Euphrates (northern Iraq), Rome had a host of client kingdoms. Further east still was the subject kingdom of Armenia which acted as a buffer state between the client territories and the kingdom of Parthia which had proved such a thorn in the Roman flesh in the past. (Only a few years before Augustus' accession to power, Crassus, a wealthy but inept aristocrat who fancied his chances as a rival of Julius Caesar, had led an army of some 40,000 against the Parthians – with disastrous results.) To the south lay the province of Syria and the kingdom of Judea ruled by Herod the Great and his sons. This presented such problems that it too became a Roman province in AD 6. The Romans were rather sensitive to Jewish religious susceptibilities, but this did not prevent them from baring the iron fist when necessary, especially against the resistance fighters in northern Galilee. Arabia, and much of the north African coastline also came under Roman control, and Egypt – so valuable as a source of grain and gold – had, since the death of Cleopatra, become a special kind of protectorate.

Augustus' successors inherited a state with considerable wealth and stability, but a state which was organized in such a way that it gave rise to untramelled autocracy. Power had passed from the Senate, a select oligarchy, to a single ruler who, in some cases – like Nero – was little more than a self-deluded tyrant. Matters came to a head in AD 68–9 when Rome had had four emperors within the space of a single year. At the accession of Vespasian (AD 69), a realistic and competent general, the senatorial ranks which had been depleted by executions were restored.

The exchequer – bankrupt from imperial extravagances – was gradually replenished by taxes from the rich Asian provinces, though many other provinces were too financially exhausted from the exactions that had been necessary to bankroll the civil wars which had wracked the state over the question of succession. Such conflicts were not helped by the overweening claims of some of the rulers, especially their insistence that they were more than mortals. Vespasian's son, Domitian (AD 81–96) – probably the 'Great Beast' of the Book of Revelation – self-styled 'Lord and God', was not above executing those that dared to question his divine status. As part of his religious 'revival', he even enforced the death penalty for Vestal Virgins – almost the Roman equivalent of nuns – who were found guilty of commiting adultery. Needless to say, his exalted status did not save him from the assassin's knife. Rome had become temporarily impatient with arbitrary rule.

Despite much autocratic incompetence, the empire – under able administration – continued to flourish, and during the next hundred years reached its greatest territorial extent and material prosperity. This period in the early second century vies with the 'reign' of Augustus as the golden age of Roman imperialism. Its high point is often seen as the reign of Trajan – himself a provincial – who did much to beautify the city, and improve travel facilities in the provinces. His was a system of benevolent paternalism which did little to change the basic structure of Roman society. The empire still relied primarily on the support of the upper classes, and failed to initiate the social and economic reforms which would have benefited the lower orders of Roman society. Likewise with the provinces: subject peoples were brought within the Roman fold, though it was only gradually that they were admitted to Roman citizenship.

For a variety of reasons, the situation in the provinces was often uneasy. The Romans had to be on constant alert, especially on the extensive frontiers where there was bound to be trouble; if not against Roman rule, then against neighbouring subject peoples with whom there was some grievance. A case in point during Trajan's reign is that of the Jews in Cyrenaica (North Africa) in AD 115. Here there was a religiously inspired insurrection which was directed against their Hellenized neighbours and their gods. It spread to Cyprus, Egypt, Israel and even Mesopotamia, and developed into a challenge to Roman authority itself. Both sides perpetrated horrible massacres until the whole affair was ruthlessly crushed by Trajan's legions. More problems arose with the Jews during the reign of Trajan's son and successor, Hadrian, who unnecessarily prohibited circumcision – which he regarded with abhorrence – and imprudently had an altar to Jupiter built on the site of the former Jewish Temple at Jerusalem. The Jews, under Simon Bar Kochba, seized the city and defied the Roman armies. The struggle lasted for two years (AD 132–4) by which time the Jewish population of Judea had been largely exterminated.

Hadrian exemplifies, yet again, one of the great anomalies of Roman rule. It could be beneficient in the extreme. Hadrian expertly managed the imperial finances, and was able to lavish money and energy on the provinces, especially Egypt and Greece, as well as Rome itself. But it was a generosity that would brook no opposition. Any challenge to its right to control, any questioning of its ultimate authority was met with overwhelming force.

By the time of the philosopher–Emperor Marcus Aurelius (AD 161–80), evidence of decline was obvious, and this was most evident on the frontiers. A whole series of circumstances conspired to cause consternation in Rome: lack of adequate troops due to plague; depletion of the treasury and the legions because of the expense of the ubiquitous Parthian wars. The tribes along the Danube were in revolt. Elsewhere in the Balkans, tribes had moved south and reached the Adriatic and the borders of Italy. Roman armies had been weakened because contingents had to be sent to counter further troubles in the East of her empire. The emperor had to recourse to the expedients of hiring mercenaries and recruiting gladiators and even slaves to supplement the legions. Roman armies succeeded in bringing these peoples to heel, but only by large-scale population transfer and a wholesale annexation of lands.

And so it went on. If it wasn't the Danube, it was Gaul or Parthia, and if it wasn't the Moors it was the Caledonians. The Roman armies had little respite. If they were not engaged in provincial or border wars, they were involved in some kind of internecine strife at home usually because of warring contenders for the throne. There were, it must be stressed, some energetic and enlightened emperors, such as Septimius Severus (AD 193–211) who certainly did a great deal for the provinces. By contrast, there were autocratic – indeed, despotic – emperors such as Caracalla (AD 211–17) who actually brought in far-sighted measures such as conferring Roman citizenship upon all free members of the empire who, in law, had previously had the status of aliens. Yet even here there may well have an ulterior motive – to widen the franchise in order to increase the tax revenues. When authoritarian rulers introduced more humanitarian legislation it often cost them very little, and actually increased their popularity with the masses.

The empire was to continue for another two hundred years in the West, and for considerably longer in its Eastern form centred on Byzantium (Istanbul). The Western Empire would endure many important changes before its ultimate demise, especially in its literary and religious traditions with the 'conversion' to Christianity in the fourth century. But the cultural legacy lived on; in its own particular way the empire made a lasting contribution to Western civilization. Despite all its shortcomings, it had a number of advantages over the republic. It developed a civil bureaucracy with permanent salaried officials, previously a practice foreign to the state, but which made for greater efficiency of administration. The early emperors, especially Augustus, had tended to run the state as a private fiefdom through secretaries and assistants – rather like a medieval English king. The establishment of ministries went a long way to tidying up these rather informal procedures. Under Hadrian, the old system of tax collection was largely discontinued, and instead of farming the revenues out under private contractors, the monies were collected by government officials. This was generally a much more satisfactory arrangement as far as the provincials were concerned because the earlier system had given too many opportunities for exploitation and the expropriation of funds. The system was not foolproof, and nepotism and sycophantism were still rife, especially in the later empire. Rome had originally flourished under its leaders; it now managed to survive because of its superior organization and administration.

In the second and third centuries, promotions to higher ranks within the state became more open, and equestrians particularly came to be recruited from provincials, especially from the Eastern areas of the empire. Furthermore, the practice of conferring honorary titles came into being, with those of the senatorial class being hereditary.

As far as the military was concerned, probably the most important feature of the empire was the growing provincialization of the army. By Trajan's reign, four out of five legionaries were drawn from the provinces, though their officers were still largely Italians. Often the men were recruited to serve in garrisons on their home territory. This served to reduce resentment about foreign services and also acted as a powerful Romanizing influence on the soldiers themselves and the subjects under their jurisdiction. The auxiliaries – as provincials – also profited from this relaxation in the rules. At first, as we have seen, they were not granted citizenship until they were discharged, but by Hadrian's time about half had been made citizens while still serving with the colours. During the second century they were receiving much the same training as the legionaries, and after the extension of the franchise in AD 212, there was virtually no distinction between them. Another innovation in military organization was the formation of contingents of *numeri* early in the second century. These were non-Romanized and barbarian peoples – officered by Romans – who were allowed to serve in a supporting capacity with the legions, and retain their traditional methods of warfare. This augmentation of the army was particularly valuable as times became more difficult on the borders.

28

By the third century the Roman army may have totalled more than a half a million men; many of them engaged in a defensive capacity, manning the numerous garrisons and fortifications on the frontiers. The army contributed considerably to the provinces by building roads, bridges and aqueducts which were extensively used by civilians as well as the military. The great disadvantage was that in establishing large fortified camps which then became municipal centres, the Romans indirectly facilitated the relative *im*mobilization of the army – a practice which proved very costly in the later barbarian invasions.

In general, though, the policy of assimilation worked; first in Italy itself, and then in the provinces. The number of provinces increased from twenty-eight early in the first century to over fifty by the middle of the second century, although this came about largely by sub-division rather than any extension of territorial boundaries. Each province was divided into communities (*civitates*) many of which developed into municipalities capable of ordering their own administration. And where native towns were granted their charters as Roman colonies they were usually granted exemption from land taxes. Under the empire, the taxation system was reorganized – as we have noted – to make it more equitable for subjects. There were direct taxes (*tributa*) including both land and personal taxes, and indirect taxes. In some provinces, these were still in the hands of the corporation of tax collectors (*publicani*) but they were supervised by the imperial procurators.

In the ancient world, life was a very uncertain affair for most people, and war was one of those necessary evils which sometimes ensured some measure of temporary stability in society. The wars on Rome's frontiers helped to ensure relative peace for the majority of people in the provinces. In many ways, Rome was quite relaxed in its demand on subject peoples. No kind of uniformity was imposed on subjects; they were not compelled to conform to Roman cultural traditions – perhaps one of the great strengths of the Roman system. But they had to respect its authority and comply with its political and fiscal regulations. Direct domination by Rome became muted with time. The assimilation process became more effective, and the empire gradually took the form of a hegemony in which the provinces were encouraged to develop independent administrations, but never their own brands of nationalism. That would have been too much – even for Roman expediency.

3

Re-education: British colonialism in India

The gradual occupation of India by Western traders, missionaries and adventurers was part of a wider expansionist policy which was really under way by the sixteenth century. Ostensibly it began as exploration with a little economic dealing on the side. But with the creation of joint-stock companies (in England from 1553) the way was open to raise venture capital to finance risky but potentially lucrative markets abroad. Probably the most important of these new trading companies was the East India Company founded in 1600. This was really formed to tap resources of the Orient at a time when Portugal, then united with Spain, was in serious conflict with Dutch and English privateers. English appetites were whetted when, in 1592, they appropriated a Portuguese vessel laden with 'spices, drugges, silks, calico quilts, carpets and colours' (quoted in Weech 1945: 573). With the ungarnered wealth of the East waiting to be had, the English wanted a major share of the action.

India had been invaded many times in her history, from the incursions of the Aryans in *c.* 1500 BC to the much later devastations of the Mongols and the Muslims. But India had never experienced anything like the economic invasion of the Westerners. This was more subtle and less obvious than the attacks from her covetous neighbours who confined their attentions mainly to the north. The Western invasion was also backed by force, but – for the most part – it was used only when felt to be necessary. Originally, the Westerners came to trade, but they stayed to govern.

The British settled in Surat in 1612, after a successful naval engagement against the Portuguese; in Bengal from 1630, Madras in 1640; and in Bombay in 1668. The Dutch had been warned off by this time and, except for small settlements in Ceylon (Sri Lanka), had departed for alternative pickings in the East Indies.

The dominant power in India during these initial ventures was that of the Moguls whose most famous emperor, Akbar the Great (d. 1605), was probably the richest and most powerful monarch of his day. He and his successors were great patrons of the arts, and built a whole series of palaces and mosques. Many of these still excite the modern traveller, most notably the Taj Mahal at Agra which was built by Akbar's grandson, Jehan, as a mausoleum for his wife. The Moguls were also tolerant of certain Western ideas, particularly religious ideas, and the rulers often debated issues with the missionaries. Akbar, himself, though illiterate, decided to promulgate a new religion, the Divine Faith (Din Ilahi), which he felt incorporated the best features of other religions, and involved worship of the sun as a symbol of universal light. It was hardly a new or innovative idea, but it was well-intentioned; he even thought it might bring Hindus and Muslims together, but it did not survive his death. In general the Muslim hierarchy tended to despise the religious pretensions of its subject peoples, especially the Jains, Hindus and Buddhists. Foreigners were the exception. Their ideas were different and they were still something of a novelty to the indigenes.

The decline of the Mogul Empire in the early eighteenth century was attended – as is so often the case – by growing autocracy and arbitrary rule. This gave an opportunity for the more martial of the disaffected subject peoples, such as the Sikhs, Rajputs and Mahrathas to rebel against their overlords. The situation was further exacerbated by the depredations of Persian and Afghan invaders from the North. For good or ill, the subject peoples sought the help of the Western merchant adventurers in their bid to cast off Mogul rule. The British, in particular, by a system of shifting alliances, were not slow to seize the opportunity to win a greater stake in the game. Indeed they justified their interference in terms of social necessity. Their mission was to bring peace and stability to this great land – at a price.

As these early European settlements consolidated, so imperialistic ideas began to develop. The British, especially after the establishment of their colony at Calcutta, became increasingly empire-conscious. Trade flourished; spices were in constant demand, and the importation of cheap cloth very soon came to be seen as a threat to home-produced woollens. By this time the French too were in on the act, and the scene was set for the playing out of one of the most dramatic themes of the eighteenth century – the maritime rivalry between Britain and France.

At first, the settlements were little more than coastal trading stations. But with their increasing acceptance by the indigenous population, the Europeans built small factories and warehouses. These modest enterprises were run by a cadre of merchants and clerks protected by small contingents of native troops in case of emergencies. Later both the English and the French raised levies of Indian troops (*sepoys*) who were armed and drilled in the European fashion. It has been suggested that initially the English and French companies wanted to keep relations with Indians on a purely commercial basis. But soon it was no longer just a matter of trade; both nations were in the game of establishing power bases on the sub-continent.

With the outbreak of the Seven Years' War (1756–63) in Europe, hostilities began between the rival companies in India. French ascendancy was neutralized by a military parvenu – a former clerk in the East India Company at Madras – Robert Clive, who defeated the French native levies at Arcot, and later reduced the French to two minor trading posts. This meant that French influence in India was all but extinguished.

As the native princes awoke to the possibility of foreign domination, preparations were made to oust the intruders who had now outstayed their welcome. The Nawab of Bengal attacked the British settlement at Calcutta and imprisoned the inhabitants in a tiny room – 'the Black Hole of Calcutta' – where most of them died from suffocation. Clive hurried from Madras, and his army defeated the Nawab's forces at Plassey in 1757 capturing all their animals and military equipment. This made the British masters of Bengal. The Nawab's successor – a British appointee – later rebelled and massacred some two hundred Europeans, but he too was defeated, and the Company was then granted the right to supervise the revenues of much of South India, specifically Bengal, Bihar and Orissa.

It could be argued that the British had never actually intended to conquer India, but having successfully waged war against the French and against some Indian princes in order to defend their trading rights, they now decided to exploit the situation. The Company annexed some territory which was then divided into eleven provinces, and ruled directly by the Company. This became British India. The vast remainder of the territory, consisting of about 550 princedoms, was left under the control of the traditional Hindu and Muslim autocrats who deferred to British Government policy in certain conditions. These autonomous states were largely untouched by the changes and reforms that were introduced in British India.

The Company's 'servants', as they were known, were technically responsible to the Court of Directors in London. But the directors – being somewhat removed from the actual operations of the Company abroad – were able to exercise only limited control over their employees. Young men went to India to make their fortunes. The result was sometimes corruption and speculation on a disturbing scale. There developed an inverse relationship between the prosperity of the Company and the increasing wealth of some of its employees. This culminated in the impeachment of Warren Hastings who was governor of Bengal in 1772 and the first governor-general of all India in 1774, a post which he held for eleven years. This was the period when Britain was still having to counter the effects of various French schemes to undermine her influence and, worse still, was at war both in Europe and with the colonies in North America. The Company's affairs had come to attract criticism by this time. A scapegoat was needed and Hastings was charged with cruelty and oppression, an allegation which seems particularly ironic in view of the fact that he seems to have been a concerned and enlightened civil servant. Yet he was not particularly well-liked by his own council, perhaps because he actually did try to limit the degree of corruption that was so obviously rampant at the time. His efforts to tighten up the administration and reduce injustice were not calculated to make him too many friends. His impeachment before the House of Lords became something of a *cause célèbre*. It took seven years to complete the case and he was eventually acquitted. It cost the then astronomical sum of £70,000, and resulted in the abandonment of the system of company-oriented government. The Company was brought under the control of Parliament in 1784; in future, the governors-general were to be chosen from men outside the Company's service.

It is probably true to say that this was not altogether alien to the Company's wishes. Although some personal fortunes had been made, overall, the Indian venture was not proving that profitable. In fact, the costs of administration were such that the Company was possibly glad to relinquish its responsibilities. The real profits were coming from the tea trade in China; tea was exported to the Company in India in exchange for opium which was officially proscribed by the Chinese government. Military and civil expenditure in India became exorbitant, but economic interest – especially in the private sector – was kept alive by the prospect of potential rather than actual revenues. The thinking was that such a vast sub-continent must surely yield profits eventually. India was a kind of 'futures market'; something that would pay off in time.

These economic hopes began to be realized. Between 1839 and 1859, India's exports doubled, and her imports from England increased proportionately. She was both a market and a source of raw material, especially cotton. In the 1860s almost all of India's trade was with Great Britain. Politically, on the other hand, it was a different matter. Unlike so many of Britain's possessions, India was virtually impossible to colonize successfully. Its sheer size, particularly the size of its population, meant that the British were always in a tiny minority. In retrospect it is amazing that they maintained control as long as they did.

This was the high-water mark of British imperialism, and she still wanted more despite the tenuousness of her hold on what she already possessed. Treaties were made with native princes, and garrisons established in their territories. The Punjab was secured after two years; and some states were actually annexed on the unlikely pretext that their late rulers had no children, therefore, these lands automatically 'lapsed' to the Crown.

Of course, it couldn't last. The East India Company maintained three armies in India: the Madras army, the Bombay army and, the largest of the three, the Bengal army which numbered about 150,000 of which only some 23,000 were British. There had been trouble in the 1840s when some regiments rebelled over the issue of extra pay for 'foreign service'. This had been a bone of contention for some time. Normally, the army was considered a desirable profession even by high caste standards, but overseas travel was believed to be a source of contamination by high caste personnel, and might lead to ostracism by their families. These ritual imperatives of the caste system led to further conflicts with the Army Command in the 1850s. These arose when a new Enfield rifle was issued to the *sepoys*, the cartridges of which had to be greased with beef or pork fat, and the tip removed before it was loaded into the rifle. In practice, this usually meant that it was actually bitten off – an expedient highly polluting to high caste personnel. In April 1857, eighty-five *sepoys* mutinied, and refused to use the new cartridges. This sparked off a more widespread rebellion in which the soldiers were joined by men from other garrisons together with some members of the civilian population who had been nursing particular grievances against British rule. The rebels tried to rally popular support by appealing to the descendants of the old Mogul nobility, but with very limited success.

The rebellion entered its most serious phase when the mutineers were joined by some of the minor aristocracy who had been dispossessed of their lands by the British, namely, Maratha leaders Nana Seheb, and the queen (*rani*) of Jhansi, a small Maharejhan state in which there had already been a massacre of British civilians. There was considerable savagery on both sides and in the summer of 1858, when the rebellion had gathered some momentum, one of the most notorious incidents took place. The town of Cawnpore was besieged by rebellious *sepoys*. Hopelessly outnumbered, the garrison – which included women and children – negotiated a surrender. They were guaranteed safe conduct and escorted to boats in which they were to sail to Allahabad, but as they were about to leave the trap was sprung, a signal was given and they were fired at from all sides. The survivors, some two hundred women and children, were ordered to be killed. This was too much for the *sepoys* who refused to obey the instructions of their new leaders so the gruesome task was handed to some butchers who hacked them to death and threw their bodies down a well.

Meanwhile, a force had been sent to relieve Cawnpore. Its commander, General Neill, had already spread terror among the native

34

population by the seemingly indiscriminate killing of civilians and burning of villages while en route to the massacre which he was unable to prevent. When the British caught up with the murderers they were made to clean up the scene of their crime, forced even to lick up the blood of their victims, after which they were summarily hanged. When the mutiny was finally put down, rebel *sepoys* were tied to the barrel mouths of English cannons and blown to pieces. This particularly horrific form of execution was deliberately designed as an example to others. And it was also intended as a final spiritual punishment for the natives who believed that the nature of their eternal destiny was dependent on having a complete body at death.

The mutiny had broken out for a number of reasons. The cartridge issue was only the immediate precipitating factor, but it was an important one in that it involved trained military personnel. There were also other sources of social unrest. Once powerful landlords were irate because their lands had been confiscated by the British when they could not show documentary proof of ownership. Others regarded the rents they paid the British as too exorbitant, and had thus run themselves into debt with money-lenders. Very many Indians had religious grievances, but usually these were directly related to identifiable political and economic policies and practices. A few months after the outbreak of hostilities, the king of Delhi issued a proclamation alleging that the British had also monopolized the trade in the most valuable merchandise, and had also generated unemployment and poverty by the importation of English goods to India.

Against all this must be set a number of qualifying factors. The mutiny failed largely because of its limited appeal for the bulk of the native population; here we are not dealing with anything like a war of independence. The Sikhs of the Punjab did not rebel, and the areas most closely supervised by the British, especially Bengal, did not give the mutiny much support. It was mainly confined to the northern provinces, and – by and large – was not aided by the independent princedoms. Furthermore, it needs to be stressed that in some areas events generated internal upheavals, caste turned on caste, and some people took it as an opportunity to settle old scores. Indeed, there is good evidence that, in part at least, the impetus behind the revolt was not so much resurgent nationalism as political ambition. It is interesting that when the British took the Punjab some ten years before the mutiny, no help had been given to the Sikhs by the present rebels, and the Punjab could then have been seen as the last bastion of Indian independence.

It is almost certainly true to say that whatever the justification for the mutiny from the Indian point of view, revolt would not – perhaps could not – have turned into a full-scale rebellion if the territory had not been so denuded of English troops owing to the exigencies of the Crimean War. Once the British authorities had stemmed the initial tide of the rebellion and had reinforced their garrisons, it is difficult to see how they could lose, given that they controlled the arsenals and could deploy their troops to the best advantage with incomparably better communications systems and superior military equipment.

The cause of the British in India was not helped by various discriminatory practices such as separate compartments for whites and Indians on trains and steamers. But these were mere niggles compared with the problems in employment. The many educational advantages introduced by the British proved to be something of a two-edged sword. They put many Indians on a competitive footing with their white counterparts, something which did not always endear them to their overlords. But, at the same time, it fostered a sense of unrealized – and sometimes unrealizable – social ambition for these new educated classes. Over the years, this resentment found many expressions, not least that of an increasing desire for national independence.

The first step was to try to obtain some real participation in the machinery of government. In 1885 the Indian National Congress was founded, which consisted mainly of lawyers, journalists, teachers and doctors, and members of the landed and commercial classes generally. The British argued that it was unrepresentative of the people as a whole, and more or less ignored its demands. After the turn of the century, an extremist faction developed within the Congress. Its members had become impatient with British intransigence and with what they regarded as the pussyfooting of the moderates within their own party. They tried to organize boycotts of British goods, and revive patriotic festivals and old traditions. Some even resorted to terrorism. Bombings and assassinations took place, particularly in Bengal. Revolutionary cells were established as far afield as London and Paris.

The British, however, were far too strong to have to surrender to this kind of intimidation. In order to counter the influence of the extremists, they introduced some reforms in the 1909 Councils Act, which meant that Indians could be elected to various legislative bodies. But they also took repressive measures against the revolutionaries whose leaders were arrested and deported. Native terrorism really had very little chance of success all the time the people did not support its activities. This is exemplified by one president of the National Congress who asked in his inaugural address (1886) 'Is this Congress a nursery for sedition and rebellion against the British Government? (cries of No, no)'. In the same speech he talked of 'our good fortune that we live under a rule which makes it possible to meet in this manner. . . . Such a thing is possible under British rule and British rule only (loud cheers)'. There may be just a hint of deliberate obsequiousness here, but the sentiments were obviously endorsed by the majority of the audience (quoted in Ashton 1988: 70).

Some measure of Indian co-operation with British rule can be seen from the fact that nearly a million Indians served with the British forces during the First World War, more than half of these being engaged in the Mesopotamian campaigns. At the same time, however, trouble was brewing in parts of India itself, notably in the Punjab. There was an attempted rebellion in 1915 led by Sikhs who were re-emigrants from America and had been supplied with money and arms by the Germans. Again, it failed, largely through lack of general support.

The interesting thing is that there were contrary pressures at work in the sub-continent at this time: pressures for reform and pressures for firmer action against recalcitrants and would-be extremists. The British recognized the enormous contribution India had made to the war effort and in 1917 the government issued a declaration that, by stages, they were going to introduce self-government to India. But in 1919, perhaps because many Indians found the pace of change too slow for their liking, there were a number of disturbances culminating in the Amritsar massacre in which Indian troops under British command fired on a crowd of demonstrators, killing 379 and wounding a further 1,200. The disturbances themselves were partly a reaction against the Rowlatt Act which authorized special tribunals to mete out summary punishment for political offenders, and partly against the deportations which had followed upon a series of 'hartels' (strikes). Mahatma Gandhi, who had returned from South Africa in 1915, led a campaign of peaceful disobedience in 1919 but in Delhi, just a week before the Amritsar incident, his followers clashed with police and a number were killed. Later in the year, martial law was lifted in the Punjab but the inhabitants were left with a memory of repressive measures and the knowledge that the man who had ordered the shooting, Brigadier-General Dyer, though effectively pensioned off as an embarrassment to His Majesty's Government, had been applauded by well-wishers in Britain who had started a fund which made him a wealthy man. Apparently, nothing was too good for the soldier who had 'saved' India from untold anarchy.

Gandhi went on to achieve both fame and notoriety as leader of successive movements to undermine British authority in India. Although his early Non-Cooperation Movement had only limited success, the Civil Disobedience Movement had a much greater influence on public opinion. All these activities were tolerated by the British until Gandhi began a Quit India Movement when Britain was at a particularly low ebb in the war against the Japanese in 1942. The then Commander in Chief, Field-Marshal Wavell (later, as Lord Wavell, to become Viceroy from 1943–6) never forgot what he regarded as an act of treachery by this 'shrewd, malevolent old politician' (Ashton 1988: 108). Gandhi was thought to have been behind the rioting and sabotage, and he was detained for two years, by which time the threat of invasion had slowly diminished. The British could not understand why Gandhi, who had been rewarded for his services to the Crown during the First World War (as he had also supported the British side earlier in the Boer War) could even contemplate the prospect of a much less accommodating occupying power such as the Japanese.

It is probably true to say that Gandhi was much more of a social reformer than a political agitator and for this he has been severely criticized by Indian radicals. His greatest lasting influence has been in his teaching on non-violence and peaceful self-sufficiency. His impatience with modernization has gone largely unheeded and his last venture into politics – that of resistance to partition – ultimately led to his assassination in 1948.

Partition in India in 1947 has to be regarded as something of a mixed blessing. The Muslims were India's largest minority, comprising about a fifth of the total population. They regarded themselves as markedly underprivileged by Hindu standards, and in 1906 formed the all-India Muslim League. This gave them the beginnings of a political organization – a move that was generally approved by the British government, perhaps because it would reduce the power of the Indian National Congress. But in giving more power to minorities and fostering a form of provincial autonomy, the British – while retaining central authority – indirectly encouraged rivalry and sometimes open hostility between these ethnic and religious groups.

The Muslims actually regarded the prospect of partition with ambivalence. On the one hand, they were anxious to have their own independent state(s), but on the other, they were anxious that this did not put them in a position of obvious economic and political inferiority in relation to the Hindus. The League flourished during the Second World War when so many of the Congress leaders had been either goaled or outlawed because of the Quit India agitation. By 1946, the Muslim leadership was able to call for a day of 'Direct Action'. This was meant to be a day of peaceful protest, but its promotional literature enjoined a 'Pledge of Sacrifice' and a vow that Muslims must dedicate their lives and all they possess to the cause of freedom, by might if necessary. The action was attended by such violent clashes that it is estimated that there were some 4,000 deaths in Calcutta alone.

When partition did come, it was vitiated by many unsatisfactory compromises about minority rights and suitable territorial boundaries. These were determined by a British Commission, and on the official announcement of their findings, all hell broke loose. The Sikhs were particularly incensed; clashes were inevitable and it is calculated that in the Punjab in the following weeks somewhere in the region of half a million people died and over eleven million became refugees. After the paroxysms which attended the birth of the two nations had lessened, the last British troops left in 1948, and a constitution was agreed in 1949. The consolidation process took rather longer in Pakistan which had the disadvantage of being divided into two widely separated territories, and it was not until 1956 that the new state finally settled down to its new constitution.

At this distance in time from these momentous events, it can be seen that British rule, for all the criticisms that have been levelled against it, did have some advantages. The British introduced some fundamental – perhaps necessary – changes to Indian society. In some areas of life, considerable toleration was exercised, for example, in relation to religious beliefs, but in certain critical respects, the influence of British rule was enormous. First, there were important changes brought about by the system of government itself. British rule was autocratic, yet this was really only a continuation of the form of government that Indians had always known. Power was vested in the viceroy and his officials. In the very early days all these officials were English, but in 1853 the Indian Civil Service was established. Appointments were made subject to open competition, although it was ten years before any Indian passed the examination. By 1914, 90 per cent of all Civil Service posts were still held by the British, and it says something for the gradual relaxation of British rule that by independence in 1947 the majority were Indians.

It should be made clear that the Indian Civil Service was always infinitesimally small compared with the vast numbers that it adminis- tered, possibly no more than 4,000 excluding clerical grades. Its British complement was drawn very much from the upper and middle classes, and although it has become a commonplace to think of these men as living lives of privileged insouicence, it should be remembered that the rigours of climate and disease meant that many died before their retirement age. As far as one can assess, they were an honest breed, something of a novelty in a land where corruption and incompetence were rife.

The provinces of British India were divided into districts, and these, in turn, into smaller territorial divisions each with its Civil Service officials. From 1848, the governor-general and the provincial governors were assisted by legislative councils composed of representatives from industry, the landowners, etc. In 1861, Indians were included, and in 1892 the councils were allowed to discuss – and question – government legislation. They met in some splendour, but their effectiveness is open to question. Real power was always vested in the British government.

There were also considerable changes in the economy, especially the land tenure system. Traditionally, India had a peasant economy where workers paid their dues – often in the form of produce – to the local lord in return for protection. It was a simple structural system based on the relative autonomy of the village. The land was held in common with no transferable individual titles of ownership. In the south, the dues were usually collected directly from the village headman, whereas in the largely Muslim north, the taxes were collected by tax farmers and recognized hereditary officials (*zamindars*) – a system which lent itself to all kinds of abuse.

Under British rule these revenues had to be increased in order to pay for the army and the costs of administration. This amounted to an average of 56 per cent of the total revenue between the critical years 1913 and 1932, after which administration costs – but not defence costs – gradually reduced. These extra monies were raised by highly questionable economic expedients which were supported by the courts. Those who collected the taxes were able to own land themselves in return for increased revenues to the Crown. Ownership also naturally included the right to buy and sell property, and the money that was creamed from tax collecting was often used to buy out small farmers who found themselves in financial difficulties, especially if they had borrowed to meet these dues – now payable in cash rather than in kind – at exorbitant rates of interest. So the villagers often found themselves dispossessed of their land, and could do little else but become either tenants or landless labourers or members of the already burgeoning urban proletariat.

The change from a largely barter economy to a predominantly money economy often had disastrous effects on the peasants, as did also the transfer of manufacturing from village handicrafts to heap factory-produced goods. The closely integrated social structures based on caste position and local allegiances gradually broke down as population increased, making it highly doubtful – at this level, at least – whether the advent of British rule had really done anything to alleviate the lot of the masses. In contrast to the very high percentage of the revenues devoted to defence and administration, between 1913 and 1932 only an average of 10 per cent was spent on capital works (railways, roads and irrigation) and a mere 1–2 per cent on medicine and public health. But beside this, one must consider the slow beginnings of the independent state. The distribution of the Indian workforce in 1951 after independence was hardly different from 1901: about 75 per cent in agriculture, about 10 per cent in industry, and even less (about 2 per cent) in trade and commerce.

The legal system too was revolutionized. Hindu and Muslim law was essentially religious law. It was based upon traditional norms and precepts. The caste system, and the Muslim distinction between believer and non-believer ensured that there was no equality before the law. The British introduced the important distinction between personal law concerning such matters as family, religion, etc., and civil and criminal law. A system of courts was set up which tried to ensure equality before the law, although again the occupying power claimed the ultimate authority in important matters of jurisdiction.

Lastly – and in some ways most critically – the British made really momentous changes in education. These really affected everything else. Although generally tolerant of the native religions, the British saw them as reactionary forces which were not conducive to the acquisition of new knowledge and Western practices. For example, the custom of *sati* – where women committed ceremonial suicide at their husbands' cremations – was abolished in 1829, a move that was precipitated by the fact that in Bengal in just one year, some 700 widows had burnt themselves on their husbands' funeral pyres.

Higher education was introduced in 1835 for the Indian upper classes. There were understandable prejudices to be overcome at this stage; the character and uniqueness of traditional Indian culture were not appreciated by the British who, at first, simply wanted to anglicize their students. But by the middle of the century about two hundred schools and colleges provided Western-style education, though only for about 30,000 privileged students. From the Indian point of view, there was an initial ambivalence about Western literacy and scientific culture, but among the young, particularly, it had certain immediate attractions. In time, a Western-style education became the mark of an elite stratum of Indian society. In a strange way education both pierced the old caste system by adding a new criterion of exclusiveness, yet, at the same time, reinforced it in so far as the new literati were mainly drawn from the upper echelons of Indian society anyway.

Gradually and inevitably Western ideas began to permeate other strata as well. It became *de rigueur* to think in Western terms, although with increasing education, came a nostalgia for certain older Indian cultural ideas; these were recaptured and refined by Indian scholars and re-introduced to Indian society. A more-or-less successful syncretism had taken place. It was as though Shiva still reigned, yet in a highly philosophized form.

In a sense, the West had won. Convergence meant a meeting of cultures, but it was a merger made on unequal terms. The Indians realized – like the Japanese at about the same time – that if they were going to have a place in the modern world, they needed Western expertise and technology. Western political ideas introduced the idea of freedom – remote as it still is from every Indian's experience – and Western science gave the potential whereby this freedom might be achieved. There were many faults in British colonial policy; it was often highly paternalistic and even exploitative, but it did introduce ideas to subject peoples characterized by attitudes of passive resignation, the possibilities for change, and – in theory, at least – the opportunities for the realization of those possibilities in terms of new political horizons and a better standard of living.

4

Culturation: The neo-colonialism of the United States in Latin America

It could be argued that the world is not only becoming a smaller place, it is also becoming a similar place – a place of identikit culture. Sociologists speak of a process of convergence. They maintain that whether we are primitives or sophisticates, whether we are ideologically wedded to the East or West, we are all moving in the same general direction. All want to industrialize or at least experience the benefits of industrialization. It is argued that Third World transitional societies are experiencing the growth of scientism, and the extension of technical knowledge and education. They too are experiencing the breakdown of the old extended family system and its replacement by the mobile, nuclear family which is so adaptable to the needs of modern industrial societies. Gradual capital accumulation is making possible a greater variety of investment opportunities, and there is a developing value-consensus about the intrinsic worthwhileness of the modernizing process.

Of course, there are discordant voices which remonstrate about the runaway world, about green issues, especially pollution, over-population, and the profligate waste of scarce resources, etc. but by and large it has to be admitted that in advanced societies people are better housed, better fed and better medicated than ever before.

This claim that industrialization produces uniform, or near-uniform socioeconomic structures has been contested on the grounds that:

  i) definitionally, the term convergence is ambiguous. It is conceded that there are partial convergences, but it is argued that there is never likely to be complete convergence.
 ii) empirically, not all societies do conform to a basic pattern; that culturally and historically some societies are so different that it is difficult to foresee their eventual convergence.
iii) ideologically, many societies seem to be poles apart, such as those with Eastern (marxist) orientations and those dedicated to Western-style capitalism. But the evidence suggests that

43

free-market ideology is beginning to dominate both types of society.

iv) practically, Western forms of rational action are not necessarily the only – or best – modes of economic behaviour, and morally it is presumptuous to assume that the West knows what is best for others. But yet again, the adoption of some form of the Western model appears to have been empirically validated as the most 'direct' means to rapid economic progress (Scott 1979). This certainly seems to have been the case in Latin America.

In the inter-war years, Latin America had an unenviable reputation for economic deprivation and political instability. It was also infamous for the frequency and violence of its revolutions. The term 'revolution' can, of course, sometimes connote merely peripheral change, or it can mean the fundamental upheaval of the current social and political structure. In Latin America, most were usurpations of power, of one kind or another, conducted according to well-understood and generally acknowledged sets of rules. But in most cases the masses were *not* directly involved; this is what made the Mexican revolution early in the century such an exception. After 1911, Mexico underwent changes that were fundamental to the accepted social order. Few revolutions involved a basic re-structuring of society as, say, with the Cuban revolution of 1959. Much more common has been the violent or otherwise enforced overthrows of governments which – more often than not – have resulted in a continuation of the old system. It is estimated that since 1900 there have been seventy-six 'revolutions' in Latin America. Bolivia, for example, had no fewer than eight between 1920 and 1952. Most revolutions during the pre-Second World War period had little popular support – and little popular opposition either. Usually they were precipitated by movements in the allegiance of key groups in the armed forces, and had little effect on the structure of government or, indeed, on the condition of the governed (see Tomasek 1970: 344–5).

The whole issue of neo-colonialism goes back a long way, and has all sorts of anti-American implications. During the Second World War, many Latin American states became associated with Nazi espionage activity. Some authorities – quite mistakenly – saw certain states (Argentina for one) as favourite centres of German spy-rings (e.g. Khan 1978: 317), whereas the main German activity at this time was in Brazil (Hilton 1981: 4). There was undoubtedly quite a lot of pro-German feeling if not actual support in Latin America. This may be a reflection of the interests of the German minorities residing there, some of whom had sympathies with the aspirations of Latin America's totalitarian regimes, particularly in Argentina. On the other hand, it may be interpreted in part as a reaction against the increasing influence of the United States.

The war confirmed the United States' position as a world power. She had been able to mobilize enormous reserves of manpower and, even more impressively, her vast potential for the generation of wealth. And she was, as yet, unrivalled in her capacity for technological expertise and development. It is not entirely an overstatement to say that she was seen as the world's banker and the world's leader, and, in the aftermath of the war, as quite simply the richest nation on earth. To those lesser nations in Latin America, particularly the smaller states in Central America – what the United States parochially referred to as her 'own backyard' – her very presence was intimidating. They began to feel themselves to be part of an unacknowledged 'empire' where all political negotiations were subject to pressure, and where even diplomatic suggestions could assume the force of directives.

All this generated a powerful and worrying sense of economic dependency on the United States, coupled with a growing desire for real national autonomy. The motivating factor here was not primarily ideological. For these people the crucial division in the world was not between capitalism and communism but between the rich and the poor, between the developed and the undeveloped nations, between those who were technologically advanced and those who were not.

The real problem was one of living standards. In the six republics of Central America during the post-war period, a few hundred families owned most of the land. There was no thriving middle-class to speak of, and the majority of the populations lived in poverty and squalor. Probably something like half the people were illiterate, struggling to eke out a living in dessert (coffee and bananas) export economies. And none of this was helped by demographic factors. Taking a quite dispassionate view of population problems, we find that the death rate in Central America fell from 25.6 per thousand in 1930 to 9.9 in 1970 while the birth rate remained at over 40 per thousand – a figure that is much too high to sustain any real hope of economic betterment.

The key to the eradication of these differences between the rich and the poor was seen in development and industrialization. These would make it possible to 'achieve social equality, educational opportunity and minimum standards of health ... in short a ... welfare state' (Sigmund 1969: 11). But in their efforts to do this, many of these nations appeared unable or unwilling to follow the examples set by the United States, Japan, and their European counterparts, and chose instead the socialist model of development which they thought to be quicker and more suited to their needs. Capitalism was rejected for moral as well as economic reasons. For good or ill, the Soviet bloc model was preferred by many states, particularly Cuba, despite its inconsistencies and ambiguities. This was almost certainly because of the identification of capitalism with colonialism, and its purported preoccupation not with the welfare of the people or their economic advancement, but with exploitation and the maximization of profit. Yet it is interesting that in some states such as Brazil, the drive towards economic independence has come not so much from political leaders as from those with keen commercial interests.

Neo-colonialism, then, was seen as a mere extension of old-style colonialism. Foreign aid was regarded as just another form of oppression in so far as it functioned as a bribe to the underprivileged. It was simply another way of buying support – a stratagem for securing political allegiance, a source of raw materials and an outlet for manufactured goods. It was a method for ensuring that poorer nations stay dependent, a device for making certain that these dependencies remain compliant – a fact which seems evidenced by the support the United States received in the 1950s and 1960s in the United Nations from Central and South American countries.

It is important, though, to appreciate that by no means all Latin American nations took this stance. Indeed, some, in the formative years of United States' neo-colonialism, took a quite different position, either by welcoming United States' aid, as Guatemala did, or by assuming an almost belligerent and reactionary nationalism, as seen in Argentina and Paraguay. And even where marxism has been espoused it has been done with suitable modifications. It is doubtful whether marxian doctrines – if such they can be called – are ever adopted anywhere, they are always *adapted*. The 'pure milk of the word' is invariably too strong to be taken in its pristine form, it has to be adulterated or used selectively to suit local situations. And even so it may still only act as a 'midwife' to what is really an incipient nationalism (Gellner 1963).

Modern nationalism implies a transition from a traditional type society to one characterized by a rational-legal order. This means that the new order must come to terms with – and perhaps must actually accommodate – the traditional system of status differentiation and hereditary privilege. It must also reassess the ideological supports for such a system, and determine whether there is any way in which these can be modified to serve the interests of the new regime. The ambiguous nature of religious policies and practices are interesting in this respect. In some situations, religion has been positively de-emphasized and even rejected as an adjunct of national renewal. Cuba would be a case in point. In some states, there has been an endorsement of religion, while in others including Chile and Brazil, the situation has arisen whereby religion is differently regarded by opposing groups. Even the priesthood has been involved; some adhering to traditional forms, and others embracing liberation theologies which urge radical reform.

Leadership too in these developing nations is an intriguing issue. Some leaders, such as Stroesner in Paraguay, adopted a traditional stance in order to preserve the existing autocratic or oligarchic order, and were even hesitant about introducing technological know-how as a potentially subversive influence in society – though this hardly applied to military hardware. Others, notably Castro in Cuba, opted for a radical revision of existing society. They tried to destroy the influence of traditional status groups and wealth based upon privilege, and have been prepared to use force in order to create what they regard as a new and more equitable society. But the most common type has been those leaders who have tried to introduce reforms while retaining those institutions and practices which might still serve the new order. In this way, they have tried to utilize traditional loyalties as a basis for further social development.

In order to get a clearer idea of the nature of what is termed neo-colonialism, it might be illuminating to look at two typical societies in which similar responses were generated in quite different ways during the post-war period, Cuba and Bolivia.

Although United States' influence is felt throughout Latin America, it is the countries of Central America and the adjoining islands that feel it most. Not long after Cuba's liberation from Spain – something in which the United States played a significant role – its potentially coercive presence was evident. Limitations were imposed upon Cuba's right to conduct her own foreign relations, and the United States reserved the prerogative – where necessary – of intervening militarily in Cuba's affairs. United States' military occupation ended officially in 1902, but by what is known as the Platt Amendment, it was resumed from 1905 to 1909, again in 1912, 1917 and 1920 and only finally rescinded under Franklin Roosevelt's 'Good Neighbour' policy in 1934.

United States' influence was experienced at several levels. After the struggle for freedom in the late nineteenth century, the land was devastated, and United States' bankers bought up vast interests in iron, steel, and in nickel and manganese mines. Indeed many of the extractive industries were either owned or controlled by foreign capital. Before the First World War, United States' investors owned only one-third of the Cuban sugar industry, but by the 1920s this had increased to two-thirds. By 1956, United States owned 40 per cent of the sugar industry and her interests extended to 90 per cent of the electricity and telephone industries, and about 50 per cent of the railways (W. Mills 1960: 22–3). The country was ripe for revolution.

Fidel Castro had been a revolutionary since his early law-school days. In 1947 he took part in an abortive attempt to oust Rafael Trujillo, the Dominican dictator; the following year he participated in the rioting at Bogota. It was not until he had graduated at doctoral level and was a practising lawyer in Cuba that he first embarked seriously on his anti-Batista campaign that was eventually to dethrone the man he saw as an American-supported autocrat. This began with an unsuccessful attack on a military post in Santiago in 1953 for which he was imprisoned. He was freed after two years and spent another two years, mainly in Mexico, preparing for further revolutionary activity. In 1956 he led a small band of guerrillas to Cuba and fomented what was to become a civil war. In this he earned an impressive reputation as a shrewd and courageous leader, and finally became head of a new government in 1959.

The Cuban problem was just another manifestation of the Latin American problem generally. It has been cogently argued that the factors which precipitated the Cuban revolution, and which still contribute to the lasting appeal of fidelismo are really factors which are indigenous to the hemisphere, namely, the historic political instability of Cuba, the contrasts in wealth and influence between metropolitan Havana and the remainder of the island, the socioeconomic changes in Cuba, and – particularly – the problems involved in Cuba's relations with the United States (Blanksten 1962: 113–36).

Since 1901 – really the beginning of its national career, Cuba has had its fair share of revolutions, six in all – with the odd coup thrown in for good measure. Furthermore it experienced the phenomenon of recurrent dictatorship, partly as a legacy of Spanish autocracy (Cuba had a longer history of authoritarian – even repressive – Spanish rule than elsewhere in Hispanic America) and partly because it was believed that only strong authoritarian government would work in the situation. Thus in some states that designated themselves 'republics', the same authoritarian strain is still evident and often has a potent charismatic dimension.

Needless to say, such regimes are characterized by a powerful military presence, and have not been reluctant to liquidate their enemies and otherwise undesirable elements. In this they typically repeat the crimes of their former enemies. In Cuba for example, it is estimated that Castro's firing squads executed 557 men in the early months of the new government, most of them junior officers and NCOs who were purported to have been Batista's own corps of executioners.

In Latin America generally there has been a marked trend towards urbanization, no less so in Cuba. The metropolitan areas, especially Havana, have become centres of Westernized culture, of industrial and commercial development, and – more subtly – as the breeding grounds of an increasingly secularized consciousness. Traditionally, the urban areas had been associated with elite groups and, therefore, centres of political power. This resulted in a rift between the urban population and the more 'backward' inhabitants of the rural areas –

the latter comprising some 47 per cent of the total population – from whence Castro drew his initial support. His populistic appeal gave the revolutionaries an agrarian power base which proved very effective against the reactionary forces in Havana.

Prior to 1959, the most obvious and most lucrative form of American intrusion was the tourist industry. Havana began to supersede Miami as *the* place to go for fun-loving visitors seeking pleasure in the city's colourful night-life. The luxury hotels, night-clubs and gambling casinos – often Mafia controlled – appeared to the Cubans as havens for extravagantly wealthy Yanquis. For the revolutionaries this was just one – albeit the most ostentatious – manifestation of United States' cultural and economic pressure. Foreign money and the commercialization of Cuban life generally were also suspected of generating much of the graft and corruption in high places. It was reaction to these factors that undoubtedly precipitated the nationalization and expropriation of United States' business interests in 1960, although the Americans did retain their naval base at Guantanamo Bay.

Reaction could also be seen in Cuba's selective rejection of Western aid and her increasing willingness to enter into trade and other economic agreements with the Eastern bloc, particularly the Soviet Union. This generated even further United States' hostility, especially when these agreements involved arms deals for all kinds of sophisticated weaponry. Cuba's allegiance to the Soviet Union was 'bought' for about half a billion dollars a year, but by the 1980s there had to be a serious reappraisal of these arrangements as the annual debt had risen to $12 million a day (Johnson 1983: 684).

It is little wonder that the United States found Cuba's position both politically and militarily unacceptable, and initiated plans to undermine the Castro regime. President John Kennedy inherited a scheme to destabilize the Cuban government by a military action – carried out largely by a brigade of Cuban emigrés – which became known as the Bay of Pigs. It was launched from Guatemala on 10 April 1961 and five days later part of Castro's air force was destroyed by an American strike force. But the land forces retired after two days' fighting and those who survived were taken captive by the Cubans. It was a plan that had been agreed at the highest levels and yet it was really a failure from the beginning. So what went wrong?

In the first place it was hardly a covert operation; so there was no element of surprise. It was all well known weeks in advance, and any denial on the part of United States' authorities would have been regarded as ridiculously implausible. Second, it was neither quite a military nor a political operation. If it had been left to the United States military, it is difficult to see how it could have failed. But it was carried out by 'trained' amateurs who were no match for the superior

Cubans fighting on their own soil. Perhaps most of all it was a failure of intelligence about Cuban strength, and certainly an underestimation of their determination to defend the revolution. Needless to say, the repercussions were enormous, and did nothing to enhance the United States' reputation abroad. Neither did it endear the Americans to the Cubans who were, of course, more distrustful than ever of the 'giant' on their doorstep.

This distrust was even further confirmed – if confirmation were needed – by the additional failure of Operation Mongoose in 1962, an attempt to subvert the Cuban regime by anti-Castro infiltration rather than direct military attack. In 1963 there were more attempts at sabotage and infiltration in order to generate unrest and hoped-for defections among Cubans, but again without any real success. Interspersed with all this were various bizarre plots to kill Castro himself, involving poison pills, exploding skin-diving equipment, and even Mafia hit-men. Nothing came of any of these clumsy CIA operations which again were authorized at the highest level (Rositzke 1977: 174–8; 197–8). The Cubans were able to use these 'incidents' for effective propaganda purposes to quieten the few dissident voices in their own ranks, and further unify the people.

The Cuban situation *vis-à-vis* the United States can be interestingly compared with that of Bolivia. On the eve of the 1959 revolution the Cuban standard of living expressed in terms of the Cuban Gross National Product per capita was the *third* highest in Latin America ($454). Only Argentina ($688) and Venezuela, rich from oil exports ($457), were higher. Bolivia, on the other hand, was third from the bottom of the 'league' with only $109 per capita, and therefore a prime example of a nation that was particularly dependent on the United States.

In 1952, Bolivia was

> the first South American republic with a large Indian population to undergo the upheaval of a revolution from which there was no return. The revolt was directed not only against the previous government but against the institutions that made that government possible.
>
> (Patch 1960: 108–37; 157–68)

At this time, some 54 per cent of the population was Indian. Although the difference between whites (*blancos*) and the Indians was already being eroded by mixed marriage etc., social distinctions were still observed. About 60 per cent of the population was 'pre-literate', and the numerous languages and dialects did much to inhibit ease of communications, as did also the distribution of a relatively small population over a land area as large as Spain and France combined.

The land tenure patterns and stratification system endorsed by traditional religious norms had left the nation relatively undisturbed until a war with Paraguay between 1932 and 1935 which ended disastrously for Bolivia. The significant – if incidental – result for post-war development was that Indians had been recruited for the war in appreciable numbers and had fought alongside whites on a superficially equal basis. Unsurprisingly, this generated rising expectations in the 'native' population which began to upset the socioeconomic equilibrium of the state.

Two main political forces were evident during this period. Using Mosca's terminology, there were the 'old forces' of successive governments which tried to pacify unrest by introducing more liberal legislation, and the 'insurgent new forces' represented by the MNR (Moviemiento Nacionalista Revolucionario) which had pronounced marxist leanings (Mosca 1939). The MNR was formed mainly by left-wing intellectuals in 1940, and was given some recognition when the government of the day, which had declared for the Allies, was ousted in a military coup in 1943. The United States denounced the coup as Nazi-inspired and her example was followed by all the Latin American States except Argentina. Bolivia was 're-instated' when – or because – MNR members were dismissed from the government. This provoked considerable left-wing reaction, and in 1946 there was armed insurrection during which the military President, Gualberto Villaroel, was hanged in the street. But MNR's time was not yet. Bolivia continued to be ruled by a series of somewhat indecisive right-wing governments until the revolution of 1952. This was only accomplished after considerable in-fighting in which it is estimated that about 3,000 people were killed.

The revolutionary government nationalized the tin mines and several other corporations, but at first they did little more than talk about agrarian reform. The groundswell of discontentment from the mainly Indian population was such that a plan for the total redistribution of the land was introduced to avert the near-certainty of civil war. Inevitably, this was contested by the landlords who wanted to retain a feudal-type system of tenure. The ensuing conflict with the syndicates of Indian farmers (*campesinos*) resulted in victory for the Indians who were supported in their aspirations by the more considered approach of the MNR. The farmers' initial demand was for small parcels of land for each family, but this would have led to small-scale subsistence farming with little or no marketable surplus. A more rational solution prevailed in theory – but not entirely in practice. The estates (*latifundia*) of the former landlords (*patrones*) were taken over in their entirety, including machinery, vehicles and houses, and worked by the syndicates.

The MNR was by no means united on all these issues. It too had its divisions and factions: military supporters, conservatives, liberals and especially left-wing (often university) intellectuals. And nothing divided them more than the perennial problem of land reform and the future status of the Indian community. An important decree of 1953 reaffirmed the virtues of agricultural enterprise, and stipulated that wages should be paid in cash, and that workers should have the rights of collective bargaining. Restitution of lands was guaranteed – particularly where lands had originally been confiscated from the Indian population – and holdings were organized in terms of their agronomically assessed potential. But the outcome of all this well-intentioned legislation was a tenure system which ensured the multiplication of small subsistence plots (*minifundia*) as a measure for appeasing large numbers of farmers, and it resulted in a system of agricultural production which still vitiates Bolivia's economy. Subsistence farming provided little surplus to feed the cities, and virtually nothing for export. The subsequent serious food shortages were only relieved by United States' aid and encouragement.

The one export on which Bolivia did rely to maintain a viable economy was tin. In fact metals – tungsten, antimony, gold and principally tin – accounted for 95 per cent of all Bolivian exports. But here again there were difficulties – both internal and external – which were largely outside the state's control. In 1951, the price of tin became highly inflated because of demands stemming from the Korean War, and the United States announced that she would not pay such exorbitant prices, and suspended purchases. The situation was exacerbated by the fact that there was a marked decline in the high-grade deposits in the Bolivian mines which also contributed to a slump in demand. During the buoyant years, the industry had become overmanned, and the necessary cutbacks naturally led to labour problems. By 1959 the production costs of Bolivian tin were about 35 cents a pound above world prices. Manufacturing itself made a very small contribution to the national income both in absolute terms and in comparison with other Latin American states. There was a serious shortage of skilled labour and raw materials – a problem greatly aggravated by high transport costs due to the difficulties of the terrain and Bolivia's land-locked location. This, plus the difficulties in the agricultural and mining industries, made Bolivia's economic future look very uncertain.

In this seemingly intractable situation, reliance on outside help became the most obvious way out. Economic aid programmes were initiated by the United States. Between 1953 and 1959 she supplied economic and technical assistance to the tune of $124 million. This represents an increase from $1.5 million in 1953 to $22.7 million in 1959 exclusive of loans – a clear indication of the United States' growing interest in Bolivia. These sums do not include export–import bank loans of $11 million over the same period, nor does it take account of $4 million from the Development Loan Fund and a $15 million stabilization loan from the International Monetary Fund and the United States' Treasury. And this is all quite apart from United Nations' assistance which had contributed over half a million dollars to survey and resettlement schemes for the Santa Cruz area alone.

In 1960, rumours were abroad – perhaps quite unfounded – that Bolivia was contemplating the establishment of diplomatic relations with the Soviet Union and the United Arab Republic and was hoping to negotiate a loan of $70 million from the Soviet Union to finance mutually satisfactory trade arrangements. Perhaps this was all simply a mild flirtation to rekindle or strengthen the interests of her current lover. Whatever the reason, in 1960 Bolivia received $2.7 million from the United States to research and possibly develop her oil-producing potential. Bolivia's benefactor had long since decided that as a marxist rather than a communist state, Bolivia could merit this kind of help.

None of this meant that the United States no longer wished to subvert the Bolivian regime. The CIA carried out all kinds of clandestine operations in Bolivia especially in relation to the early guerrilla activities of Che Guevara who was free from territorial commitments and had a particular relationship with this very discontented society. Yet in Bolivia he had to modify his own doctrine that people must see the futility of fighting for social goals within a framework of civil debate. Cuban revolutionary success was not exportable everywhere; other states obviously had to find their own answers to the problems of poverty and deprivation.

The socialism of 'new' nations, whether it is operationalized through an autocratic authority as in Cuba or through a more conventional government apparatus as in Bolivia, is largely sustained by anti-foreign attitudes. Its main imperatives are a desire for social equality – however highly qualified – and an urge towards rapid economic development. Its appropriation of marxist doctrine is judiciously selective; the ideology is important but it must necessarily be adapted to specific situations. It is often socialism ordered by an elite; popular discussion is normally allowed, but critical decisions of a politicoeconomic nature are normally the province of a carefully insulated – possibly military – executive. It is also a socialism which is usually infused with a powerful sense of nationalism. Thus it often welcomes outside aid, but defends its dependence by insisting that it must be aid without strings. Furthermore, it is frequently a form of socialism that de-emphasizes – perhaps even actually rejects – marxist materialism, and favours instead an essentially humanistic approach (Sigmund 1969: 17), seeking some kind of *rapprochement* with religious institutions rather than an outright rejection of their ideas. This may not be because it endorses their philosophies or practices, but because it knows that it must come to terms with religious systems if only out of self-interested expediency.

The anti-imperialist stance of so many Latin American states is perfectly understandable in the light of the exploitative tendencies evinced by their rich protectors. A partisan, C. Wright Mills, writing in 1960, noted how out of the $31 billion given in aid by the United States since the Second World War only $625 million went to Latin America, less in fact, than had gone to the Philippines alone. And its loans had been swallowed up by inflation-beset economies which vainly try to stay competitive while also maintaining high military expenditure (W. Mills 1960: 174–5). Counterbalancing these anti-American tendencies are programmes of political co-operation through the Organization of American States; of military alliance; and of economic assistance. But so much of this was either overtly or covertly directed towards the cause of anti-communism.

Few people give something for nothing, and this is certainly the case with world power aid whether it is from the East or the West. The recipients, on the other hand, regard the aid with considerable ambivalence; they are both grateful and resentful, they need all the help they can get, but are naturally unwilling to mortgage their futures for a temporary alleviation of their immediate problems.

5

Reconstitutionalization:
The Macedonian Empire
of Alexander the Great

In conquest situations, there are – broadly speaking – two positions that can be taken by the dominant power. It can adopt a relaxed but paternalistic stance, allowing the conquered to carry on much the same as before but with added exactions in terms of money, goods and manpower – roughly the policy adopted by the Persian Empire in the fifth and fourth centuries BC (the Classical Period); or it can try to impose new constitutions on unwilling states – with varying degrees of success – which was the position of the Macedonian Empire which took over from Persia in the fourth century BC.

The origins of the Macedonians are largely unknown. The southward migrations of these peoples were probably well underway by the seventh century BC, and their settlement in what is now northern Greece and southern Yugoslavia had taken place by the next century. The literary evidence for these early years is sparse, but what there is seems to accord with archaeological opinion that the Macedonian tribes ousted the indigenous peoples of the area and established them-selves at Aegae near the Thermaic Gulf where they coalesced into an identifiable nation. Scholarship has long been divided on the question of whether these people were really Greeks – certainly the Greeks at the time were reluctant to give them status as true Hellenes. The Macedonian language has not survived in any extant text, but their personal and place names, and the names of their gods strongly suggest a Greek dialect. Scholars are now more or less agreed that they were one group of many Dorian tribes that had made their way into Greece from the Balkans in successive waves probably from as early as the eleventh century BC. By the fifth century we can definitely think of Macedonia as a kingdom. The remarkable finds at Vergina in 1976, which centre on what is almost certainly the tomb of Phillip II (father of Alexander the Great), testify to its magnificence and importance by the following century.

The Macedonians appeared somewhat archaic to the Greeks who by this time had largely abandoned monarchical systems. Instead they had developed a system of *poleis* or city-states where – in many states at least – their social and political organization reflected an increasing desire for more participatory government. The contacts between the two peoples were rather tentative and spasmodic until the late sixth century, at which point the Macedonians came into indirect conflict with the Greeks. The Macedonian king, Amyntas, had become a vassal of Darius the Great of Persia, and subsequently, his son, also an Alexander, was obliged – or forced – to join Darius' successor, Xerxes, in his campaign against the Greeks in the early fifth century. Interestingly, we find that later this same king applied to participate in the Olympic Games by claiming that he was connected with an early esteemed dynasty of Argos. And it is a symptom of the uneasy relations between the Greeks and the Macedonians that some Greeks tried to exclude him as a barbarian (technically a non-Greek-speaking foreigner). He won his case with some difficulty, but his claim to 'genuine' Greek lineage was suspected of being a myth that was conveniently contrived for the purpose.

It is to Alexander that tradition ascribes an important innovation in Macedonian military organization. Previously, the Macedonian forces had consisted mainly of cavalry drawn from members of the leading families. Alexander extended the military franchise by incorporating trained companies of infantry (*pezhetairoi*) drawn from the lower orders of society. This effectively broadened the basis of the military system and had important status implications for Macedonian society generally. It is doubtful, though, whether this was done in the interests of democratization. Rather it can be seen as a function of the fratricidal wars that increasingly plagued the Royal House, and the unending campaigning that took place against either alien or non-compliant peoples on the borders.

As far as we know, the social and political institutions, and particularly the general principles of military organization of the Macedonians of the fourth century had been in being for some time. Apparently all Macedonian land was deemed to be the property of the king. Some was retained for the use of the royal family, and much was distributed to the aristocracy who, as supporters, were regarded as the 'companions' of the king. In return for estates and allotments of land, these men were under an obligation to render military service when required – and from all accounts this was pretty often. The system seems to have worked rather like that of medieval Europe where nobles held land as fiefs from the king in return for military duties, except that in Macedonia the companions (*hetairoi*) seem to have had greater social equality and therefore greater accessibility to the monarch, especially when it came to decisions about affairs of state.

The majority of the people, as in all peasant societies, were farmers,

artisans, etc., who worked the land as free labourers, and who presumably paid their dues – ostensibly for protection – in the form of
service and produce. What happened to the poor and the dispossessed
indigenes is anybody's guess; their status was probably only one rung
above that of slaves. They lived out their lives in some kind of bondage,
and worked on roads, in mines, and performed other menial – often
unpleasant – but necessary tasks for the state.

The Macedonians did their best to modify the impression of their
more civilized neighbours by conforming more and more to Greek
standards. They were great admirers of Hellenistic culture, and many
of their kings, in particular, adopted ideas and practices which they
felt would make them more acceptable to those whom they liked to
think of as distant cousins. Some inaugurated games and festivals, and
invited artists and poets, including the elderly Euripides, to the still
rather unsophisticated Macedonian court. But it remained difficult
to dispel entirely the barbarian image, especially when the monarchy
itself was marked with violent and bloody dynastic struggles.

Macedonian instability was exacerbated by threats and incursions
from tribes on the borders, and sometimes the Macedonians were
forced to call on the Greeks for military assistance. This hardly worried
them because internecine warfare was a favourite preoccupation of the
Greeks. Once spring – the campaigning season – arrived, armies were
on the march to somewhere or other. There was always a dispute here
or a territorial issue to be resolved there. Indeed, it was not unknown for
reasons to be invented, often on the basis of some assumed or mythic
incident or insult, in order to justify invasion of another's territory.
And this was characteristic not only of avowedly militaristic states
such as Sparta, but also of subtly expansionistic states such as Athens.
By the mid-fourth century, the more powerful Greek states had virtually
fought themselves to a standstill. Warfare, particularly between the two
most aggressive states, Sparta and Thebes, had not only left the country
exhausted, it had also left it with a dangerous power vacuum. No one
was strong enough to lead. So the way was obviously open for any
enterprising would-be dynast who had sufficient military muscle to
impose his will on the others.

At just this time, family feuding among the Macedonian nobility had
come to a head, and in 359 BC, the throne was seized by Philip – a man
bent on conquest. From the beginning he seems to have been intent
on controlling the entire disunited Greek world. Who better, therefore,
to lead this vigorous new nation against these admired but impotent
squabbling states of the south? Philip was a man who combined
resolute energy with calculated cunning; a leader who had learned
his trade well. He had enjoyed a Greek education; he had studied the
speeches of Isocrates who had tried to muster enthusiasm for a united

campaign against Persia; and, what is more, he had learned much of the art of warfare while a hostage years earlier in Thebes.

Philip was well aware that the first essential for success was not so much military strength as military expertise and unquestioning loyalty, so he created a standing army of professional soldiers from the Macedonian peasantry. His inspiration was the late Epaminondas, the Theban general, who had crushed the previously invincible Spartan army at Leuctra in 371 BC. Greek warfare had always been a cumbersome affair. It consisted mainly of opposing lines of heavily armed infantry (*hoplites*) of varying depth 'leaning' on one another until one line broke. All this was aided and abetted by the peripheral services of light-armed skirmishers and cavalry. It was obviously time for a change. Philip adopted and adapted the deep phalanx formations of the Thebans, arming his troops with even longer spears (*sarissas*) and training them in new and innovative methods of attack. The phalanxes presented an echeloned 'hedgehog' effect which the enemy found extremely difficult to counter or disperse. This, combined with strong formations of highly disciplined cavalry working to carefully pre-arranged plans, gave the Macedonians an edge over any of the other Greek states.

After securing his position at his capital Pella by a few judicious assassinations, Philip launched his model army first against the unmanageable hill tribes on his borders and then against his neighbours, the Thessalians. This had the effect of subduing a potential menace and giving his troops some necessary experience; it also increased the resevoir of manpower he needed for his further expansionist policies in the future. His campaigns in the north brought him into inevitable conflict with the Greeks themselves who feared for their gold supplies from Thrace and their corn supplies from the Black Sea.

Philip was now in a delicate situation. He wanted to command the whole of Greece, and could probably have done so by force alone, but he did not want to alienate the rest of Greece unnecessarily. He needed their co-operation to further his long-term ambitions. So by a mixture of guile and diplomacy he made further encroachments into central Greece. His main problem was Athens. He had a grudging respect for her history and traditions, but also a growing impatience with her imperial arrogance which could no longer be supported with military power. Furthermore, there was the unquenchable eloquence of Athens' most famous orator, Demosthenes, who did his best to warn the Greeks about the political intentions of this barbarian upstart. He encouraged the Athenians to unite against the enemy; but his 'Philippics' failed to stir them and their allies to mount any effective resistance. The Athenians voted all kinds of patriotic resolutions but were either too weak or too listless to carry them out.

An uneasy *modus vivendi* was arrived at, but it couldn't last. Philip saw an opportunity to gain an advantage at relatively little cost by intervening in a sacred war which had been going on and off for years in central Greece. Philip and his Thessalian allies routed a Phocian army, slaughtering some 6,000 as they fled to the sea in the hope of being rescued by friendly Athenian triremes. By posing as a defender of Apollo, Philip had led a 'crusade' against the sacrilegious Phocians, thereby justifying further conquest, yet also alerting the rest of Greece as to his intentions. At last the Athenians woke up to the danger, and united with others to defend themselves against the Macedonians, but were hopelessly defeated at the battle of Chaeronea in 338 BC.

Only two years later, Philip was assassinated, possibly at the instigation of his wife, Olympias, just as his plans for a Persian expedition were about to mature. The assassins themselves were quickly and conveniently dispatched – so the true nature of the plot was never revealed. It was now left to his gifted and, arguably, pathological offspring, Alexander – who may also have been implicated – to put his grand design into effect.

Barely 20 when he came to the throne, Alexander determined to make an immediate impression upon the Greek world. He set out to subdue the ever-recalcitrant hill tribes and then turned south to enlist the cities of Greece itself. A league of co-operative states was formed with Macedon as the dominant partner, but it was a precarious alliance. Some states became restive, and Alexander had to apply the pressure. Athens he treated with comparative leniency, but Thebes which he regarded with deep suspicion as a treacherous 'medizing' (i.e. Persian-aiding) state he attacked with almost unparalleled ferocity. Almost the entire city was razed to the ground and those who were not massacred – mainly women and children – were enslaved. In a manner characteristic of arbitrary despots, he spared some temples and – so it is said – the house of the long-dead poet, Pindar, whose work he so admired.

It was an outright military victory but only a qualified political success. The traditional enemies of Thebes, the cities of Orchomenos, Plataea, Thespiae and Phocis had actually joined in the slaughter in which some 6,000 people perished and another 30,000 were sold into slavery. Other cities were suitably cowed into co-operation; in Arcadia they actually condemned to death those who even suggested giving aid to Thebes. The only notable exception appears to have been Sparta which retained a predictable aloofness. The whole sorry affair did little to win friends and influence people. By this action, Alexander merely generated an abject fear of reprisal. A deep-seated resentment developed among the Greeks which was to show itself time and again while he was on his campaign in Persia.

In 334 BC, after leaving garrisons at key centres in Greece, Alexander took a modest army of possibly 40,000 men across the Hellespont (Dardanelles) and won an early victory on the river Granicus – not far from the site of ancient Troy. He then led his forces through Asia Minor and either received or forced the surrender of the cities along the coast which owed nominal allegiance to the Great King Darius. At Gordium he cut through, rather than unfastened, the famous knot, and the oracle appropriately predicted that he would win an empire.

By this time, the Persians were becoming thoroughly alarmed. A vast but unwieldly force including many Greek mercenaries was mustered to meet the Macedonians at Issus in Syria (333 BC) but it was completely routed. The captives included the Great King's wife and mother, and Darius offered peace terms which included his Western territories plus a huge ransom, but these were contemptuously refused. Alexander's strategy was to cut off the Western *satrapies* (administrative districts) of the Great King's empire before driving into the Persian heartland itself. He moved south, and on his way received homage from the coastal towns of Syria and the Lebanon. Here, some proved to be obstinate. Tyre, in particular, a seemingly impregnable island state, he besieged determinedly by building a mole from the mainland to the island. Again, a kind of calculated cruelty took over. The city had taken seven months to subdue; it had delayed his programme; it was an affront to his invincibility; *ergo*, it must be taught a lesson. When the city fell, his troops – equally frustrated by such a long siege – killed everything in sight. A similar massacre took place at Gaza where resistance held Alexander up for another two months. This time – as reported by the historian Quintus Curtius (Burn 1973: 100) – Alexander personally executed the acting governor, Batis, by lashing his body to his chariot and dragging it round the walls in imitation of his hero, Achilles, in the legendary battle of Troy.

Then came a deliberate diversion to Egypt – but this presented no problem. Alexander was simply received as a new version of the god-king. This was 'confirmed' by his visit to the oracle of Amon at the Siwa oasis, where it is said his divine status was reaffirmed. He could now afford to be magnanimous, and he founded the city of Alexandria – only one of the many to bear that name – and in 331 BC swept on towards Babylon and defeated another huge army of Darius at Gaugamela in northern Mesopotamia. This time the Great king fled to some of his furthermost territories in the remote north-east of his empire where he was eventually murdered by his own officers. The way was now open to the royal treasury at Susa and the royal cities of Persepolis and Ecbatana with their almost unimaginable wealth. Both were looted, and during a drunken orgy at Persepolis, possibly in revenge for the Persian sack of the Athenian Acropolis some 150 years before, Alexander instigated or indirectly caused the burning of the magnificent royal palaces – an act of vandalism which history has not yet excused.

The Macedonian soldiers really believed that they had arrived. They had conquered the greatest empire the world had ever seen; they thought that they could now take their ease and enjoy the fruits of their labour. But Alexander was restless. He spent little time in organizing his hastily won empire. The Persian *satrapies* and provinces were allowed to continue under their existing governors, but with the oversight of Macedonian financial and military supervisors. These were just temporary arrangements. Alexander then pressed on eastwards. Ever curious, and always eager for conquest, he led his victorious army out of Persia into the remotest parts of Asia; to Bactria, to Turkestan, and then southwards to the Punjab in India, establishing settlements and organizing military outposts which would one day become tiny incongruous pockets of Greek culture.

By this time, his troops had had enough. They had braved great dangers and fought uncomplainingly for their insatiable commander – until now. Their march had taken them 11,000 miles to what seemed to be the edge of the world, and they refused to go any further. Alexander remonstrated ineffectively with them, sulked, and eventually gave in. The army turned back, and the return journey through the inhospitable deserts of Baluchistan was a nightmare – much worse than anything they had previously experienced. They arrived back in Susa in the spring of 324 BC after enduring enormous privations. The victorious expedition had lasted just six years and had taken a terrible toll, as much from the conditions as from the battles themselves.

It was now a time of reckoning. Those officials that had been left in charge while Alexander was away and were judged guilty of neglect or abuse of their duties were summarily executed, as were also those that were believed to be implicated in plots against the king's life. This was extended to faithful retainers and one-time generals, and eventually to some who dared to question the king's authority. When confronted with complaints from some Median nobles, for instance, about the behaviour of certain Macedonian generals, Alexander took a particularly grave view of the accusations. Rape and sacrilege amounted to more than mere misconduct; they were acts of gross insubordination. The generals themselves did not take the matter that seriously, but the king had them imprisoned and executed, together with 600 of their men.

Intrigue became rife when Alexander made plans to create a Persian–Greek Empire by a series of enforced marriages which he believed would cement relations between the previously alien cultures. Noble or expedient as the intention was, it did not endear him to his own troops. Still less appealing was his adoption of Persian style dress and manners, and his insistence that erstwhile friends should now prostrate themselves before him as though he were divine (*proskynesis*) – an act which they found intolerably servile. Those who had formally been companions now found themselves to be mere subjects – indeed, unwilling devotees of a resuscitated cult, that of Alexander the god.

The government of so vast an empire was no easy matter. The entire campaign of conquest had been such an unrelenting and hurried affair that all sorts of *ad hoc* provisions had to be made. But, in general, these arrangements were very different for most of the Greek states, whether on the mainland or in Asia Minor, than they were for the territories of the one-time Persian Empire.

The pattern had been set by Philip after the defeat of the Greek coalition at the battle of Chaeronea. At last, the Macedonians were able to dictate their own terms, and were now free to intervene in Greek affairs any time they wished. The states were allowed to maintain their traditional autonomy as long as they gave all necessary co-operation to their Macedonian overlords. Conditions were agreed with Philip, and the Corinthian League – a Macedonian hegemony – was formed. In broad terms, Philip confirmed their existing constitutions, but he undoubtedly favoured and encouraged oligarchic regimes.

At Alexander's accession, a number of states decided to express their disaffection with Macedonian hegemony by expelling their Macedonian garrisons, moves which the young king countered decisively with an effective amalgam of persuasion and coercion. The work of the League was consolidated and plans for the Persian expedition were laid. Participation in the campaign was mandatory for all members of the League, and the size and cost of the states' respective contributions to the campaign were assessed on the understanding that their powers were carefully circumscribed. There was to be no internal dissension. Executions were totally prohibited – unless, presumably, they were sanctioned by higher authority – and there was a ban on any revolutionary measures such as redistribution of land and the cancellation of debts, or the freeing of slaves.

Once the expedition was under way, Alexander found it both expedient and ideologically more acceptable to favour democracies, especially in the newly liberated Greek cities of Asia Minor. Except that now everything was all going to be done on command. The Persians had encouraged oligarchies and tyrannies in these states, which therefore almost obliged the Macedonians to reverse the order. It paid to identify liberation with democracy.

With successive victories, Alexander increasingly came to see himself as the arbiter of fortunes. The cities would be whatever Alexander wanted them to be. On the island of Chios, for example, he insisted on the return of the exiles, contrary – apparently – to popular wishes, and commanded the imposition of a new legal constitution which he decided personally to scrutinize. He saw fit to resort to the authority of the League only when it suited him.

> As far as we can tell, the synedrion [the council of the League] played no part in the regulation of the Aegean islands. Alexander acted autocratically and issued orders without reference to any other authority . . . Macedonian suzerainty was a mockery of any concept of Greek autonomy.
>
> (Bosworth 1988: 194 and 197)

War, of course, requires quick decision-making, but legislation demands careful reflection and considered judgements. Alexander made wide-ranging political changes and sometimes allowed revolutionary innovations which often violated both the spirit and the letter of the League's constitution. The League, *per se*, could only act when the council was convened, yet in many instances Alexander acted independently – the League was never actually invoked. The basis of his settlement with the League was far removed from the concept of first among equals – it was really a form of faintly disguised military repression.

The Greek cities of Asia Minor were in a particularly anomalous position. They were going to be liberated whether they liked it or not. Most of them welcomed the prospect of freedom from Persian domination, but they came to realize that they might be exchanging one kind of unfreedom for another – and one that really wasn't that different. If cities failed to surrender they suffered the predictable fate of sack and enslavement. And even if they did, though without the appropriate alacrity, they might be fortunate to escape without actual slaughter. Admittedly, Alexander was in a difficult situation here. He could hardly ill-treat those he had ostensibly come to save; on the other hand, his dignity could not endure the humiliation of fraternal indifference or ingratitude. Liberated they might be, they were still the spoils of conquest, and were still subject to tributary status. They might be fellow Greeks, but they were still going to be governed by Macedonians. Their futures were within the gift of the king. Alexander alone would decide on the degree of their autonomy; only he would judge the nature of their constitutions, and particularly how much they would have to contribute to his exchequer. And he had expensive military tastes. These exactions were meant to be systematic and rationally administered, but were, in fact, often quite arbitrarily assessed. For instance, Ilium (Troy) was exempted altogether and actually given new buildings. Sentiment prevailed here in view of the city's legendary historical associations. In some favoured cities, the potential tribute might be diverted for the increased adornment of the temples, as at Ephesus, but others, especially if in any way tainted with medism were fortunate if they were not reduced to penury.

In some cases, Alexander made populist appeals to the *demoi* of the cities. Oligarchy was not usually that popular among the poorer citizens, and in order to win support, he liked to make a direct appeal to the masses to encourage them to oust and even execute the oligarchs, and settle for a more democratic – Macedonian approved – form of government. How much actual difference such a change of government made to ordinary people is difficult to guess, especially where they were really only exchanging one kind of *de facto* overlordship for another – Persian for Macedonian. If there was remission from tribute – as an inducement – it had an obvious and immediate appeal, but the operational laws of the community would probably not alter that much. Perhaps – as in our our time – people are primarily interested in the 'goodies', not in the niceties of particular constitutional arrangements. A city might be treated with extreme generosity, yet it could lose its privileged status any time – this was the prerogative of the conqueror. In the case of Aspendus, Alexander imposed a significant but not entirely unreasonable levy of fifty talents to defray some of the expense of maintaining his forces. The city agreed, but then decided to renege, whereupon Alexander applied a little intimidation. The city gave in, but he chose to double the impost and added an annual tribute in the bargain. Petty states soon learned not to play games with Alexander.

Alexander was quite instrumental in all this. He made his arrangements to suit the occasion – even if this was sometimes subject to whims and fancies. His principal aims were to win allies, raise funds and further his military ambitions. Everything conduced to this end. What he could not do by favour, he did by force. By and large, his actions were popular with the Greek cities. They welcomed liberation and voted him honours, but they knew that freedom was precarious; he could revoke it whenever he pleased. Perhaps it is significant that when he left the Aegean region with his main forces, the garrisons in the coastal area took two years to put down the Persian counter-offensive there. One suspects that the Persians could not have sustained their offensive for so long without a little support from their erstwhile subjects, who were now theoretically Alexander's new-found friends.

The Macedonian administration of previously Persian-held territories in the East was another matter altogether. The only precedents were those of the Persian administration itself. Alexander, therefore, took over the patterns that had already been set, and in the preliminary stages of his campaign, installed his own men in place of the displaced Persian *satraps* (military governors). Their tasks were mainly of a military nature. They took charge of the garrisons; and their subordinates were sometimes appointed to look after matters of finance and organization.

This system had certain obvious drawbacks. It pre-supposed a large number of competent Macedonian commanders who were both able enough and dispensible enough to remain in the newly conquered territories while Alexander and the army moved on to further fields. It further pre-supposed that the king had enough high-grade troops to leave with them. In each case, they would constitute a trusted core of the *satrapal* army, the rest being made up of hired mercenaries – an arrangement made possible by the enormous revenues that were being amassed with each successive conquest. Another disadvantage to this system was its relative inflexibility. With troops concentrated in 'fixed' areas, emergencies such as possible tribal attacks and insurrections could not always be quickly and decisively countered.

A more fluid arrangement was obviously called for. So Alexander decided to leave tried and competent *satraps* in post, providing they took the appropriate oaths of loyalty. But as a back-up, there would be Macedonians not too far away. In practice, this arrangement was rather uneven. Only in certain areas were there the necessary heavy concentrations of troops that could be deployed as the occasion demanded. This worked well in the case of Caria where the government was delegated to a local princess, Ada, who had ruled as *satrap* for four years. She surrendered herself and her territory to Alexander, and subsequently 'adopted' him as a son, no doubt for dynastic reasons. But as a necessary expedient Alexander left a most experienced general, Ptolemy – one of his eventual successors – with an army of over 3,000 men to ensure that his back was nicely protected. Ptolemy acted in a semi-independent capacity; his military brief was such that he could operate, if required, in more than one province.

In short, Alexander took an entirely pragmatic attitude to matters of administration. Different situations demanded different solutions. He ratified some men in office, and dismissed others. As with the Greek cities, in some cases it was little more than a matter of whim or inclination, in other cases, it was a much more rational decision based on his current military situation. While he was still in the Persian provinces he was often dealing with native rulers and peoples such as those of the Lebanese coast who might evince genuine pleasure at being allied to the Macedonian cause. These, he hoped, could therefore be trusted to be loyal to their promises. But sometimes this proved to be false. Alexander made a number of misjudgements especially with petty rulers of states physically closer to Persia who had been forced into submission. He found that some of those that pledged support transferred their allegiance once the army had moved on. So like other conquerors in a hurry he found that he had to leave substantial numbers of troops behind for the 'pacification' of the territories.

Some territories comprised discrete geographical entities with reasonably clear-cut boundaries, such as Egypt, where Alexander was welcomed as a liberator, but others, including Syria, were extremely difficult to administer effectively because they contained such a diversity of peoples and cultures. A fundamental move that Alexander made to unify his empire was to insist that the various cities and provinces must abandon their old money systems and adopt Macedonian coinage stamped with the image of the conqueror. This had the effect of neutralizing local identities, and also of symbolizing an open acknowledgement of Macedonian overlordship. As with the Greek cities, they were allowed to enjoy a form of autonomy – but at a price.

The coinage question raises the interesting issue of provincial administration generally. Broadly speaking, Alexander left the Persian fiscal system intact. The *satraps* collected the tribute, covered the day-to-day expenses of administering their provinces and deposited the surplus in central treasuries. The bullion from Alexander's victories was eventually concentrated in Ecbatana and amounted in sum to a fabulous 80,000 talents. Financial administration was therefore often confidently left to the local rulers and governors, though in particularly rich provinces the financial experts were often appointed directly by the king. Egypt is a case in point. The appointee, Cleomenes, a Greek immigrant, was put in charge of the entire fiscal system which he administered with considerable skill and shrewdness. In fact, he became a real power in the land – a *de facto satrap* – and almost a ruler in his own right. The situation was ripe for corruption and peculation. Cleomenes lined his own pocket as well as that of the Macedonian treasury and when finally exposed was executed by Ptolemy who took over Egypt as a 'legacy' after Alexander's death.

Once Alexander had finally defeated the Persian king in 331 BC, he appears to have taken the view that the mandate had been transferred, as it were, and now that he was king, he should try to cement relations by appointing Persian nobles to positions of authority in the new empire. But in key centres such as Babylon, he was still astute – and possibly suspicious – enough to appoint his own Macedonian military representatives. These clearly exercised the real power. Once Alexander was again on the march towards the north east and the Hindu Kush, not every Persian *satrap* proved to be that reliable, and some used their positions to expand their nominal forces and foment rebellion in the occupied territories. Some even had the Macedonian garrisons massacred and then proceeded to carry on guerrilla war against the insurgents. The more the Macedonians tried to consolidate their gains in the remoter areas of the old Persian domains, the more precarious became their positions. In Bactria and Sogdania, for instance, the tribes refused to be pacified, and it took two weary years to tame them. In fact, the situation was so volatile that Alexander left a defence force of over 13,000 men – in those days, an army in itself – to contain the possibility of further insurrection. He also pursued a calculated policy of undermining the military potential of the area by a combination of massacre and military settlement. Except for his own Graeco-Macedonian reinforcements, he denuded the territory of its military – and, therefore, rebellious – potential by conscripting native levies for his future Indian campaign and establishing a network of military colonies controlled by a Graeco-Macedonian elite. As a final gesture, Alexander and a number of his officers were even prepared to resort to the expedient of marrying native women to further the interests of unity, although some of these – often extra-marital – arrangements were later repudiated by the men.

In the territories outside the former Persian Empire, especially in India itself, Alexander was generally prepared to allow the squabbling native princes to stay in place providing they acknowledged his royal authority and were willing to pay the requisite tribute. Sometimes Alexander chose to intervene in these 'domestic' disputes as a way of reinforcing his control and impressing others with the strength and ability of his own forces. But these victories were really rather hollow. The hold on these far regions was, at best, tenuous; they could not really be contained by the manpower at Alexander's disposal especially with the rash of insurrections and conspiracies taking place behind the lines. It was enough to have a nominal allegiance, and to have planted the embyronic seeds of European culture in these 'barbarian' lands.

It is the opinion of some authorities that there was no really coherent strategy behind Alexander's campaigns, and that everything he did was determined by relatively short-term considerations. 'It is difficult to see any permanent policy beyond his primary requirements that the *satrapies* once conquered should remain peaceful with the minimum expense of manpower and that his kingship should be universally and unconditionally acknowledged' (Bosworth 1988: 241).

After the rigours of years of campaigning, Alexander retired to Babylon and spent months planning further conquests in Arabia and the Western Mediterranean where he hoped to include Italy and Carthage within his empire. He was a brave and gifted commander whose military ingenuity was only matched by his personal impetuosity. Despite his cultural and organizational achievements, it is perhaps fortunate for the world that he died when he did (323 BC), ostensibly of a fever possibly aggravated by drink – though poison was suspected. He was a victim of his own 'imperative yearning' (*pothos*), an urge that was 'a dominant feature of his tricky, adventurous, alluring, frightening character' (Grant 1982: 4).

It is impossible to know what would have happened had Alexander not died so young. Some principles can be discerned from the fragmentary measures which he had already decreed. Posterity had generally applauded the fact that he wanted to integrate various racial and ethnic entities within the empire – a doubtful and complex mono-cultural undertaking that met with only limited success. He is said to have founded seventy colonies, and certainly took steps to introduce Greek as a universal language, and to train non-Greeks in the ways of Greek life. So his intention seems to have been assimilation rather than integration. Whether he would also have instituted a co-ordinated economic system as an extension to a common coinage must remain very uncertain. A more cynical view would be that, despite his far-sighted innovations, the organization of this immense empire had all the characteristics of haste and improvization, and that it was really a form of oriental despotism to the glory of the cult of the god–emperor.

6

Malintegration: Japan and the Greater East Asia Co-Prosperity Sphere

Japanese imperialism is usually associated with the 1930s and the invasion of Manchuria and northern China, but perhaps we should look for its beginnings in the nineteenth century. It was at this time that Japan was initiated into the mysteries of Western technology, though one could hardly conclude that this was the cause of future Japanese expansionism. Aggression was certainly not 'generated' in the Japanese by the occidental world; as we shall see, the martial spirit was very much part of their traditional culture. Their contact with the West merely fed that spirit by introducing them to modernity with all its capacities for waging war more effectively. They quickly grasped the potentialities inherent in industrialization, and saw the feasibility of appropriating and developing the technology which could make them into a significant colonial power.

Until 1853 Japan was a discrete civilization virtually cut off from the rest of the world, although there had been some contact with Westerners since the sixteenth century when some Portuguese landed there from a ship that had blown off course. Another similar accident occurred in the next century and this brought the Japanese in touch with the English. Inevitably, some traders and missionaries ventured to this fascinating land which had borrowed much from Chinese culture but had, over the centuries, added unique ingredients of its own. At first, the foreigners were something of a novelty, and were reasonably well-treated. The Japanese were particularly intrigued with their guns which they saw as an interesting possible addition to their armoury. But they soon became disenchanted with the newcomers, and before long the persecutions began and anyone professing Christianity was liable to face the death penalty.

Eventually, the barriers were set up. The Japanese wanted no more intrusions. There had, of course, been attempted invasions before when the Mongols under Kublai Khan tried unsuccessfully to conquer them. Since then they had been free, so they were certainly not going to entertain the possibility of a Western takeover. An edict was therefore

69

issued in the early nineteenth century that no Japanese were to go abroad, and all those that had done so were forbidden to return. Furthermore, no foreign ship was allowed to dock at a Japanese port on pain of death. A partial exception was made in favour of the Dutch who were permitted access to Nagasaki where they attempted to carry on a dwindling trade with a few merchants. Continuing contact was kept to a commercial level only; the Japanese had seen enough of the Europeans to appreciate the potential dominance of Western culture.

Japan remained effectively sealed against the rest of the world until the middle of the century. Then came the arrival of some American warships under Commander Perry, an efficient but reluctant emissary, who carried a letter asking for a treaty. He gave the Japanese a year in which to make up their minds, and the Japanese were so impressed by the hardware and the absence of any immediate ultimatum that they decided to accede to the request. Predictably, other nations then began to ply their particular wares. Everyone it seemed was on the oriental bandwagon. China had already succumbed to Western commercial pressure, now Japan was faced with the stark alternatives: surrender *to* the West and go under, or appropriate from the West, and beat them at their own game. The Western world now knows just how successful their choice was.

The traditional feudal order in Japan which was sanctioned by religion and unified by the cult of the emperor, was effectively governed by the hereditary body of military vassals, the samurai. This whole order swiftly but agonizingly adjusted to the modern world. Yet changed was not without its repercussions. The power of the shogun – the man behind the throne – was virtually abolished in 1867, but contrary to the expectations of some of the reactionary groups, the emperor decided to continue on the path of Westernization. Emancipation for the peasantry brought its own particular problems. They were freed from one burden only to find themselves faced by others. Feudalism went by decree in 1871, but in 1872 a system of military conscription was established. By 1890 or thereabouts there was a general determination to develop along Western lines not only to increase national prosperity, but also to ensure national security and reduce Western encroachment by the hasty build-up of the nation's forces. Nationalism generally was encouraged, it was a unifying principle which enhanced and facilitated centralization – so necessary to rapid industrialization.

In retrospect, it is interesting to ask to what extent the desire for increased prosperity was the key element in all this, as with so many other industrializing nations, or whether the real motivating factor was the will to power. Certainly the military authorities played a predominant part in the social revolution that took place, and the fruits of economic improvement were 'guided' towards military development. Perhaps motives were not always clear to the Japanese themselves. Indeed, it might be that there was (is?) a duality in the Japanese character itself. The ambiguity of their whole industrial and economic enterprise is curiously exemplified by the fact that they produced some of the finest swords in the world, *and* inaugurated a festival for the appearance of the first cherry blossoms. They lavished care and thought on landscape gardening which they brought to a fine art, but also concentrated much energy on producing cheap mass-produced goods in order to finance their programme of territorial expansion.

The awakening of Japan was attended by some notable political convulsions. By 1894, she felt herself strong enough to make claims in relation to Korea and her old enemy China. The war which resulted was short and decisive. A number of territories were ceded to Japan including Formosa (Taiwan), in addition to which she received extensive commercial concessions and a large indemnity. These gains were contested by the great European powers who were also scrambling for what they could get in the newly opened-up Far East. It was a time of shifting allegiances; people sought friends where they could. This brought Japan into alliance with Britain (1902) but into direct confrontation with Russia. Territories were occupied and vacated, and sometimes reoccupied – all to the consternation of the map-makers. Russia and Japan could not resolve their difficulties over Korea and Manchuria, and Japan resorted to the lightning strike. It was clever in conception and execution. Indeed it was a portent of things to come, and is neatly summarized in the old samurai maxim, 'win now, fight later'. Contrary to all expectation she defeated the Russians on both land and sea (1904–5) – a humilitating experience for a traditional great power, especially as it was occasioned by a small upstart nation. Russia lost much of its Baltic fleet and too many of its ill-motivated troops. On the other hand, Japan, regardless of her strategic brilliance, was left virtually bankrupt. Both were consequently ready for terms; Japan's interests in Korea were recognized, and Russia evacuated Manchuria.

This victory confirmed for the Japanese not only their *right* to rule, but also their *ability*. Japan's prestige increased, and the European powers now dignified her court with ambassadors instead of mere ministers, and her fellow Asians looked with respect at a sister nation who had turned the tables on the white intruders. Japan now consciously embarked on a programme of expansion. She was all too aware of the European claims to colonies, but she was determined to make sure that she never became one of them. Indeed, she now set out to become a colonial power herself.

The outbreak of the First World War really facilitated the first phase of Japan's programme of expansion. With the great powers embroiled in a life-or-death conflict, Japan took the opportunity to render a little assistance that netted large rewards. By declaring war on Germany in 1914, she was able quickly to confiscate enemy holdings in China. She then made demands upon China itself which, had they been carried out, would have made China a Japanese protectorate. These demands were partly upheld by Britain and France, despite the fact that China was also a wartime ally. In fact, so anxious were they to maintain something like a Far Eastern status quo while they got on with hostilities in Europe that they granted Japan even more territory in the Pacific in exchange for her continued support in the war. Japan would have liked more still but was frustrated by the objections of the United States which joined China and the Soviet Union on Japan's not so secret list of potential enemies.

On the home front, Japan had been spared the horrors of war, and her development was phenomenal. Her industrial output doubled during the war itself, and afterwards her technical expertise, high investment and low-cost productivity made her the workshop of the East. In two generations her population had doubled, and just about all the cultivable land in her islands was being utilized to feed the masses. Her great deficiency was in raw materials for her industry. Most of these had to be imported, and had to be paid for by banking and shipping services, and a vast output of manufactured goods. How else could she fund her expansionist ambitions? Little wonder that she began to cast covetous eyes on other peoples' property.

Japan's economic policy was largely shaped by the *zaibatsu*, the political-commercial cartel system. This brought together the financial requirements of the great industrial concerns and the imperial aspirations of the government. It was a happy coincidence of interests. Together they made possible Japan's emergence as a leading military power. But this all necessitated a government with the right political complexion.

During the 1920s, Japan had found it profitable to adopt a reasonably low political profile. She adopted a form of parliamentary democracy, and universal male suffrage was introduced in 1925. But underlying all this remained an implicitly repressive system. Radical parties formed and protested, and the Peace Preservation Law was passed which gave virtually unlimited powers to the police to suppress any 'dangerous thought' movements – a Japanese euphemism for communism. Even membership of such a party could carry a term of ten years' imprisonment.

For many these were lean years, but usually the last to suffer were the military. Defence budgets had to be cut, and – true to tradition – the army and the navy vied for what there was. One can, for instance, understand the consternation of the army when the projected naval expenditure for 1922 was a third of the national budget. The Japanese – like many others – struggled through the 1920s, but in 1927 there was severe economic depression. The silk trade collapsed, farmers were badly hit, and only a fifth of university graduates could find work. The prevailing feeling, as in a number of European states at that time, was that democracy had failed. The solution, argued the generals, was a military adventure which would distract the public, bring honour to the nation, and open up a territory which was rich in grain, coal and iron ore. In short, the 'conquest' of Manchuria. They maintained that this would be a natural extension of Japan's already considerable interests there, and would also provide a base for possible further military incursions into China and Mongolia. But the Japanese had to act quickly. Manchuria had been part of China for centuries and had been relatively sparsely populated until recent times. They wanted no more Chinese migrants in the territory, nor did they want Russia to extend her interests there either. Japan wanted the economic monopoly in Manchuria, and thus decided upon annexation. An 'incident' was therefore arranged in 1931 which would give them the necessary pretext to occupy the entire area which was then controlled by a Chinese warlord. Within a year Japan had a new colony which she established as the 'new' state of Manchukuo, despite the ineffectual protests of the League of Nations.

The next target was Shanghai – but this time it wasn't so easy. In 1932 there was another incident which, in this case, sparked off a conflagration that lasted for nearly fourteen years. The Japanese already had a large naval force based in this rather cosmopolitan city, to which they added a large contingent of troops. The Chinese responded by sending in their 19th Army. An as yet unofficial war began. The Japanese bombed the Chinese quarter; many thousands died, and many more were made homeless, but the Chinese still held on. The Japanese poured in even more troops to redeem the situation – after all, the reputation of the Japanese army was now at stake. There was no giving in. It was part of the samurai code that if a warrior drew his sword two inches from its scabbard, it could not be replaced until blood had been shed. For a while the battle was undecided. Sometimes, the Japanese even had to retreat, something which was an affront to their honour and which therefore had to be redefined as a 'strategic withdrawal'. At the time, there was a purportedly true story of a wounded Japanese officer who had been left behind during the withdrawal and who was rescued by a Chinese officer and then taken to a Chinese hospital. When he recovered, he went back to the battlefield – the scene of his shame, and committed *seppuku* – ceremonial disembowelling – to restore his honour (Hoyt 1987:101).

Incidents such as these appear to have fuelled Japanese patriotism. The code of *bushido* seems to have percolated down from the military to society in general. Stories were told of dying soldiers whose last words were in praise of the emperor or of Japan itself, of bereaved mothers who publicly stated that they had other sons to give. Military endeavour appears to have had complete endorsement at the social level. Supernationalism – the passion for empire – seems to have replaced mere nationalism in Japan's psyche, and was encouraged by economic arguments about the possibility of wider markets and more living space. It was justified ideologically by a kind of religious-cum-racial revivalism that was markedly anti-European and which stressed the virtues of traditional Shintoism and the cult of the emperor.

All this generated various crises of confidence at government level. It was the familiar story of the old forces versus the resurgent new forces, except that, in this case, unlike so many other societies, the new forces were not those of radicalism but of reaction. There was plot and counter-plot, and even the judicious use of assassination by the military in order to maintain their dominant position within the system – a privilege that was made easier by the fact that the heads of the army and navy were directly responsible to the emperor rather than to Parliament. In 1933 a group of young officers murdered a previous prime minister, and there was a public plea for clemency, some petitioners even sending their severed little fingers as a sign of their sincerity. At the naval court-martial there was not one death sentence, and eventually even the prison sentences were commuted. In 1936, another group of young officers mutinied and killed a number of high-ranking officials, but this time the emperor disapproved; the revolt collapsed and its leaders committed suicide.

But turbulence at home did not inhibit Japan's persistent aggression in China. This brought her into conflict with public opinion, especially in Britain and the United States. In 1933, she withdrew from the League of Nations, and gravitated more and more towards her eventual European partners, Italy and Germany, who were also bent on expansionism, and who adopted a very similar stance in relation to world opinion.

By this time, the Japanese had developed a definite technical superiority in certain types of weaponry. Their Zero fighters and Mitsubishi twin-engined bombers were certainly in advance of anything the Chinese possessed, and in some respects this superiority even extended to the weaponry of the Anglo-Americans. It has actually been claimed that 'ton for ton their warships were faster, more heavily armoured, and better armed than their British and American counterparts. Their torpedoes were the best in the world, and their torpedomen the most efficient.' Their I class submarines were also superior, and 'could cross the Pacific and return without fueling, an achievement the Americans did not manage until after 1945' (Hoyt 1987: 137–8). It was the refusal of the British and the Americans to allow any substantial (i.e. proportionate increase) in these naval forces under their existing treaty that exacerbated relations with Japan.

By 1937, the 'China incident' was recognized as a full-scale war. As the Japanese made further advances, eventually taking Peking and Hankow, in Japan herself military training was stepped up. Virtually everyone from the emperor down now recognized that Japan's destiny was to be the leader among the Asian peoples and that the nation must therefore prepare for a wider conflict in the Far East. Their industry was geared towards armaments production and their conscription system ensured that they had huge reserves of manpower that could be called upon when hostilities began on a wider scale. Meanwhile, China was to be the proving ground for the Japanese forces: it would test their mettle, and show up any necessary modifications that had to be made in weaponry and tactics.

The China experience also pointed the way to Japanese occupation policies. This can be seen quite clearly in their treatment of prisoners. Some were obviously required for interrogation, so they could be allowed to live – at least, temporarily. It was customary to shoot other captives including the sick and the wounded. This was obviously intended to instil fear and respect, and was justified in terms of 'countermeasures' and retribution. Campaigns were conducted with scant regard for either civilian lives or property, and their supremacy in the air meant that the Japanese could bomb and strafe cities and refugees at will. Nowhere is their pitiless treatment of the conquered seen better than in what has come to be known as the 'Rape of Nanking'. The ferocity of the massacre there amazed even some of the Japanese military when they came to hear of it. In the main it was perpetrated not by hardened veterans but by young conscripts. It is not known for certain just how many died, but the generally accepted estimate is about 150,000, very many of them women and children. War can be horrible at the best of times, but it is here more than anywhere that the Japanese army picked up the reputation for being savage and uncivilized. Interestingly, the emperor and the civilians in the cabinet claimed later that they did not know anything about these events until after the war. The position of the emperor has always been seen in the West as somewhat equivocal. Perhaps it was analogous to that of Albert Speer who, when interviewed about the Nazi Holocaust programme, insisted that he didn't know but added that *he could have known*.

When, in July 1941, the Nazi-dominated Vichy regime in France allowed the Japanese to occupy French Indo-China (Vietnam), relations with the Americans went from bad to worse. There were half-hearted attempts to reach some kind of understanding and negotiations were still taking place when the Japanese initiated the Pacific War by bombing Pearl Harbor on 7 December 1941. Franklin Roosevelt, the American President, pronounced a 'day of infamy', but for the Japanese it was the recognized name of the game. They were impatient for a share of Second World War action, having been impressed by the astounding military successes of their Axis partners. They naturally felt that the pickings in the Far East were too easy and too good to miss. Despite their initial successes throughout the whole area the Japanese had now created a situation that was ultimately to prove their undoing. As the price for their aggression, they now had to face declarations of war from Britain, the United States, from the exiled government of the Netherlands, Australia, and, rather inconsequently, from several Latin American states. They irony in all this was that Japan felt herself to be the injured party, and public support for the war became even more enthusiastic.

Much of 1942 was a time of almost unmitigated disaster for the Allies. The Japanese successfully launched land and sea operations against their territories in South East Asia. They overran Burma, Malaya, Singapore – an ignominious surrender which is still a matter of debate – the Philippines, and the Dutch East Indies (Indonesia). They knew that they had to fight a short war because their resources could never match those of their enemies, particularly the Americans. But they hoped that the benefits of these new conquests would make up for their natural deficiencies, especially rubber from Malaya and oil from the Dutch East Indies.

It was their intention to establish a 'New Order' in Asia based ostensibly on the principle of Asia for the Asiatics. Superficially it was all very convincing. They were going to free their 'brothers' from European subjection and usher in an enlightened epoch of South Eastern culture. People would be summoned, as it were, to participate in a new and glorious venture for the promotion of their mutual interests. This organization for the political and economic development of these territories was given the grandiose title of The Greater East Asia Co-Prosperity Sphere. It was not exactly a new idea, such visions had been entertained by some Japanese officials and intellectuals for some time, but now it was being given physical expression. At first, many of the peoples they 'liberated' were receptive to the idea. They welcomed the Japanese as fellow Asiatics who had now emancipated them from the rigours of white colonization, and they were prepared to co-operate in a far-sighted scheme which had to be to their long-term advantage. All over the South Pacific and South East

Asia there were initial expressions of joy. From Taiwan to Thailand the Japanese were hailed as deliverers from Anglo-Saxon bondage. A new era had dawned.

The Japanese made much of their liberating intentions. At the fall of Singapore, their commander proclaimed that they were there to do away with British 'arrogance . . . and promote social development by establishing [an] East Asia Coprosperity Sphere' which would respect the rights and talents of individual as well as racial entities (Thorne 1985: 144). Later in 1942, a fuller statement was made to try to allay suspicions by assuring the conquered that

> Nippon has no thought of establishing any regimented sphere of imperialism in East Asia. This would be contrary to her principles. Fundamentally, it is to be a union of neighbouring states, sharing to a greater or lesser degree common racial and cultural origins . . . founded by their voluntary agreement for their common happiness and prosperity.
>
> (quoted in Thorne 1985: 144–5)

The Japanese were keen to emphasize the aesthetic and ethical nature of Asian traditions, and felt that with their unique blend of oriental culture and occidental know-how they could make a significant contribution to the welfare of their Asian 'brothers'. They insisted that racial divisions which had been keenly upheld by their former white overlords were now a thing of the past, and that under the 'New Order' all this would change. In short, it was to be something the East had never experienced before, an order that would bring lasting peace, social development and cultural enrichment.

The Japanese exploited every tactical angle they could to foster these ideas. Religion particularly was employed to advantage. Christianity, Islam and Buddhism, naturally alien to the nationalistic Shinto faith of Japan, all proved to be grist to the ideological mill. There were no attempts at syncretism, rather an emphasis on the liberal broadmindedness of the Japanese who could see virtue in all these philosophies, and who wished to see people pursuing their own cultural and spiritual interests. To further this idea, they also encouraged nationalist aspirations in their subject peoples – always providing that they continued to recognize the dominant role of Japan in Far Eastern affairs. This was done through educational institutions such as the School for Free Indonesia in the former Dutch East Indies and the encouragement of political parties with 'co-prosperity' orientations. Needless to say, this was all in addition to the more practical expedients such as the formation of collaborative police and military units where possible, and the introduction of members of the indigenous population into the administration of the respective territories.

By and large, these subject states were not so much pro-Japanese as anti-white and anti-colonialist in orientation, and Japan played on these sentiments. The key incentive to collaboration was the promise of independence which in some cases, was actually 'granted'. The Philippines, for example, was given independence in October 1943 when the tide was beginning to turn against the conquerors, and in September 1944, when the war was really lost, the Philippines actually declared war against the United States – a fruitless gesture prompted by the US bombing of Manila during their advance. Other states such as India hesitated because they realized that it would be independence in name only, and waited until they felt they were in a position actually to administer the territories in question. The Japanese liked to involve the natives if it cost nothing and made them happy. So they gave India's Chandra Bose a key appointment in the administration of the Andaman and Nicobar Islands, but it could be little more than a token authority.

These were the avowed intentions of the Greater East Asia Co-Prosperity Sphere – a term used officially for the first time in January 1941 (Iriye 1987: 131). But things didn't quite work out as expected. The first territory to experience the delights of this New Order – other than the already well-exploited state of Manchukuo – was French Indo-China. Its government had been left paralysed by the defeat of France, and throughout 1941 the Japanese had been able to secure greater and greater concessions for not taking it over entirely. But the Japanese were not there for the good of the natives, they were looking for rice. The northern part of the territory was made into a protectorate, and Japanese garrisons were sited in key areas. It is arguable whether what the Japanese required was co-operation from ostensible partners, or collaboration from acknowledged subject peoples. High-sounding, and even high-minded, as the Co-Prosperity Sphere was intended to be, it was in reality a form of imperialism, with Japan exercising an hegemony over the rest of the 'equal' states who were expected to make generous contributions to the Japanese economy.

The Japanese were able to mobilize quite substantial forces in a number of their subject states. Somewhat atypical in this respect was the Indian National Army organized by a Sikh ex-prisoner of war, Mohan Singh. India was not yet a subject state, though it was next on the agenda, and the Japanese were able to attract exiles and prisoners to the 'Asian' cause. Its political leader was Chandra Bose, a former president of the Indian Congress Party, who had escaped from house arrest from the British early in 1941, and who now shuttled between Berlin and the Far East drumming up support for Indian independence. He boasted that when he eventually appeared in Bengal, the people would rise up in revolt – something of an overstatement, although between 1942 and 1943, some 25,000 Indian prisoners of war in Japanese camps in Malaya did volunteer for service with the Indian National Army. About 2,000 died in battle and through starvation and disease, but some hundreds also deserted, and the Japanese began to distrust their staying power, as did the Indian Army on the other side of the lines.

Many subject states also raised appreciable armies in support of the Japanese. In Burma, Japanese-trained patriots rapidly recruited a Burma Independence Army of 200,000 men which in August 1942 was reorganized into seven battalions. And in Java, the Peta, a volunteer force of 34,000 men called the Army Defenders of the Homeland, was also quickly mustered in 1943 to counter the revived and advancing Allied forces. Similar smaller units were raised in Japanese-dominated Micronesia and in French Indo-China where, surprisingly, the Japanese did not try to exploit nationalist sentiments against the French. Ironically, what were intended as forces of de-colonization actually became the unwitting agents of re-colonization by the Japanese.

The outstanding victories of the Japanese forces in 1941–2 netted them an impressive variety of economic booty: some 80 per cent of the world's rubber, 54 per cent of its tin; 19 per cent of its tungsten, large supplies of manganese and iron ores, bauxite, and the oil wells of the Dutch East Indies with their huge reserve stocks. But curiously enough – possibly due to the immediate needs and exigencies of war – the Japanese were not able to harness and utilize these resources in ways that alleviated the urgent shortages in their war economy. A Greater East Asian ministry was established whose brief was to prepare schemes for economic co-operation between the various conquered territories. Meetings were held, conferences arranged, and plans for the extraction and utilization of materials discussed. But no programme was finally agreed, nor were any reliable statistics ever forthcoming. So much for the much-vaunted benefits of the Greater East Asia Co-Prosperity Sphere.

The Japanese puppet governments in their dependencies were administered in such a way as to allow things to go on much as before. Shrewdly they encouraged these aspirations of eventual independence, and found many native factions particularly responsive. Conferences were convened for representative parties. In November 1943, when Japan's best war days were over, a Co-Prosperity Sphere conference was called in Tokyo to reaffirm her lofty aspirations for her 'allies'. Representatives attended from the subject states and the puppet governments, and even Australia was enjoined by radio to consider that its 'proper place' was within the Japanese sphere of influence. All the appropriate sentiments were expressed, and then everyone was encouraged to renew their efforts in the moral crusade against the Anglo-Americans. But with the turn of the year, the appeals to these Asian partners took on a more desperate tone; the emphasis shifted from Japan as founder of a New Order to Japan as protector against the encroachment of the West. The slogan was now 'live or die with Japan' (Thorne 1985: 147).

At times attempts were also made to promote a fellow feeling among the lower echelons of their populations, but often the propaganda exercises and fabrications were little short of ludicrous. To take a relatively trivial example, in Bangkok a boulevard was constructed of which nine-tenths of the buildings had false fronts. It was only built to be photographed, for propaganda purposes. In its own way, it represented the Co-Prosperity Sphere itself – intention without achievement, shadow without substance. The Japanese-proclaimed 'independence' of some states, such as Burma and the Philippines, was little more than notional, although deals struck with unlikely local leaders such as Sukarno, the post-war dictator in Indonesia, can be seen now to have had a future significance. But in general the Co-Prosperity reality proved something of a sham. The indigenes were often insulted and abused, and their native customs flouted. The presence of the Japanese army was bad enough, yet this hardly compared with the ominous activities of the secret police (the Kempeitai). The reality was not only political and economic incompetence, it also became a pervasive combination of extortion and brutality.

In reaction against the Japanese, various rebel armies also formed in some of the subject territories. A classic example was the HUK movement in the Philippines which operated in central Luzon. It began with a membership of a mere 300, and reached something over 10,000 by 1944, and is said to have been responsible for the deaths of as many as 5,000 Japanese and about 15,000 Philippino collaborators. It was this communist-inspired movement that became the core of the later People's Liberation Army which revolted against the post-war government in 1948. Quite unintentionally, Japan had made a significant difference to the political alignments in the Far East, and generated movements which were to have considerable importance in the coming years.

Some idea of just how the New Order operated can be seen from the ways the Japanese treated their defeated enemies, the 'foreign devils', and also their fellow Asiatics whom they often despised. In the initial success phase of their operations, in the interests of what their War Minister General Tojo grandiloquently called 'a holy war', they were determined to show their contempt for the conquered, especially if they were Anglo-Americans. They meant to impress upon everyone right from the beginning who were the new masters in South East Asia. In Hong Kong humiliations and cruelties were inflicted on Europeans and Chinese particularly. Nurses were raped and wounded prisoners were bayoneted to death. In October 1943 a member of the British Army Aid Group was hanged for smuggling medical supplies into the camps and encouraging prisoners to escape. And on the same day in north Borneo local Chinese and native Suluks revolted and killed forty of the invaders. In reprisal, the Japanese burnt villages and arrested and tortured thousands of civilians, and machined-gunned many others (Gilbert 1989: 468–9). This sort of thing was repeated elsewhere, especially in Malaya. To be fair, not all Japanese followed local commander instructions and were reprimanded for doing so. But the pattern of terror and repression was commonplace. Sometimes the soldiery obviously got out of control, but this does not explain the systematic ill-treatment of those whom the *bushido* code regarded as inferior, notably prisoners of war. For example, when the Japanese captured Bataan in the Philippines after what for them was something of a struggle, they forced the prisoners to undertake a long march in gruelling conditions. Many of them were sick and wounded, but any who lingered or collapsed were summarily dispatched by either a bullet or a bayonet. Some 7,000 died on this march alone, about one-third Americans and two-thirds Philippinos – people who, in theory, came within the Co-Prosperity ambit, but who had made the fatal misjudgement of aiding Japan's enemies.

Japanese field orders repeatedly stressed that prisoners who were of no more use were to be killed, and there is some evidence that fatal experiments were carried out on still live patients by medical officers. Apparently, even cannibalism was authorized when food was desperately short. The statistics show that the Japanese killed more British troops in prison camps or 'work projects' than in battle; for instance, of the 50,000 prisoners who worked on the Siam (Thailand) railway, 16,000 died of torture, disease and starvation. The Japanese prison camp record is, in fact, much worse than that of the Germans. Strictly speaking, prisoners were not supposed to exist, to surrender was the ultimate in degradation as far as the Japanese were concerned. Of the prisoners held in German and Italian camps only 4 per cent died, whereas of those held by the Japanese 27 per cent died (Gilbert 1989).

Ultimately, the Japanese were to suffer themselves. The bombing of Japanese cities wrought havoc, especially among civilians. Perhaps as many as a million died in the fire-storms in 1945 alone. On the military front, the Allies reclaimed the islands one by one with terrible losses among the Japanese. In a very real sense, their own military code conspired to bring unnecessary destruction to their armies. At the fall of Saipan, for example, which the Japanese had vowed to defend at all costs, some 50,000 Japanese soldiers and civilians died – virtually the entire population – many of them by suicide. Some literally threw themselves at their opponents with explosives strapped to their bodies. In just one night, 3,000 wounded soldiers, in a ritual of self-destruction, died rather than be captured, and when the Americans were finalizing their operations, scores of people – including women and children – killed themselves by jumping off the cliffs rather than face the humiliation of falling into enemy hands.

After the war, in retaliation for the atrocities committed against both soldiers and civilians, the Allied Tribunal sentenced twenty-five Japanese to death as war criminals; seven were actually hanged. Local military commissions condemned another 920 to death and a further 3,000 to prison. Some Indian opinion insisted that the sentences were too harsh – after all, the Allies had committed atrocities too. But then there was a great deal of anti-British feeling in India at the time. On the other hand, there were Philippinos who thought that, if anything, many of the sentences were too lenient – an interesting sentiment, considering that they too were supposed to be among the beneficeries of the Japanese New Order. In fact, the atrocities against Indian and Philippino soldiers, and non-white civilians among the Chinese and Malays were more numerous – and possibly more savage – than those inflicted upon the hated Anglo-Americans (Johnson 1983: 428). For instance, when the Japanese wanted to 'punish' the Chinese after assistance in a token American bombing raid on Tokyo early in the war, in the space of three months they killed a quarter of a million soldiers and civilians.

With hindsight it can be seen that the Japanese committed two classic errors. The first was essentially a military error, although it had strong economic implications. It was the mistake of taking on a power whose resources were infinitely greater than their own. Much as they despised the Americans, there was no way – in the long term – that they could defeat a nation which could mobilize such vast reserves of manpower and material. They also underestimated the extent to which the Anglo-Americans were eventually prepared to match them for ruthlessness and efficiency. The second great mistake was really of a more implementational kind. Having had what some may still regard as the laudible conception of uniting the Asian peoples, the Japanese operationalized that conception in the worst kind of imperialism. They purported to free South East Asia from white domination, and then substituted for it a form of repression that was far worse. It is all very reminiscent of the Spartans of classical times who were going to free Greece from slavery only to impose an imperialistic slavery of their own. But then the world never learns. In retrospect, it is not difficult to endorse the view that search the world how one will, it is almost impossible to find anything good to say about the Japanese Empire. . . . A reluctant admiration for Japan's military feats must not block out the consciousness [of her] sinister shadow. In the years before the conflict, Japan had an opportunity to develop its empire in miniature – in Korea, in Formosa, and in the parts of China which it came to dominate – and in this exhibition of the Japanese spirit it failed to show any virtues. . . . The liquidation [of this empire] was an unqualified benefit to the world.

(Calvocoressi and Wint 1972: 479)

7

Arbitrary repression: Mussolini and the Italian African Empire

In the aftermath of the First World War, the re-constructed Europe comprised some twenty-eight states, of which twenty-six could be generally described as democracies. Yet by the eve of the Second World War in 1939, sixteen of these had surrendered to dictatorship of one form or another. Parliamentary forms of government had been abandoned, the range of political parties had been severely circumscribed, and the normal constitutional restraints had become largely ineffectual.

Theories still proliferate as to why this should have come about, but there is some consensus on the view that this retreat from democracy can be correlated with the changing fortunes of the middle classes. The First World War with its widespread devastation and thirteen million dead had resulted in social and economic hardship on an unprecedented scale. Everyone was affected, the poor and the unsupported most of all. The problems seemed insuperable. The old leaders were largely discredited, and scapegoats were sought to blame for the evils that had befallen society; Jews, bankers, capitalists – indeed, anyone who had not been directly involved in the conflict, and who appeared to have profited from the general misfortunes of others.

There were student appeals for reform; socialist agitation was rife, and communist experiments were the order of the day, especially in Germany and Hungary. But it was the middle classes who responded to impoverishment in the most reactionary political terms. Poverty and the threat of unemployment was a new experience for them. They had shared the ideals of the old conservatives, and like them were now undergoing a loss of both security and prestige. The lower echelons of the middle classes, clerical workers, artisans and those with modest commercial interests, were particularly badly affected by the economic effects of the war, and it was among these that fascism was to find some of its most ardent supporters. Indeed, for them, fascism became an instrument of bourgeois resurgence (see Lee 1988).

The resurrection of Italian nationalism in this century is particularly associated with Gabrielle D'Annunzio, a romantic poet-soldier figure who had become prominent in Italian radical circles after his much-heralded exploits as a pilot during the First World War. After the war, the peace conference had ceded part of the Dalmation coastline to Yugoslavia; the Italians protested that it belonged to historic Italy, and in September 1919 D'Annunzio organized a precipitate seizure of the port of Fiume with the help of a motley array of ideologues and army deserters. It all smacked of Balkan high drama, but ended in something like farce when the Italian government ordered the bombardment of the port.

Nationalism revived under the somewhat unlikely leadership of Benito Mussolini. Before the First World War, Mussolini had been an avant-garde socialist and was effectively exiled to Switzerland. The war turned him into a rabid nationalist, and a fervent opponent of German oppression. This was ironic in the light of future events. Mussolini was something of a political chameleon, and had adopted all kinds of 'positions' at different times in his life. He has been described as an intellectual poseur and cultural exhibitionist, someone who could be variously a monarchist, socialist, fascist and/or anti-cleric – all to suit the occasion. In short, an ideological opportunist.

After the war, Mussolini built up a fascist organization which appealed to many of the more idealistic Italian youth and especially to war veterans. These black shirts carried on a vigorous street war with socialists and communists, and in October 1922, after a cabinet crisis, Mussolini led them on a self-advertising – and possibly unnecessary – 'March on Rome'. This abortive uprising saw the eclipse of Italian liberalism and the birth of cult-figure authoritarianism. In its own way it had worked – Mussolini was now in power.

Thus was set the fashion for modern fascist dictatorships. By the mid-1920s, there were fascist movements blossoming all over Europe. But fascism, *qua* fascism, remains something of an enigma. Except for its strong authoritarian and nationalistic character, it is difficult to define. Indeed, re-examination of the phenomenon shows it to be no one kind of a thing (Lacquer 1979), and some writers have actually gone so far as to insist that it is actually a form of marxist heresy (Johnson 1983). Certainly, fascism could – depending on the circumstances – be considered to be either reactionary or revolutionary, and could adapt as necessary to either class war or class co-operation (Mack Smith 1981). Mussolini suggested that fascism was a form of authoritarian democracy on a national basis. In effect, a despotic utopia.

In Italy fascism took the form of the Corporate State. This aimed to lessen – indeed, eliminate – economic discontentment. Industry existed for the good of the state; private enterprise, like private property was allowed, but if it was inefficient it came under the management of the state. The Ministry of Corporations (somewhat like an industrial parliament) also ensured that workers, although members of trade unions, had their hours and conditions of work strictly controlled by state agencies. And strikes and lock-outs were largely obviated by state-organized Labour Courts.

In effect, the Corporate State was, in theory at least, a cradle to grave affair. It provided state benefits, holidays, pensions, and the like for its employees, and they in turn were supposed to reciprocate with lifetimes of unstinting labour for the cause. As a utopian blueprint it had something to commend it, but the actuality fell far short of the intentions of the ideologues. The system was riddled with inefficiencies of all kinds; these became particularly evident later when Italy was testing her military mettle. And, unsurprisingly, the system had its darker side as well. It was not at all like the dreams of the would-be political visionaries. The system was vitiated by recourse to violence. Repressive measures were used against malcontents and free thinkers who were understandably hesitant about the doubtful benefits of this Brave New World.

From its earliest days Italian fascism showed signs of incipient expansionism. It was also inordinately conscious of its status, and sensitive to its image in post-war Europe as a radical, upstart movement with an uncertain future. Only a year after coming to power, an incident occured which challenged the dignity of the new regime. An Italian frontier commission consisting of a general and four staff officers who were engaged in demarking a boundary between Greece and Albania were killed by unknown assassins. Mussolini insisted on an apology and the capture and execution of the killers. So far, these were not unreasonable demands, but he also demanded a huge compensation, all within five days. The povery-stricken Greeks were unable to meet these conditions, and Mussolini ordered the bombardment and occupation of Corcyra (Corfu) in violation of the wishes of the League of Nations. In this instance, the Italians only backed down and evacuated the island with the threat of British intervention. But they had shown that the League was only as strong as its powerful member nations; if they were reluctant to act – as later proved to be the case, the League, as such, was impotent. This may be seen as a cynical dress rehearsal for more serious expansionist excursions later on; a try-on to test the will and determination of the League to do anything about anything.

Italy had already made extravagant claims for extra territories, presumably as a reward for joining the victorious allies in the war, and to mark her status as a rising European power. In 1925, she was granted Jubaland (between Italian Somaliland and Kenya), having already been given – with some hesitation – the official title to the Dodecanese Islands, an occasion which Mussolini intended to celebrate dramatically by sending in a naval squadron to re-possess that which Italy had already possessed for ten years.

In retrospect, historians are not sure to what extent Mussolini should be regarded as an astute and forward-looking military planner or an ambitious political opportunist. There is some evidence for both views. Whichever theory is adopted, it is reasonably clear that by the early 1920s, he had found it vocationally expedient to abandon his previous republicanism and anti-clericalism and adopt a more eclectic approach to political programming. Perhaps an essential ingredient in Italian fascism was his own bid for personal power. Elizabeth Wiskemann has indicated that he was probably feeling his way half-blindly towards a dictatorship, the implications of which even he did not fully understand and which evoked widespread but not general enthusiasm (Wiskemann 1966b). Whether what was developed in Italy in the name of fascism was actually totalitarianism is also still disputable. Mussolini's compromises with other institutions such as the Church and the monarchy suggest not. Until 1938 – despite all the repression and intimidation – there were no official race edicts as in Nazi Germany, and there were no actual deportations of Jews until the Germans took over after the Italian surrender to the Allies in 1943.

As an aspiring dictator, Mussolini set about trying to establish good relations with selected neighbouring states. The Locarno Treaty in 1925 was intended to settle the issue of existing frontiers between Germany, Belgium and France, but nothing significant was done to secure Italy's border with Austria over whom she claimed to exercise her rights as protective (and covetous?) neighbour. In these pre-Axis days, she regarded Germany's prior claims to Austria with nervous impatience. Perhaps more important were Italy's attempts at political penetration of the Balkans, especially in relation to Yugoslavia *vis-à-vis* Albania, the tiny state with which she now made economic treaties but which she would successfully invade in 1939.

It was really Africa that Mussolini felt offered the most promising imperialist possibilities. Italy already controlled Tripolitania and Cyrenaica (reconstituted as Libya in 1934) which gave her much of the North African coastline, as well as Italian Somaliland and Eritrea in East Africa. But in trying to expand – especially in North Africa – he had to contend with the *in situ* opposition of Spain and France (the latter, according to Mussolini, a nation ruined by alcohol, syphilis and journalism). In both North and East Africa, Italy also faced problems with the British. The Italians wanted a slice of the colonial cake, especially where there were already large concentrations of Italian residents, but their territorial ambitions soon outstripped the political realities of the situation. At first, Mussolini's claims were reasonably modest, a few oases here, or a strip of borderland there, yet these were soon to increase with demands for substantial territories in the Cameroons and in Tunisia, which generated French anger and indignation. Even Turkey, another loser in the 1914–18 conflict was regarded as a likely prospect. The Allies' asset-stripping after the war had given hope to all those who felt that they had a legitimate claim on the spoils. But nothing worked. The only real concession that was made was in 1928 when Italy was granted a consolatory share in the international administration of Tangier.

From 1934 onwards, Mussolini became increasingly preoccupied with the possible annexation of Ethopia (Abyssinia). A victorious invasion would serve several purposes. It would recover lost territory and would also be an act of revenge for the defeat of Italy by the Ethiopians at the battle of Adowa in 1896. Furthermore, it would give a boost to the cause of fascism and provide an outlet for the pent-up enthusiasms of Italian youth, and might even up-rate Mussolini's dictatorial status in the eyes of his fascist competitors in Germany. The League in general and the British in particular were anxious to appease Mussolini and tried to satisfy his colonial ambitions by promises of alternative territorial concessions. They offered him parts of the Ogaden bordering Italian Somaliland, and the port of Zeila on the Gulf of Aden. To the British these were mere scraps thrown to the wolves, and to Mussolini they were simply titbits of territory that nobody particularly wanted. He had said rather contemptuously at the time that he was not in the game of collecting deserts (Collier 1978).

Ethiopia was the only large independent African state – in fact, it was the only area of Africa left for Europeans to colonize. It had a common frontier with Italian Somaliland, and Mussolini, therefore, found it convenient to pick quarrels with Ethiopia – in effect, to continue a *casus belli* which would justify an invasion and result in an early conquest. Planning for the campaign began some three years before the actual outbreak of hostilities in 1935. And by the spring of that year reinforcements had begun arriving in Italy's African territories in preparation for the initial attack. By the end of May, Italy may have had as many as a million men under arms, but it took a full year before the capital, Addis Ababa, was captured. This effectively ended the campaign.

Although the conquest of this rather backward and divided country had at last been achieved, it is arguable whether the Italians were really successful in realizing all their original aims. Furthermore, it had aroused the ire of the League which half-heartedly tried to impose sanctions on the aggressor. It was all rather ineffectual, mainly because the member states could not agree on exactly how or to what extent this should or could be done. Mussolini had chosen his victim carefully. Nobody – as it turned out – was going to lift a finger, let alone a rifle, to save this semi-civilized backwater of Africa. In the end, although 50 out of the 54 member states were opposed to the invasion, Mussolini got little more than a slap on the wrist for this act of unvarnished aggression in which modern technology had been used to crush ill-armed tribesmen.

Having savoured the fruits of victory in Ethiopia, Mussolini felt confident enough to indulge in further adventures in Spain. In the summer of 1936, Franco had decided to lead this troops against the struggling forces of the republic, and in doing so had enlisted the aid of the sympathetic Axis powers. Hitler and his Reichsmarschall, the Air Chief Goering, wanted to test the capacities of the newly developed *Luftwaffe*, and Mussolini, having adopted the mantle of military conqueror, was keen to enhance the cause of fascism and satisfy his growing need for martial glory. Hitler had little confidence in the military prowess of the Italian troops, but Franco needed all the help he could get. Increasing supplies of Russian arms and the mobilization of an international volunteer force for the Republic equalized the chances of the combatants. The whole operation was originally intended as a military push-over, but it settled into a protracted and bloody conflict marked by fearful atrocities on both sides. By 1939, however, despite the doubtful quality of the Italian contribution, the combined weight of the fascist forces made a Franco victory inevitable.

Triumphs of this kind merely whetted Mussolini's appetite for further military excursions – if only to keep up with his Nazi stablemate who had now progressed from his former supernumerary status in the fascist firmament to being its admired but much feared luminary. Hitler now called the shots. His political triumphs in the Rhineland, Austria and Czechoslovakia both incensed and embarrassed Mussolini who liked to think of himself as someone cast in the warrior mould. Many of the carefully posed photographs and newsreels of the time show him strutting and posturing in ways which enhanced the heroic image. He once remarked that the British who 'made a religion of eating and games' could not begin to understand the warrior ethos. In an article in the *Encyclopaedia Italiana*, he describes fascism as believing 'neither in the possibility nor in the utility of perpetual peace. . . . War alone brings up to its highest tension all human energy and puts the stamp of nobility upon the people who have the courage to meet it' (Baer 1967: 248).

But Mussolini could not hope to emulate the deeds of his more powerful partner, and so he assumed the new persona of honest broker. During the Munich crisis in 1938, he gave the impression that he was the only person who could mediate between the opposing fractions – the man who held the balance of power, the saviour of Europe.

It was all little more than political affectation – but in this case it was a profitable pose. If only he had maintained it he might have survived but, greedy for a share of the spoils, he finally threw in his lot with Nazi Germany during the impending fall of France in June 1940. Italian forces became insignificant and even distrusted cogs in the Nazi war machine. They were humilitated by the Greeks in 1940–1, and by the British in the Western Desert and East Africa (1940–3). The contingents that contributed to the Russian campaign, which the Germans launched in 1941, also had a singularly undistinguished record. One can only assume that their hearts were just not in it. This became all too apparent when they surrendered to the Allies in 1943, only to find much of their country taken over by their erstwhile German friends who then treated them as virtual enemies.

So much, then, for the broad outline of events in fascist Italy. We must now look at the ways in which the fascists administered their subject territories and see how their actions were often arbitrary and certainly not always consistent with their policies. In some areas, their intentions were wholly admirable in conception but often badly flawed in practice. Grandiose reclamation and building schemes were planned and begun not only on the Italian mainland but also in Sicily, Sardinia, Albania and Africa. Huge numbers of labourers were employed on ambitious projects which were sometimes never completed, and monies were not uncommonly creamed off by graft and corruption. This was all admirable advertising for the fascists, despite the poverty and squalor which still plagued many Italian cities.

In the subject territories the balance of development was often uneven. Some areas came in for much more investment than others. And at the administrative level, some governors treated their subjects liberally, if somewhat paternalistically, while others simply regarded them as ripe for exploitation. One crucial factor in all this was the constraining nature of fascist ideology. As we have already noted, it had strong nationalistic overtones, so development had to reflect this new image; Mussolini himself suggested that his objective was to make Italy great, and by that he meant respected and feared.

As far as the subject territories were concerned, policy – no matter how well-intentioned – was vitiated by pervasive racial ideas. These developed slowly and uncertainly in Italy. For instance, in the early days of fascism they had no clearly defined racial policies in relation to the Jews. In 1932 Mussolini had actually referred to anti-semitism as 'the German vice', and to the idea of an Aryan master race as 'arrant nonsense, stupid and idiotic'. He repudiated Nazi racial superiority theories and after his first meeting with Hitler in 1934 spoke of him variously as 'mad', a 'silly clown', and a 'garrulous monk' with whom he had little in common. Things changed however after a further meeting three years later when Mussolini decided that he had found a friend with whom he could 'march ... to the last'. It was this 'categoric promise of loyalty, that marked the beginning of ... disaster [and] for Italians the beginning of disillusion. ... Until now ... [they had seen fascism] as unadulterated by the grosser barbarisms of National Socialism' (Hibbert 1965: 98; 100).

Mussolini was now particularly impressed by German efficiency and military development, and not least by the adulation of the German crowds, and decided to adopt a more stringent racial policy for political reasons. Jews were banned from certain key professions and some were expelled; they could not become members of the Fascist Party, and their children were required to attend special schools. Marriage and sexual intercourse with Jews and Africans were forbidden on pain of imprisonment. But until the German take-over in 1943, these policies never seem to have been consistently implemented; there were none of the large-scale massacres and deportations that one associates with Nazi racial policies. However, these practices do not seem to have been condemned when they took place elsewhere.

Actually, the fascist position on race is full of anomalies and contradictions. There is some evidence to suggest that it was not the growing *rapprochement* with Nazi ideology that influenced Mussolini, but the closer experience of tribal peoples occasioned by the Ethiopian war. Racist ideas were already implicit in certain aspects of fascist doctrine, and were already being promoted in academic circles. The noted anthropologist Professor Lidio Cipriani advocated policies akin to apartheid and maintained that Italian racial superiority was 'biological and unchangeable' and that natives had an 'irreducible mental inferiority'. It was not the task, therefore, of Italians to try to raise that level or even impose their own civilization – the natives were quite incapable of receiving it. Progress, for them was quite impossible; evolution and emancipation were condemned as democratic (i.e. non-fascist) ideas. Thus – in true Periclean manner – it was argued that conquest was justified by right of sheer supremacy.

These ideas, which had very limited currency before 1935, became more popular with increasing contact with native peoples. By 1936, the minister for African affairs ordered that whites and blacks must live separately, and in 1937 penalties of up to five years' imprisonment were imposed upon any Italian citizen living with a black subject. As one writer acutely observes, 'the reason given, the purity of race, was entirely hypocritical' because fascism was actually inconsistent about having sexual relations with African women. 'The real sin was living alongside the natives as equals and thus damaging the image of the master race' (Mack Smith 1979: 113).

Natives, then, were to be treated like children with whom they had a kind of intellectual affinity. Integration was to be discouraged, education was to be strictly limited, and any kind of cultural assimilation abjured (the Italians regarded this as the great error of the British administration in India). Any contravention of the rules would be met with the necessary sanctions. Indeed, any infringement was covered by a general law introduced in 1939 prescribing a penalty of up to three years' imprisonment for any act harming the prestige of the race.

Racialism and ethnicity, making distinctions between people on the basis of colour and culture, have always been with us. But *racism*, the intellectualization of the idea that some people are inherently inferior or superior to others is a relatively modern phenomenon (Carlton 1990). Racist ideology – like propaganda – uses myths to supplement or replace reality. In fascist Italy the seminal prejudices were all there, barely recognized let alone articulated until the needs of empire merged ominously with the insidious influences of Nazi ideology. Racism had an elective affinity with colonial ambition.

In the early days, Mussolini had railed against the unjust treatment of colonial peoples, but the later imperialist demands of fascism neutralized these former concerns. In fact his governor in Somalia, Cesare de Vecchi, openly avowed his intention of obliterating the cultural orientations of the indigenous peoples, and demonstrated his contempt by burning villages that were centres of rebellion, and shooting prisoners in hundreds. He made it very clear that colonies were there for exploitation; territories were seen as potential sources of economic wealth. Thus colonial expansionism became confused with patriotic duty, and materialism was disguised as development. The irony was that the colonies never did pay their way. Until 1941 when the Italians effectively lost their African Empire, they were always dependent on subsidies from the central government. In some areas, particularly Libya, money was poured into various projects though with only patchy returns. Much good work was done: slavery was legally abolished, inter-tribal warfare reduced, and famine and disease controlled, but at no time did the balance of trade run in Italy's favour.

There was further disappointment for those that saw the colonies as havens for would-be Italian immigrants. It was hoped that these territories would draw off some of the surplus people from Italy's poor and overcrowded urban areas, and it became a practice in Libya and East Africa to confiscate uncultivated land for potential Italian residents. But the colonies were never able to attract them in large numbers despite Mussolini's prediction that one day they would 'house' some ten million people. In fact, in all the colonies put together, there were probably no more than 50,000 – less than the number of Italians in New York City. As a solution for Italy's overpopulation problems, imperialism was singularly unsuccessful in both material and human terms.

The colonies could not be fully developed partly because of this dearth of Italian workers, and partly because of the shortage of willing native workers. There was no clear educational policy for these people until the mid-1930s. After all, it did not pay to give them ideas above their station, so they often became the victims of conscripted labour practices, especially on the large banana plantations in East Africa – reminiscent of the ancient Roman *latifundia* – where they were often very badly treated. Rations were short, and beatings and imprisonment were common for those who did not fulfil their quotas. The policies and practices pursued in Tripolitania and Cyrenaica were not wholly dissimilar from those in East Africa. Willing co-operation in the task of development was encouraged, but any infringements were often met with extreme harshness and even gratuitous cruelty.

Mussolini did not exterminate whole populations in the interests of bogus racial pseudoscience, or even out of military expediency, but he was hardly squeamish in pursuit of a chimerical 'pax Romana'. He was not above using concentration camps, population transfers and even mass executions to further his purposes. For instance on 5 June 1936 he sent a telegram to Graziani, his commander at Addis Ababa, instructing him that all rebels held as prisoner were to be shot. Two days later he was insisting on the use of gas against the rebels, and urging the same commander to carry out a policy of terror and extermination. The rebels in question included civilians and clerics, in fact anyone who hindered the total subjugation of the territory prior to the anticipated influx of industrious Italian settlers.

It is disputable whether the Italians ever set out really to understand African tribalism. This was particularly true of the Bedouin peoples of North Africa. Nomadism seems to have been incomprehensible as a way of life; people who did not lead settled lives were regarded as little more than uncivilized barbarians. Consequently, the Italians were not above using troops recruited from one colony to help repress rebellious tribesmen in another. This occurred, for instance, when native levies for Eritrea were brought in to quell minor insurrections in Tripolitania. Sometimes these tribes wrought trouble out of all proportion to their numbers, as was the case with the Senussi in Cyrenaica. Because they had the help and sympathy of the people, they were able to continue sporadic warfare against the Italians for ten years, much to the exasperation of Mussolini who was at a loss to explain how these uncouth tribesmen could frustrate the efforts of modern fascist forces. Ultimately, the natives were largely starved into submission: property and lands were confiscated ostensibly as 'compensation' for the cost of the war, shrines were closed, and remaining resistance crushed with extreme cruelty. The population was driven into camps together with their herds; in these intolerable conditions perhaps as many as 20,000 people died – about a quarter of the population – and their leader publicly executed.

Eventually, with the territories more or less pacified, an uneasy status quo was achieved. Education was maintained at an elementary level only for most, with Italian as the main language of instruction. The fascists insisted that they had a moral and intellectual superiority over other peoples and therefore had the right to rule. A few vain cries of protest were heard, but by and large even liberal officials went along with colonialism as a policy, and repression as a painful necessity in dealings with recalcitrant tribesmen.

With the amalgamation of the North African territories to form the territory of Libya in the mid-1930s, something like normality was established. Under a more humane governor, conditions improved and Italians were once again encouraged to migrate to the colony. Fifty acres each were given to white families and up to ten acres to others. They were supplied with seed and stock and, in general, they all tried to make a go of things, but the Second World War came too soon to prove the success or otherwise of this socially adventurous experiment.

In the Dodecanese Islands, the development of policy and practice was virtually the reverse of that pursued in Libya. Here the Italians ruled a Greek people upon whom they attempted to impose their special brand of fascism. But even so, there was in the 1920s a policy of enlightened government which gave considerable freedom, particularly to religious minorities. This changed in the 1930s when the governor of Somalia, De Vashi, was transferred to the Aegean, taking with him some of the repressive practices he had introduced in his former colony. Personally, he lived in style, but he did not bring any profit to the motherland through his administration – much to the chagrin of Mussolini.

All in all, colonial endeavour had been rather a worthless venture. By 1938, the cost of administering the empire ran to about one-tenth of the total foreign reserves, while the imports from the colonies in return amounted to only about 2 per cent of her total imports. The colonies, on the other hand, had to import all their industrial equipment, and about half their food supplies. It is little wonder that the Italians in general and Mussolini in particular began to lose interest in the very concept of an African Empire. Certain fascist entrepreneurs undoubtedly made money from it, but overall it was proving to be more trouble than it was worth – a fascist black elephant. More and more, as the 1930s drew to a close, Mussolini and his intimates saw their imperial future in the

Balkans – a Mediterranean Empire to complement (or counterbalance) that of the Nazis in northern Europe.

The creation, then, of an African Empire proved to be an expensive gamble that did not pay off. It was intended to benefit Italy both economically and politically, but instead it drained the motherland of much-needed resources and exacerbated her relations with most of Europe. The entire project was fraught with contradictions. Mussolini, as self-styled protector of Islam, gave the impression that he would make generous concessions to the subject peoples, and Italian newspapers rather grandiloquently proclaimed this to the world – but little was actually done to further the policies of assimulation and development. There were strong hints that the reward for compliance and co-operation would be Italian citizenship, but for the vast majority this was a prize that never materialized. But then could the Italians really have done anything else? To give parity of esteem to those who were considered to be of inherently inferior status was totally alien to fascist principles. It really should have surprised no one that these promises would never be fulfilled. The Italians had reasonably clear objectives, it is true, but only the haziest ideas as to just how these were to be achieved. And even when real possibilities did present themselves, for example the oil-producing potential in Libya – so important for the burgeoning Italian war-machine – little exploration was actually carried out, mainly because the fascist administration was too proud to permit the necessary investment of foreign money and technology.

The fascists also found themselves involved in inconsistencies at the ideological level. The whole idea of taking over the mantle of the Muslim caliphs as defenders of the Islamic faith was completely at variance with the view put about in Italy that they were the new missionaries in a Catholic crusade against pagans and unbelievers. This almost Jesuitical stance led them to close Protestant missions and proclaim the virtues of the 'true faith' while at the same time, repairing mosques and even building a Muslim theological school in Tripoli. All this was done ostensibly in the interests of the subject peoples, though one may be forgiven for cynically thinking that it was actually done more out of expediency than conviction.

It is really difficult to escape the conclusion that there was little real focus to Italian colonial policies, and that this extended to their practices as well. The whole enterprise went sour from the beginning, subject peoples are slow to forget just how they have become subject. Despite the largesse, the technical gadgetry, and the political sops that were thrown their way, they did not easily forgive the oppressive means of their own subjugation. Furthermore, they were too well aware of the broken promises and the unfulfilled intentions of their overlords. The fascists could not ultimately win because they lacked the support of the people. They did not lose this support; they never really had it in the first place. They thought – and announced – that they had a civilizing mission to the barbarians, yet they rejected the possibilities for absorption and assimilation which might have brought success. These were outlawed as degenerate ideas peddled by weak-minded colonial powers such as the British and the French. Instead, they pursued an arid and ultimately unproductive policy of arbitrary repression which, by its very nature, had very little chance of success.

The war ended the whole vainglorious dream. Colonial expansion was implicit in fascism. Mussolini had found it possible to reconcile his early socialism with the demands of fascist ideology by transferring the class struggle to the international stage. Loyalty to class was superseded by loyalty to the nation. Proletarian Italy was to become the 'employer' of conquered colonial labour; colonialism was justified in terms of its mission and its economic advantages, besides being a convenient compensation from the miseries at home. East African expansion, especially the conquest of Ethiopia, had been achieved with the necessary acquiescence of the monarchy, and the willing endorsements of the Vatican which had declared that it was not powerful enough to prevent the use of poison gas against the natives. All this was part of an anachronistic colonial enterprise which could never have been achieved without the implicit connivance of the Western powers – especially France – who had seen these African encroachments as an inexpensive diversion from possible European intentions. At the time, Italy had been seen by others as the main menace to world peace – mistakenly, as it transpired. Far from strengthening Italy, these adventures had, in fact, pinned down substantial forces and consumed significant proportions of the Italian budget, all to little avail (Lowe and Mazari 1975: 289).

All this was effectively lost when Italy entered the war in June 1940. Mussolini had belatedly – and perhaps ignominiously – been offered yet further colonial concessions if he would remain neutral, but he had his eyes on bigger prizes. He wanted to be in at the kill yet he should have sensed Italy's unpreparedness when only a few days before the armistice with France his forces were repulsed by weak and dispirited French units.

In North Africa, however, the situation was much more to Italy's advantage. Indeed, the British were in a seemingly hopeless position. In Africa, they had barely 50,000 men to face about half a million troops, counting regular Italian forces and their colonial levies. In Eritrea and Ethiopia the Italians had some 200,000 men and could easily have invaded the Sudan where the British could only muster about 9,000 troops, or moved southwards to Kenya where the British had similar numbers. The remainder of their troops were stationed in

Egypt where they faced an Italian army about ten times their size. And in support, all they had was a pathetically small assembly of antiquated aircraft. Their desperate plight at home after the retreat from Dunkirk, and the imminent threat of invasion meant that they were reluctant to commit forces to the Middle East to counter the anticipated Italian onslaught. Even the small reinforcements they could afford now had to take the long journey round the Cape because of powerful Italian naval forces in the Mediterranean. The situation was further exacerbated by the ambivalent attitude of Egypt who dutifully broke off diplomatic relations with both Germany and Italy, but having no great love for Britain, announced that she would not go to war unless she was actually attacked. And this despite – or perhaps because of – the fact that there were great concentrations of Italian troops on her borders, and perhaps also because she had a large and potentially subversive Italian population.

The Italian advance in North Africa was hardly as expected. It was cautious to the point of virtual inactivity. In the face of such hesitancy, the British, now reinforced with much-needed armour, attacked in force and achieved a series of amazing – and unexpected – victories. What had begun as a large-scale raid to test the Italian defences, had soon netted over 100,000 prisoners and enormous amounts of materiel.

There seems to be no doubt that the Italians would have suffered much more serious reverses had it not been for the fact that precious men and equipment had to be withdrawn from Libya in a futile, but understandable, attempt to help the Greeks to stem the German invasion early in 1941. As it was, the Germans were able to come to the aid of the Italians in both North Africa and Greece with notable success. At first, Mussolini was unwilling to accept German help on the scale suggested, which was modest enough. He had been humiliated already in Greece; he didn't want to feel that he couldn't handle the African situation alone. But this professed independence got him nowhere. If he had been prepared to argue for the reinforcements that the task really required and had Hitler been disposed to give them – unlikely in view of his Russian plans – almost certainly the Axis forces could have taken Egypt. Instead, the Allies slowly assumed the ascendency while Mussolini, in his frustration, dismissed and appointed commanders, as if this would really make any difference to the ultimate outcome of the conflict. North Africa was finally lost in 1943.

In East Africa it was a less complex and even more dismal story as far as the Italians were concerned. Again, they were extremely hesitant about making a move, ostensibly because they were afraid of running out of fuel due to the British naval blockade. This gave time for the British to build up their forces consisting largely of

Commonwealth troops and, although still greatly outnumbered, they were able to inflict crippling losses on the Italians who, this time, had no Germans to come to their rescue, and seemingly no stomach for the fight. Many had apparently heard about the Ethiopian treatment of Italian captives, and were more than happy to surrender to the British. The East African-Ethiopian campaign was over in less than a year.

Within three years of Italy's entry into the war, her empire had disintegrated. Mussolini began to lose all sense of political reality, and when Italy itself surrendered to the Allies in 1943, he was dismissed by the king with whom he had long had ambivalent relations, but who had endorsed the original intention to join the war, even to the point of declaring himself nominal head of the Italian forces. Freed by the Germans Mussolini conspired with them to have executed many of the 'traitors' on the Grand Council who had condemned him, including Ciano, his own son-in-law. He and his small entourage also co-operated with the Germans in the government of a forlorn puppet state, the misnamed Salo Republic in the north of the country, which commanded very little public or military allegiance. But time was running out. The fascists were intimidated by their masters, threatened by the Allies, and menaced by a growing army of Italian partisans. They vainly clung to the tarnished trappings of power, but were finally overwhelmed by those whom they had once presumed to command.

8

Exploitation: The Spanish in Peru

The story of the Spanish in Peru is an anomalous combination of boldness and duplicity, of reckless courage – especially during the conquest phase – coupled with almost unexampled treachery. In the post-conquest period, there was a considerable disparity between theory and practice; between the ideology and the actual administration. Some of the conquerors evinced serious paternalistic concern while the majority maintained a regime of ruthless repression.

The Spanish explorers arrived in Mexico in AD 1518; a year later Hernando Cortés with less than 500 troops (*conquistadores*) together with their native allies began their campaign against the Aztec peoples of Mexico. In three years, the kingdom was theirs. And so began a systematic exploitation of its gold and silver deposits to swell the coffers of the Spanish king, Charles V, who was always looking for further revenues to finance his innumerable wars in Europe and North Africa.

But this was only the beginning. Rumours began to reach the Spanish of still greater wealth to be had further south in the fabled land of the Incas. It was even said that the streets of Cuzco, the Inca capital, were paved with gold – a slight exaggeration, of course, but containing just enough truth to whet the insatiable Spanish appetite. They were looking for El Dorado – the land of gold – and their search was well-rewarded in Peru.

The Inca Empire, centred in the Peruvian heartland, actually extended over much of the Western coastal strip of South America. The land area was only about 200 miles wide, but it stretched some 2,500 miles, from Ecuador in the north to Chile in the south. It included all kinds of tribal groupings which had come under Inca authority largely by conquest and, in later years, partly by attraction – a policy that was sometimes considered more effective than warfare. Subject peoples were allowed to retain their own languages, but were also required to adopt the Inca tongue (Quechua). They were also free to keep some of their own native traditions, providing they made the necessary contributions to the state.

So although we are going to look primarily at the ways in which the Spanish subjugated and exploited these peoples, we must also take a critical view of the Peruvians themselves. It is necessary to get a sense of perspective in these matters. The Incas were not exactly amateurs at military repression themselves.

From c. AD 1200 the Incas began to expand their domains along the Western coastline. Actually the history is a little hazy here; the sources – which are limited anyway – contain obvious mythological material. But from the middle of the fifteenth century, things become a little clearer and much of the historical detail for this period is now generally agreed by scholars. We know that the Incas set out on campaigns in both the north and south, persuading or forcing other tribal groups into alliances, and dealing repressively with those who resisted their authority. The first 'historical' emperor, Pachacuti (1438–71), set the style for the dynasty; in some cases, whole tribal groups – except children and old women – were exterminated, and in other instances wholesale population transfer was practised. Some authorities – as an exaggerated and doubtful compliment – even liken Pachacuti and his son Topa Inca to other 'great conquerors' such as 'Philip and Alexander' (Mason 1964: 117).

This policy of expansionism continued until the Spanish Conquest. Peoples were either killed off, subdued – as with many tribes in the hinterland – or incorporated into the Inca state. And when the Incas were not fighting other peoples, they were contesting power among themselves. Almost coincidental with the beginning of the conquest, Atahuallpa, the last 'true' Inca ruler, secured supreme authority for himself by fighting his own brother for the throne. When this civil war was over, Atahuallpa had his brother's whole family and supporters killed in front of his eyes. Some eighty people were fastened to poles and exhibited on the highway to Cuzco.

The term Inca is actually a little confusing. It can refer to the tribe in general, and is often commonly used in this way, but it is probably more accurate to use it for either the emperor, the Inca himself, or, by association, the ruling class who in one way or another were usually related to the emperor. This 'family' controlled a system that might be classified as one of collective absolutism. The authority of the Inca was unquestioned. He ruled through a hierarchy of officials who constituted the state literati – trained administrators with a monopoly of formal knowledge. Their training was rigorous and demanding, and took place in special 'schools'. Even the Inca himself had to undergo this preparation for office, which had a strong monastic flavour and took four years to complete. There were only four chief officials who each had charge of a quarter of the empire. Under them were four further officials, each chosen by those above them, and so on throughout the ranking system. Authority therefore always flowed downwards from level to level with no permitted contact between officials of equal (i.e. horizontal) rank. Control was thus maintained by both a delegation and separation of powers.

The state was organized on the basis of the endogamous clan (*ayllu*) who lived in small village units and, in effect, constituted small states within a state. These were ruled by a headman (*curaca*) whose authority was hereditary. Indeed, the whole empire was run on a rationally conceived numerical basis. Every ten households were under an official chosen by his superiors, and this was continued for units of fifty households, a hundred households (under a *curaca*), five hundred, one thousand, ten thousand and finally forty thousand households. All were governed by appointed officials, and from the *curaca* upwards, all officials were of the nobility, and the very highest officers were of the Inca family itself. This required large numbers of Inca relatives, but then the Inca had many wives – chief of whom might be his sister or half-sister – and hundreds of concubines.

The Inca administered the empire without a written language as such, though officials did have the use of a mnemonic device – the *quipu*. This was simply a series of coloured knotted strings which they used as a memory aid for accounting purposes. There was a very well-organized communications system which helped to maintain control throughout the empire. One method was the use of smoke signals by which one authority, Garcilaso de la Vega, insists that it was possible to send a message 2,000 miles in two hours. But they also had an extremely advanced transportation system without the use of the wheel (which, curiously, was a feature of children's toys). It worked on a relay basis with take-over points for runners every mile. It is estimated that the average speed of a message/delivery was 140 miles a day – perhaps better on good roads. In fact, it was reported that the emperor had fresh fish brought to him from the coast every day, and Cuzco is 300 miles from the sea.

The Inca land tenure system has been much admired by posterity. The irrigation and terracing techniques were probably superior to most other pre-industrial societies in their skilful use of land and their conservation of water. Indeed, the system may have supported a population in the heartlands that was probably twice that of modern Peru. The land distribution system itself was quasi-communistic in form. The land was divided between the royals, the priesthood and the people. The basic unit of land, the *tupu* (possibly 60 / 50 paces), was considered enough for a couple without children. With each boy born the family was given an extra *tupu*, and with each girl, half a *tupu*. It was not much, but it was enough. Individual initiative was discouraged and the common people were not allowed to own luxury goods – even if they could afford them – but the system did ensure that everyone, including the old and disabled, were provided for. Extra lands were sometimes given as rewards for military or civic service, and it was a condition of the gift that it could not be disposed of at the holder's discretion.

This whole economy was without money of any kind, and also largely without metals except the wealth of silver and gold. Taxes had therefore to be paid in kind, either as merchandise or work. Taxation in the form of work was organized on an annual corvée basis from which there were certain exemptions. Predictably, these included those of the royal blood and the nobility, and priests of the Sun. But they also included army personnel of all ranks if they were on active duty; all males under twenty-five and over fifty; all women, and all sick and incapable persons. Apparently all were regarded as equal in this, regardless of their skills. Normally it lasted two to three months a year, and in some ways must have resembled the annual mobilization of labour that took place in ancient Egypt for construction of major works of various kinds. In Peru, work was mainly on temples, aqueducts, bridges and palaces, but those recruited might well be expected to function as miners, litter-bearers, post-runners etc. Raw materials were provided as were also food, clothes and medicines. Depots and stores were organized on a village basis, and were regularly inspected by the royal tax officials.

By our standards, the administration of law under the Incas would appear to be inordinately severe. Quite minor offences were often punishable by death. As we might expect, much depended on the focus of the offence, whether it was commoner to commoner, or noble to noble, or – more pertinently – commoner to noble. For example, commoners stealing from another's land could be pardoned without too much difficulty, but commoners who stole from royal or priestly lands might well be executed. Even officials were not exempt, and anyone who displayed unwarranted incompetence and incurred the Inca's displeasure might fare no better than a poor stumbling litter-bearer.

As was the case in so many pre-industrial systems, Inca society was suffused with a theocratic ideology. Religion pervaded the whole state apparatus and informed all its activities. It was well documented in early post-Conquest times by Catholic clerics who were often quite sympathetic to native beliefs and practices even if institutionally their treatment of the Peruvians was little short of abysmal.

The religious system was state-established and state-supported, and was the closest approximation to a 'church' to be found in aboriginal America. Strictly speaking it was a henotheistic system, having a principal deity, Viracocha, and many lesser deities plus what can only be described as a motley assembly of animistic spirits. Viracocha was said to have created all things including the other deities. He had many titles (the evidence suggests that the name was too sacred to be spoken) and was believed to have taken human form and descended to Earth to teach others how to live and eventually left Ecuador, walking on the waves. In this he closely resembles the Aztec culture-hero, Quetzalcoatl, who was seen as a white-bearded stranger who left the Yucatan in similar circumstances, promising to return. Little wonder, therefore, that initially both the Incas and the Aztecs thought that the Spanish were the gods come back to their people. And it is just possible, of course, that these myths are actually vestigial folk-memories of trans-Pacific and trans-Atlantic voyages. Tales still persist that the Americas were visited in ancient times long before Columbus or even the Norsemen, but the evidential support for these is very thin and ambiguous.

Viracocha was regarded as a rather remote and austere deity who could be approached not so much by the people but by the Inca nobility. Operational religion for ordinary Peruvians centred on the nature deities, particularly the sky gods, most eminent of whom was Inti, the Sun, who was believed to be the progenitor of the royal line. The Inca himself was thus regarded as a quasi-divine being who was a direct descendant of the Sun. The principal Inca temples were built in honour of the Sun, and lands were set aside to support the religious officials and attendants. At the main worship centre at Cuzco there was the greatest of the many images of the Sun, thought to be about six feet in diameter and made entirely of gold. The Moon was both a sister deity and a consort for the Sun, and together they produced Venus, the morning and evening star. There were hosts of other planetary and nature deities some of whom were regarded as benign, while others were seen as positively malevolent. In addition, there were disembodied spirits who had not gone to 'heaven' to be with the Sun or even to 'hell' – a cold subterranean world.

Despite their involved cosmological speculations, it may well be that most Peruvians were more interested in the application of religious ideas to the everyday concerns of the state. 'Religion was organised to serve practical ends which were complementary to economic and social policies reflecting the reality of Inca power' (Kendall, 1973: 181).

The Inca was the chief custodian of the Sun cult, and he was served by an established hierarchy of priests which conducted all necessary rituals. The upper echelons of the priesthood – especially the High Priest himself – were all related to the Inca. They held their position on a hereditary basis. The lower orders of the priesthood could be both hereditary and by election. Commoners could be priests of this class, but usually their term of office was for a limited period only, and they did not enjoy the privilege of state support.

The cults were also served by various orders of priestesses. Some were dedicated to the Moon goddess, others to the Sun, and all were expected to maintain the highest standards of chastity. They began as 'chosen women' at about the age of 10, and were often recruited from the daughters of the nobility, but other girls who satisfied the exacting standards of beauty and disposition might also be included. They were educated by nun-like older women (*mamacunas*), and then some were given as brides to selected males, usually officials as a reward for their services, or if they were particularly attractive the girls were earmarked as servants and concubines for the Inca himself. Others might be sent to 'covents' to become *mamacunas* themselves, or chosen as priestesses of the cults. The most privileged were those that served the central cults of Cuzco; those not so esteemed were to be 'distributed' to serve the same cults in the provinces. Their vows of perpetual chastity were solemnly binding, but, unsurprisingly there were certain 'irregularities'. If the Inca was involved he was automatically absolved, but any infringement with others resulted in the most dire punishments. The very least these Virgins of the Sun could expect was a severe whipping; more likely they would be buried alive or hung by their hair from a cliff until they died, while the males involved would be unceremoniously strangled.

Worship mainly took place in the open air in the great plazas outside the temples or at the many wayside shrines. Divination was practised usually to discern the future (unlike the Aztecs, the Peruvians had no marked belief in lucky and unlucky days) or it might be used as a fire-test to determine guilt. The burning of coca was used to contact the spirits, and the 'reading' of llama entrails was common practice in trying to determine what was or was not propitious in a given set of circumstances. Omens were greatly respected: the hooting of owls, the howling of dogs all might be dangerous in particular situations – Atahuallpa is said to have finally resigned himself to his fate on seeing a comet. Sorcery too was well-known; the spirit world was very much the province of paid magicians, though most misfortune was attributed to the much more powerful Inca gods.

Alongside all this was the customary array of quasi-medical expedients such as blood-letting, emetics, and fasting besides mummification and embalming to preserve the semblance of life. It was little wonder that the invading Catholics were amazed to find that among this complex of rituals were the practices of confession, penance, and absolution. These close parallels with their own practices both disturbed and astonished them, and were conveniently ascribed to the agency of that Great Deceiver, the Devil.

The major difference between Inca religious practices and those of their Catholic conquerors centres on the matter of sacrifice – particularly human sacrifice. Wine and food offerings were most usual, and the wealthy often offered figurines or burnt their clothing as an act of worship. But the most common form was the sacrifice of animals which were bred for the purpose on government lands. Human sacrifice was relatively rare, and was reserved for special occasions. It could take the form of a ceremonial death of some subsidiary wives and servants of a noble, or in its more ritualistic form the sacrifice of the young. This might take place at the accession or death of an Inca ruler, during famine or plague, or departure for war. It was considered to be the kind of sacrifice most precious to the gods, so the victims had to be very special people. Usually boys and girls of about 10 years of age were chosen. They had to be physically perfect, and – so we are told – they welcomed their choice and looked forward to a life of eternal bliss. Normally they were inebriated either with drugs or alcohol and then strangled and their blood used as an offering to the implacable deities.

All this changed dramatically with the arrival of the Spaniards. In 1532, at about the same time that Atahuallpa was celebrating his victory over his brother, news was received of strangers who were approaching Peru from the coast. Atahuallpa had his brother and his followers killed and awaited the arrival of the white 'gods' from the West. The Spaniards – largely Castillians – were commanded by a soldier-adventurer Francisco Pizarro. With a mixture of guile and military ingenuity, he led an army of barely 200 men plus an assortment of disaffected rebels and tribesmen, and conquered an empire. First they captured and then executed Atahuallpa after having promised to release him if he paid a huge ransom in gold. Then they set about the task of neutralizing all effective opposition, while accruing as much booty as they could find.

Pizarro and his men took an entirely piratical approach to Peru. They had been driven on by rumours of the fabulous wealth that was there for the taking, and had braved daunting hardships to get it. And they were not going to stop now. They were not really interested in Inca culture or its institutions. Their insatiable hunger for loot overrode everything else, and their example was followed by those who came after them. The Spanish Crown too was complicit in the exploitation of the Incas. The king claimed his right to a fifth part of all treasure taken and ensured his share by sending his personal official to oversee operations.

It is impossible now to assess the worth of the immediate haul from Peru as a whole, but working from 1938 estimates (Mason 1964: 133) a 1991 figure would perhaps be about £200 million. And legends still abound that the Indians hid vast quantities of gold to stop it getting into the hands of the conquerors, especially when they heard of the death of their ruler. Even the none-too-subtle use of torture was unable to prise much more from the natives.

Within a few years all the principals of the conquest had themselves died, in most cases by violent means. They had taken seven years to penetrate the Inca kingdom and five years to secure it. And Spain was going to make sure that all that effort was not wasted; the exploitation had really only just begun. The Spaniards were determined to extort as much silver and gold as possible from their new lands. The king, though expressing due concern for his new subjects, had expensive schemes in Europe which necessitated a continual influx of Inca wealth. Having confiscated all available movable wealth, what better than to tap the unexhausted riches of the Peruvian mines? And who better to work them than a plentiful supply of compliant native labour?

The Peruvian natives were used to feudal absolutism, but it was an absolutism that assured them of regular food and modest living conditions for their families. Under the Spanish things were different. Now it was a case of misery, starvation and death. In some areas the death toll was horrendous. Two valleys near the coastal plains, for example, Huara and Chincha, which were said to contain about 40,000 Indians each were reported in the 1540s to contain no more than 4,000 all told. By 1600 the population of the valleys of Lunahuana and Huana had fallen from 30,000 to 2,000. Overall the population at the time of the conquest is estimated at about seven million; by about 1600 it was down to approximately 1,800,000. One observer, writing to the king emphasized the urgency of the problem, 'I must advise your Catholic Majesty that the wretched Indians are being consumed and are dying out. Half have disappeared, and all will come to an end . . . unless the situation is remedied'. And another, Fernando de Armelones, pointed out the tragic irony of the situation, 'we cannot conceal the great paradox that a barbarian [the Inca] kept such excellent order that the entire country was calm and all were nourished, whereas today we see only . . . deserted villages [in] . . . the kingdom' (quoted in Hemming 1974: 348).

There were several reasons for this staggering decline. First, there was disease. The Peruvians had lived in relative isolation, many of them far above sea-level, and they had little or no immunity to a whole catalogue of European diseases. Smallpox had already made itself felt just before the arrival of the Spanish, and not long afterwards, in 1546, an epidemic – possibly typhus – spread throughout the land with devastating consequences. Between 1585 and 1591, another epidemic struck which apparently resembled measles, again with tragic results.

Second, in addition to all their other privations, the natives were exorbitantly taxed; the conquerors divided the land into vast estates (*encomiendas*) which were awarded to *conquistadores* who had distinguished themselves in battle or who had otherwise rendered valuable service to the cause. The Indians worked the land for their overlord, the *encomendero*, whose demands were often unreasonable and even unrealistic. Even the transportation of the tribute presented almost insurmountable problems for some natives. For example, we hear of the Indians of Pavinacocha, men and women, who had to carry 800 bushels of maize and other goods 200 miles over mountainous terrain to the capital – an enterprise which, including the return journey, took up two months of their year. The *encomenderos* had no legal or official jurisdiction over the Indians, but in actuality – especially in the remoter areas – they had *de facto* powers of life and death over their powerless subjects.

Third, as we have seen, the natives were grossly overworked, especially in the mines. Negroes were imported, but were unable to endure the high altitudes, so the natives were forced to work in the dank underground shafts to produce the special metals that had virtually become the *raison d'être* of the occupation. Huge numbers of slave workers were needed to produce the formidable quantities of gold and silver that the conquerors – and especially the Crown – required. This, added to the mortality rates in the mercury mines, and the deaths from forced labour which occured on a whole succession of vain desert expeditions in search of yet more gold, spelled near extinction for the indigenes in some areas.

But there was yet one further factor – war, and its whole sorry retinue of privation and suffering. As one authority puts it,

> the people of Peru ... lived through a numbing series of catas-
> trophes. Their calm, rigidly-organised society was shattered in
> quick succession by a ferocious civil war [the pre-Conquest
> confrontation between Huscar and Atahuallpa], a bewildering
> conquest by foreigners totally alien in race and outlook, two
> mighty attempts at resistance, and a devastating series of civil
> wars among the invaders.
>
> (Hemming, 1974: 350)

Thousands died in these wars, possibly 20,000 in the first rebellion alone which had been led by Manco Inca in 1536–7. The Indians really had very little chance once the conquerors began to receive reinforcements from colonies in the Caribbean and from Spain itself. The second rebellion in 1539 was put down with great ferocity. In just one incident, the Spanish commander in Lima, Francisco de Chaves, wrought havoc in the valleys. At the first signs of Indian restlessness he had launched a punitive expedition in which he sacked houses, destroyed fields and hanged men, women and children indiscriminately. In fact, he is said to have slaughtered six hundred children under the age of 3 and burned and impaled many adults. Tacit admission was made about these atrocities when in 1551 King Charles ordered that schools should be founded and a hundred children supported out of the estate of Chaves who had died a decade earlier. In a quite separate incident, the Spanish tried to make overtures to the now renegade Inca. They sent some native envoys who were duly murdered and their gifts rejected. Pizarro was holding the Inca's favourite wife hostage at the time and – so it was rumoured – had sexually violated her. In retaliation, he had her stripped, tied to a stake, and shot to death with arrows. Many Spanish were shocked and remonstrated about this, but it did not stop their leader from executing more chiefs who had surrendered, and burning those who had the temerity to protest about the savage murder of the Inca's wife. The Inca himself survived in his mountain retreat, but the last significant rebellion against Spanish rule had come to an end. From this time onwards Manco Inca maintained a 'government-in-exile', and the Spanish established a puppet Inca at the capital. Another revolt was planned in 1565, but this too was nipped in the bud, and as a result Spanish rule became even more repressive.

The Spanish determined that they must be the sole rulers of Peru, and in 1572 organized what was to be a decisive campaign against the would-be independent Inca state in the mountains. The heir of Manco Inca, who had only 'ruled' for a year, was captured and condemned and surprised his supporters by denouncing his traditional religion and receiving baptism, before he was publicly executed. This really was the end; the conquest had taken just forty years.

The occupation did have some advantage for the Peruvians. The Spanish introduced numerous products such as wheat and barley, and a range of fruits and vegetables. They also brought with them a variety of domestic animals: sheep, goats, cattle and horses besides pigs and chickens. But these things were not easily accepted. For many years the natives expressed their resistance to Spanish rule by a rejection of their culture and its artefacts. To a large extent the Spanish used some existing Inca institutions to facilitate a certain continuity of tradition, though other institutions were allowed to die an unnatural death. There were, on the other hand, some marked deviations from Inca norms. Cities were established and an elaborate system of law courts was set up. Money was introduced with a consequent weakening in the custom of reciprocity. This played havoc with the traditional economy. The Indians were confused by these new ideas and were vulnerable to the exploitative machinations of their new overlords. The complement of this was that the sudden influx of wealth into Spain had upset the economic markets. It had changed price levels and induced inflation, and encouraged a more acquisitive ethos among Spanish investors and entrepreneurs.

In the upper echelons of the administration – especially in Spain itself – there does seem to have been some concern for the welfare of the natives. But this was tempered by an overweening desire for the riches of the Inca Empire, and one suspects that many in government were reluctant to ask too many questions about how these riches were obtained.

Potentially, the one great civilizing agency the Spanish brought with them was the Church. Ostensibly the main purpose of the expeditions as far as the Crown was concerned was the conversion of the heathen, and priests were commissioned for this very task. The conquerors never evinced much concern for the bodily welfare of the natives, but often showed an inordinate zeal for the condition of their souls. The truth of the matter is that even the clergy were ambivalent about the whole operation. Some endorsed the policy of expansion without question and gave their blessing to the rapacious activities of the *conquistadores* while others felt a genuine pity for their charges and did what they could to ameliorate the hardship of Spanish rule.

The Church really did not know what to make of Inca religion. This was a new world in every sense to the priesthood. Catholic scholarship had never encountered anything like the thought-systems they found in these new colonies – especially in Mexico. Cultural shock was not confined to the Indians. It was very much a two-way affair. Arriving in the New World with its strange theologies and even more bizarre practices was like descending on another planet. Priests found themselves having to revise all sorts of previous conceptions about what constituted 'true' religion and the purpose and scope of salvation. And all this at a time when there was increasing questioning and discontentment on the home front – the Reformation in Europe was just getting underway.

As far as the Peruvians were concerned it could be argued that the very benignancy of the Inca state had led to a sterilization of individuality – almost to passive mediocrity. The system was benevolent but impersonal – and ultimately this increased its vulnerability. Part of its weakness may have lain in its exploitable religious ideology. For the natives, it was the point at which the cultures could meet. Theoretically there was the basis for a possible *rapprochement* between an all-embracing state religion and a totalizing universal church. The very affinities between the two systems acted as the solvent of Inca resistance. Peruvian religion was the unwitting agency of its own destruction.

9

Subjugation: Europeans and the indigenes of North America

In recent years, there has been a proliferation of books reviewing the histories of the American Indians, especially their highly chequered relations with Europeans from the early sixteenth century onwards. Many of these have been – in various ways – reassessments which have tended to be biased in favour of Indian culture. Rightly or wrongly, the 'white man' is regarded as the villain of the piece. References to 'adventurers' and 'intrepid explorers' in earlier and popular texts have given way to more pejorative terms such as 'invaders' and 'intruders'. Europeans are thought to have no right to the Americas, and their motives are invariably seen as highly suspect. Any talk of altruism, of exercising civilizing influences, of spreading advanced European culture, is interpreted as hollow and hypocritical. The European is viewed as an essentially aggrandizing creature, really only interested in wealth and territory – in short, in anything he can take.

True as much of this anti-European criticism is, it is not the whole truth. On the basis of the new received wisdom the layman could be forgiven for thinking that North America was once an idyllic hunting ground peopled by hosts of happy, carefree natives who were then corrupted by unscrupulous, expansionist Europeans. For example, one well-intentioned popular author claims to have written a 'narrative of the conquest of the American West as the victims experienced it' and how those who read it

> may be surprised to hear words of gentle reasonableness coming from the mouths of Indians stereotyped in the American myth as ruthless savages. . . . The Indians knew that life was equated with the earth and its resources, that America was a paradise, and they could not comprehend why the intruders . . . were determined to destroy all that was Indian.
>
> (Brown 1970: xvii)

This kind of emphasis does a disservice to the actuality – in so far as

110

we can discern from the evidence exactly what that actuality was. It may simply be replacing one set of myths by another.

The white men were unscrupulous and calculatingly ruthless in their dealings with the Indians, as we shall see, but they were not all like this. Some were understanding and just – one might almost say caring – albeit paternalistic in their policies and practices. Furthermore it should never be overlooked that many of the tribes they encountered were equally ruthless not only in their responses to the intruders, but also in their fratricidal wars with one another.

The French were probably the first in the field in North America soon after 1500. Certainly the voyages of Jacques Cartier in Canada between 1534 and 1541 are well attested. But the French were not able to establish settlements of any note until early in the seventeenth century. They moved south into the valley of the Mississippi setting up more bases, and at the very end of the century (1699) claimed the territory of Louisiana. By 1718, they had expanded still further and founded New Orleans. Meanwhile, the British and the Dutch had set up colonies on the eastern seaboard of what was to become the United States. Drake, in his epic circumnavigation of the globe (1577–80), actually 'claimed' California for the British Crown, though a claim is really all it was. The British settled early in New England and Virginia; slaves were imported from Africa to work, and soon tobacco plantations were commenced in Virginia. Potential profit from tobacco called for constantly increased acreages; new fields had to be found every few years, and it was sometimes found easier to secure this by confiscation than the clearing of new lands. The Pilgrim Fathers arrived in 1620, and others seeking religious and political freedom settled the areas around Massachusetts Bay, Maine, Rhode Island and Connecticut.

The mid-seventeenth century was a period of considerable uncertainty in England. The Civil War, the rise and fall of Cromwell, and the Restoration coincided with the time of consolidation in the New World colonies. Royal charters were granted; Dutch territories were incorporated; Spain still held on to Florida and immigrants – many of them German – began to pour into the new territories. The cosmopolitan character of the United States was being established.

By this time too there had already been some preliminary clashes with the Indians. Some 'proprietors' even had their charter revoked in 1729 for their incompetent handling of Indian affairs in Carolina – a situation which eventually led to a division of the territory. This contrasts with the more enlightened approach of William Penn and his followers who settled the territory of the future Pennsylvania on Quaker principles (1681–3), making a humane and successful treaty with the Indians. The Quakers sought peaceful solutions to their problems with the Indians, and initially this worked quite well until

111

it was corrupted by the foreseeable conflict between the English and the French.

The colonial policies of the French and the English were quite different. The French colonists were fully supported by their government. Troops were supplied where necessary, either for use against other hostile settlers – effectively, the English – or against the Indians, and they were given grants of land when their service was done. Dowries were given to women who were prepared to go out and marry colonists, and seed, stock and implements were also supplied. All land was on lease from the French Crown, and in return all able colonists were liable to military service. The main weakness of this system, rational as it seems, was that it tended to discourage the formation of independent, self-reliant colonial governments, and when the parent government lost its enthusiasm (as it sometimes did in its preoccupation with European affairs) the colonists inevitably suffered. Furthermore, religious persecution drove some French to join the British Colonies, especially so after the revocation of the Edict of Nantes in 1685 which withdrew certain privileges from the Protestant Huguenots.

The British Colonies were quite different in that they were not subject to centralized control. There was comparative religious freedom; in fact some settlements – notably Rhode Island – were famed for their degree of religious toleration. Furthermore, there was relative political autonomy. This ethos of independence generated initiative and a spirit of self-sufficiency which was infectious, so much so that in sheer numerical terms the British began to outstrip the French. The British proved altogether more successful in attracting the adventurous to the New World, and by 1689 there were 200,000 British colonists and only about 11,000 French. Perhaps this actually says something for the unpopularity of the government in Britain itself, and its treatment of dissident minorities. Certainly by 1750, the number of British settlers had reached about a million whereas the French still only had about 50,000.

These figures do not necessarily indicate that all was going well in the colonies. Problems beset these infant settlements, and from about the middle of the eighteenth century, the Crown decided to exert more control over the new territories. Certain evils crept into the whole colonial and colonizing process, especially mercantilism with its exploitative view that colonies really only existed as producers of raw materials and as ready markets for British manufactured goods. After a period of *laissez-faire* in which a blind eye was turned to smuggling and other illegalities, controls were tightened to bring the American colonies into line with those elsewhere (Revill 1962: 471). But this did not rule out the slave-trade and kindred questionable activities.

Relations with the Indians also began to deteriorate, and these were not always helped by prevailing religious attitudes. In the sixteenth

112

century, the Spanish had been impressed by some of the tribes in New Mexico, particularly the Zuni. One soldier had written,

> They do not have chiefs ... but are ruled by a council of ... elders .... They tell them how to live ... and give them certain commandments to keep, for there is no drunkenness among them nor sodomy nor sacrifices, neither do they eat human flesh nor steal.
>
> (quoted in Brandon 1969: 119)

But this generous approach to the Indians was not shared by all. The Jesuits were persevering and made slow but significant progress among the tribes of the Five Nations confederacy which was dominated by the Iroquois who, initially, had been fiercely resistant to the overtures of the missionaries. Protestants too were very active in promoting the Gospel among the natives but, again, often met with a hostile response. This could hardly be unexpected in the face of European intrusion. The Indians found it extremely difficult to reconcile the pious and well-intentioned pleadings of the Europeans as missionaries with the domineering and rapacious activities of Europeans as unwelcome overlords. And none of this was helped by the assumptions of some Puritans that the Indians were destined for damnation anyway. One Puritan chronicler wrote of an epidemic of 1616–19 as 'The wonderful preparation [of] the Lord ... for his people's abode in the Western World' in that it had killed off 'the Savages' – 'chiefly young men and children, the very seeds of increase' (quoted in Brandon 1969: 167). There is little doubt that these sentiments were echoed by many earnest settlers who took the view that they were latter-day Israelites fighting for the Promised Land. This was an impression confirmed by the massacre of 600 Pequot tribespeople by an army of colonists and Indians at a stockaded town in Connecticut in 1637. The governor of the settlement at Plymouth later wrote that 'it was a fearful sight to see them frying in the fire ... but the victory seemed a sweet sacrifice [of praise]' (quoted in Brandon 1969: 168–9).

Perhaps the most successful of the denominations in these early years in their dealings with the Indians were the Quakers. They sought to come to some understanding with their new charges, and tried to influence them as much by their humane example as their actual teaching. As we have seen, this changed with new circumstances, but it was a noble experiment at the time.

The European scramble for more and more territory could only result in conflict between the main contestants. The eighteenth century was vitiated by interminable wars between Britain and Holland, Britain and Spain, and particularly Britain and France where the conflict in the New World was really an extension of their ongoing rivalry in Europe itself (the Seven Years' War). Some of the early clashes in Canada in the middle of the century brought almost unmitigated disaster for the British, but they restored the situation by the capture of Quebec (1759) and Montreal (1760), in which the commanders on both sides, Wolfe and Montcalm, were killed. This meant that Britain now controlled virtually the whole of Canada and by the Treaty of Paris (1763) became the dominant power in North America generally.

The anti-climax of all this was that at the peak of Britain's military achievements tensions developed between the mother country and her American colonies. This was largely precipitated by attempts to raise revenues for the administration and policing of the new territories – particularly the protection of the frontiers against tribal raids. There were protests from colonists and this led to more coercion by the British which, predictably, resulted in yet more agitation in the colonies. Eventually a congress was convened in Philadelphia in 1774 at which a declaration of rights and grievances was largely rejected by the British government, and war broke out the following year.

The supreme irony for the British was that, having defeated half of Europe, they were then beaten by a rag-taggle army of their own colonists. They did well at first, but their command was riddled with inefficiencies, and frustrated by the inability of the Crown to co-ordinate operations from London. But, to be fair to the British, the colonists were hardly alone against what was effectively a world power. The French (who were obviously determined to reverse their fortunes in the Seven Years' War) sent them considerable help in the form of money, men and materials. In 1778 they also 'loaned' their fleet which had a decisive influence on events. In 1779, Spain joined them; and in 1780 the British also found themselves at war with the Dutch. And just to twist the knife, other European states, notably Russia, Sweden, Denmark and Austria ganged up on Britain with an Armed Neutrality Pact. British reverses now came thick and fast, and in 1783 a general peace was signed at Versailles. This necessitated territorial concessions, but few real advantages to anyone except the new United States which was now assured of its independence.

The position of the native population in this seemingly irrelevant extension of European power politics was somewhat invidious. In theory it should have been marginal to their main concerns. After all, why not let their enemies fight it out amongst themselves, it could surely only be to the Indians' advantage? But it did not work out this way. As with the previous war between Britain and France, the Indians could hardly be left untouched by the hostilities. Many tribes found themselves sucked into the wars – often on opposing sides – by promises of rewards for their military support.

In the past, traditional inter-tribal warfare had been limited in scale,

114

though not always in severity. There were sometimes long-standing enmities between tribes living considerable distances from each other, such as the Iroquois of the eastern seaboard and the Cherokee of the Carolinas. The reason – or rationalization – for much inter-tribal warfare centred on revenge for the souls of the dead. Of course, there were political and economic tensions, and clear status competition, but ostensibly war was a matter of religious ideology. The dead would find no rest until their spirits were appeased. War was frequently urged by women who might accuse warriors of cowardice if they hesitated to avenge an insult and particularly if they appeared reluctant to 'cleanse' the shame of bereavement by inflicting torture and death on the enemy. For example, war among the Iroquois Confederacy (including the Seneca, Cayuga, Onondaga, Oneida and Mohawk tribes of the Great Lakes) often consisted of little more than raiding parties who were sent out to burn an enemy camp and take prisoners either for torture or 'adoption'. The settlement of feuds, especially when the tribes concerned were in close proximity, often escalated into more conventional warfare. War-parties could 'replace' their own dead either by adopting enemy prisoners (even white prisoners), or 'adopting' their scalps, or by bringing back prisoners to be slaves, or – very commonly – to be the victims of torture and death. Torture was a ritual, and anyone who did not withstand it with dignity and courage was usually dispatched with impunity. The cruelty inflicted could sometimes be unendurable. There is an account of an ageing Seneca warrior who was captured by the Huron, and originally marked for adoption. He was already badly wounded, and maggots were eating at a gaping hatchet wound in his hand. His 'case' was reconsidered, and he was given to a senior Huron who wanted revenge for the death of his nephew. He was subsequently tortured – by women as well as men – by slow burning throughout a whole night during which he was kept alive by refreshments. According to the Jesuits who witnessed the spectacle he refused to revile those who jeered at him while causing his agonies. In death he was finally given the respect his sufferings deserved and he was adopted into the Huron nation (Wallace 1972: 104–7).

It has been argued that with the coming of the white man 'Indian warfare enormously increased and Indian insecurity became incalculably intensified, but that profound training and conditioning, and . . . the affirmation of the will to live dangerously while living in impassioned tranquility, did not collapse' (Collier 1956: 102). Allowing for some exaggeration and the colourfully expressed sentiments, it is certainly true that with the arrival of the Europeans came increased tribal divisions. Tribes were played off against one another to the detriment of all concerned. They were dealing not with one invasion but with many, and the rivalries of the Europeans became reflected in the rivalries among the tribes themselves. The Indians became embroiled in the struggle of competing imperialisms which – at first – they sought to exploit, but which ultimately contributed to their own downfall.

The Forest Indians – the tribes of the Iroquois hegemony – made a vain desperate attempt to break free from white domination in 1763 in the so-called 'Conspiracy of Pontiac'. The plan was to attack a number of British forts simultaneously. It failed partly because it was betrayed by those who did not want to participate, and partly because of a general lack of cohesion in its actual execution. After this, the Iroquois, no longer able to manipulate French–British rivalry, and finding themselves without a firm European ally, settled for a treaty in 1768 in which they were forced to forego their territories south of the Ohio and Susquehanna rivers.

Until the early years of the eighteenth century, honours had been fairly even. The Indians that were mainly affected by the European invasion, those of the eastern seaboard, had been able to negotiate a certain amount of independence by playing off the whites against each other, particularly the French and the British. This way they were able to survive. Of course, the reverse was true as well. European national groups used the Indians to further their own interests *vis-à-vis* their opponents. But as the Europeans gained increasing dominance, so any chance of an Indian revival receded. They extended their 'conquests' to the south and especially to the West, and the natives had to retreat further and further into the less populated hinterland.

The Europeans now had control, and they began to turn the screw firmly and inexorably so that in the end the Indians were going to be left with practically nothing. From the end of the eighteenth century, the tribes were no longer dealing with rival European powers, but the European legacy, the new government of the United States. The names had changed, but not the policies. If anything, the cultural extinction of these tribal entities became more rationalized and more certain under a central, white administration.

Let us take, first of all, the case of some of the 'Five Civilized Tribes', the Cherokees, Choctaws, Chickasaws, Creeks and Seminoles. The Cherokees of Georgia were persuaded to give up seven million acres of their land for four and a half million dollars which would be paid to their credit. After three years the money had still not been handed over, and tribes people were reluctant to move. The government decided to act – in their own interests. Some 7,000 troops plus other interested non-military personnel were dispatched to clear the Cherokees off their lands. Many men, women and children were forcibly evacuated to camps, their livestock went to the camp-followers, and most of their own homes were burned. Others were compelled to embark on a long trek to Arkansas in mid-winter; and about a hundred a day died of exhaustion and cold. It is estimated that of the 14,000 or so that began the journey, about 4,000 died *en route*. On 3 December 1838, President Van Buren was able to inform Congress that these 'measures authorized by Congress . . . have had the happiest effects . . . the Cherokees have emigrated without any apparent reluctance' (quoted in Collier 1956: 124). The Indians lost out both ways. The costs of this 'long march' were cynically defrayed by the monies that the government had originally credited to the Indians for the 'purchase' of their lands.

Between 1800 and 1840 a variety of treaties were made with the tribes east of the Mississippi, but virtually all of these were either broken, nullified or modified by the government. And all this was done officially – through the appropriate statutes and enabling Acts. What was to become known as Indian Territory was created in the state of Oklahoma, and more deportations began. There was no serious resistance – possibly because many tribespeople were convinced that they were exchanging new lands for old. There were, of course, exceptions. In Florida, the Seminoles held vastly superior government forces at bay between 1835 and 1842 and, in the end, the government admitted that the effort was hardly worthwhile and left the Indians to their precarious retreat in the swamps of the Everglades. Large numbers of the other tribes also avoided deportation and found refuge in the fastnesses which so far had eluded government control.

Those that had acceded to governmental edicts and settled on the spacious, uncultivated lands in Oklahoma were told that this territory was for their unrestricted use. The government even went so far as to pledge these lands to the Indians for perpetuity – but intention and duplicity were not far apart. It seems that there was some sympathy for the Indians from many officials, but these were often far from the scene of the affairs they legislated. The army, on the other hand, which was at the raw edge of Indian–settler relations, determined that one way or another these societies had to be neutralized. It was a matter of political and military convenience to make sure they were completely subdued.

In 1849, the control of Indian affairs was transferred from the War Department to the Interior Department which continued the unproclaimed policy of dissolution. Any plausible excuse was employed for the abrogation of treaties. Retribution had not been a salient feature in the aftermath of the Civil War, but an exception was made of the 'Five Civilized Tribes'. They had aided the defeated Confederate side and were made to surrender their rights even to part of the Indian Territory they had been allocated. Dispossession was carried out as official government policy into the twentieth century; tribal funds were impounded and tribal government severely restricted. The fate of the Indians of California is a case in point. They did not fare well under Spanish auspices and when California became part of the United States, treaties were negotiated in 1851 whereby the Indians surrendered over half the state to their new masters on the understanding that they would have permanent ownership of seven and a half million acres, but the Senate in Washington – possibly under pressure from Californian officials – never ratified the treaty. The agreement was allowed to 'lapse', and eventually every promised acre was sold to whites.

A similar fate befell the Indians of the Plains, notably the Sioux, Cheyenne and Navajo. These tribes had roamed the prairies for centuries; their mode of existence was unfettered and free, bound only by economic restraints and their own rigidly held conventions. The European assault on these tribes was conducted at three levels: the economic, the religious and the military. These were not mutually exclusive; together they constituted a conscious attempt to undermine the power and effectiveness of the tribes.

Government forces not only attacked the Indians directly, they also exploited rivalries between the tribes in order to reduce their ability to resist further European incursions which were now taking place at an accelerating rate. Increasing numbers of settlers were making their way westwards by wagons, the scramble for land was on. Furthermore the imperatives of rail construction necessitated the ousting of even more Indians from their lands. Coupled with this was the destruction of the Indian economy by the devastation of the buffalo herds. This can be interpreted as a deliberate war measure against the tribes rather than a legitimate hunting activity on the part of the whites. It was often gratuitous slaughter and could hardly be justified in terms of need or even acceptable sport. What had been a hunting and warrior economy now had to be transformed into an agricultural economy, a change which was not welcomed, and a task for which most tribespeople were unprepared and untrained. Indians were compelled by government edict to live in specially designated areas – in effect, reservations – and this land allotment system was totally alien to their customary way of life.

More subtle, but just as effective in its own way, was the undermining of traditional Indian culture. Religion, in particular, was seen as a major cohesive force among the tribes; it was in religion that their culture was expressed. Religious ceremonies and rituals were severely circumscribed by government regulations, ostensibly because they were 'pagan' and inhibited progress towards eventual assimilation. But it was also seen – quite rightly – as a source of unity and inspiration. It was necessary, therefore, to curb such activities, especially the four-day ritual of the Sun Dance which was recognized as the chief integrative ceremony among the tribes. Armed force was used to prevent its enactment among the Sioux, and subsequently all such 'heathen practices' were legally outlawed by the Interior Department in 1884, and actually remained in force until 1933.

These outright assaults on Indian culture, the confiscation of lands, and the broken treaties brought about the last, tragic expressions of Indian desperation. The most significant was the well-known Sioux–Cheyenne uprising of 1876 where at the battle of the Little Big Horn in Dakota the ill-famed General Custer made his last stand. The United States forces were simply out-manoeuvred on this occasion, but it was a success that couldn't last. The Indians eventually had to bow before the superior numbers and technology of their opponents. Less well known is the rising of the Nez Percé Indians in Idaho in 1877. The Indians endured what they regarded as a series of serious provocations, and decided that enough was enough. They attacked and killed fifty-eight soldiers in several skirmishes in their attempt to fight their way to what they thought would be freedom in Canada. After a journey of about a thousand miles, the hundred or so warriors were reduced to fifty, and the women and children were exhausted. At this point – only fifty miles from the border – they were confronted by fresh troops; forty warriors were wounded and others killed in the final battle. A pledge was given that the survivors would be taken to Montana over the winter and then returned to Idaho, but, as was so usual, the promise was broken and they were sent instead to Indian territory where hunger and disease halved the band within seven years.

The military authorities reached a point of exasperation with the Indians. In some areas, especially in Arizona and New Mexico, the army found itself confronted by elusive bands, most notably the implacable Apaches who were determined to withstand white rule. Extermination programmes were initiated and volunteers were brought in from California to help kill the warriors and take the women and children prisoner. The Apaches retreated into the mountains and continued their guerrilla war against the whites. No Apache band was actually conquered, and most of their casualities were non-combatants. Settlers and prospectors lived in fear of the Apache whose methods of warfare were both cunning and merciless. Atrocity stories abounded – and they were not without foundation. Like the Iroquois, the Apaches seemed to delight in cruelty. Few of their captives died quickly; some were slowly roasted upside down, others – including women – were literally torn apart. Their reputation was such that when, in 1871, a hundred Americans and Mexicans were tried for the mob murder of 85 Apache people who had put themselves under military protection, they were acquitted by a jury after only a few minutes' deliberation.

After the anti-Indian campaign had cost some thousand American lives and a reported $40 million, the government decided on a policy of conciliation rather than extermination. But to some extent it was a carrot and sticks affair; a carrot of inducement and two sticks so that the enemies could beat each other into submission – in other words, a policy of divide and rule.

In fairness, it has to be said that government policy was not entirely cynical. There were humane voices trying to get a better deal for the Indians, even among the American military. General George Crook, a veteran Indian fighter, saw the Apaches not a 'hell-hounds' or as the 'saintly martyrs' of the Red Man sentimentalists, but as frightened people whose fear had made them past masters at terrorist tactics (quoted in Brandon 1969: 356–7). For Crook, they were honourable, if ruthless, foes who commanded respect for their tactical ingenuity and their unswerving integrity in keeping their promises.

In some ways the most poignant incident in the last days of Indian resistance was the notorious massacre at Wounded Knee Creek in South Dakota. This too was related to religious revival associated with the Ghost Dance, a religious cult which is said to have been first preached by a Paiute Indian named Wavoka and which was essentially pacific in intent. It was called the Ghost Dance because it was believed that the ghosts of dead Indians were waiting to help living Indians in their difficulties. It was also millennialistic, advocating as it did the advent of a new, utopian age for Indian culture. This gave rise to rumours of an Indian rebellion. Newspapers in the East carried stories about Indian attacks and the slaughter of white families. These fictions provoked the army to action, and on 29 December 1890, 98 disarmed warriors and some 200 defenceless women and children of the Hunkpapa Sioux were surrounded and annihilated by army troops.

The account of the settlement of America by the Europeans sounds initially like a catalogue of disaster, and yet during this entire period some real attempts were made to come to terms with the Indians. One can, of course, always ask what the whites were doing there in the first place. And why, after the initial trading settlement phase, did the migrations to the New World have to continue? These questions are obviously related to the conditions in Europe from which many wished to escape, and to the undoubted potential of the new lands which could be had at a very small price. Not least of all was the prevailing ethnocentric perception of the indigenes as inferior savages who 'deserved' to be conquered, and who needed the influence of European culture.

The ensuing occupation of America can thus be seen to have taken place in a number of loosely defined stages (see Underhill 1971: ch. XIV for a discussion of the phases of government policy). The first of these might be termed the *exploratory stage* which covers the sixteenth-century period of discovery and initial settlement by a variety of European powers. This was the period of curiosity, first contacts and no clearly formulated policies regarding the indigenes. The second or *colonial stage*, which takes us from *c*. 1600 to 1775, represents the period in which treaty and conciliation went hand in hand with outright conquest. The two cultures seemed irreconcilable; the Indians could not comprehend the land mania of the whites, and the whites did not appreciate that when they bought land they were not purchasing the freehold, only the right to use that land. Violent clashes became inevitable. The large tribal confederacies, especially those of the Iroquois, were still recognized as independent nations but by this time everyone knew that the whites were here to stay. Complete white domination was merely a matter of time.

The third or *domination stage* which takes us to *c*. 1845 is the period in which the tribes of the eastern seaboard were forced to surrender more and more of their lands, and the bitter enmities generated by the cruelties of the English–French–Indian wars continued to fester. This stage heralded the beginning of the new United States, and it was also the period in which the whites extended their power as far as the Mississippi. Settlers demanded that land should be taken from the roving bands of Indians and given to those who could use it for pasturage and cultivation. Treaties were made and broken as the population pressure increased, and antagonisms were exacerbated by the new government's inconsistency in their dealings with the Indians. In Canada, the British – rightly or wrongly – had taken the unambiguous view that the Indians were subject peoples, and consequently had very little trouble with them. The government of the United States, on the other hand, embarked on various aid programmes; they supplied tools, schools, spent millions of dollars, and organized exchanges of land further West in conjunction with the Department of Indian Affairs set up in 1824, but all to very limited avail. Despite the often good intentions, the Indians did not want to be uprooted, not did they trust the creeping conquest of their lands which entailed uncertainties and deception.

The fourth or *consolidation stage* from *c*. 1845 to *c*. 1890 saw the reaffirmation of white power in the lands beyond the Mississippi. The government acquired southwestern territory from Spain in 1848 and 1853; California in 1849, and the Pacific northwest in 1851. After the Civil War (1861–5) states which had been considered as almost exclusively Indian, such as Nebraska and Kansas, were taken over, mainly to satisfy the needs of land-hungry veterans. Many small tribes, especially those in California simply had their lands taken; the Plains Indians were subdued, and the few remaining 'hostiles' in the south-western territories were either killed or assimilated, and the reservations firmly established. Except for the occasional plaintive protest, the subjugation of the Red Man was now complete – but at the expense of what can only be described as cultural genocide.

10

Depredation: The Assyrians and population transfer

The land of Assur, later known as Assyria, in northern Mesopotamia (Iraq) has no natural frontiers, and it was therefore not possible to demarcate its boundaries; in this sense it was unlike many other early nation states which occupied fairly discrete geographical areas. Its remote history is uncertain; what we do know is that by about 3000 BC Semitic peoples moved into the area, possibly from further east, and founded some form of city-state. For the best part of two thousand years they were dominated by a succession of other powerful nations, particularly the Babylonians to the south, and the lesser-known Mitannians to the West. Their art forms and literature were also largely influenced by others, although in language and material culture they had a great deal in common with the Sumerians who, at various periods dating from the early third millennium, were the most important society in southern Mesopotamia. There was, however, some distinction in their religious pantheon which was headed by their tutelary war-god, Ashur, and Ishtar, the goddess of fertility. Gradually they developed into what might be termed a defensively aggressive people who were prepared to take advantage of any weakness in their more powerful neighbours. By the fourteenth century BC we find that they had expanded sufficiently to be recognized as a significant entity by the powerful Amenhotep III, a pharaoh of the Egyptian New Empire, and by the following century, they had become a force to be reckoned with when their king, Shalmaneser I, invaded both Babylonia and the land of Hatti (modern Turkey). It was about 1100 BC, when there was something of a power vacuum in the Middle East, that the first Assyrian Empire reached the initial phase of its ascendancy.

For a variety of now obscure reasons, including a succession of weak – possibly less militaristic – rulers, Assyria went into decline for nearly two hundred years, and was again intimidated and sometimes controlled by other ascendant societies. But she reawoke in 911 BC. Her territory had been reduced to mere strips of land either side of the Tigris river, but she maintained her free cities and a small but highly trained standing army which had been kept on constant alert by the incursions of hostile tribes. She retained her identity, maintained an unbroken line in her monarchy, and settled down to rebuild her imperial image. She exploited the captured iron mines of Cappadocia far to the north – a key factor in her future success – and gradually laid the foundations of the greatest empire that had been known up to that time.

It may be that at first her wars were primarily defensive, the object being to protect the kingdom from those who threatened its existence. There were intermittent campaigns against sundry tribes, and these expeditions became testing grounds for a much more calculated policy of terror and expansion. What began as a struggle for national survival became a determined effort to carve out a territorial empire. It seems inescapable from Assyria's own texts that there was an important ideological dimension to her militaristic activity. This is always a tricky area for discussion because it is obviously so easy for a people to try to justify aggression in these terms. But in the case of Assyria it would seem that one had only to scratch the surface of her ambition to reveal genuine religious motivations. Predatory her wars certainly were, yet ostensibly this was all done for the honour of Ashur whose enemies had to be punished, at all costs. Georges Roux writes that 'the booty collected and the tribute levied were a source of income and a means of weakening possible aggressors, as well (as being) a token of submission to the supreme deity of Assyria' (Roux 1966: 258). But it is arguable whether the regular and systematic Assyrian campaigns which appear to us as a kind of brigandage, were – as Roux insists – a form of 'crusade'.

What kind of state produced such a military system and why did it start out on this route? What were its intentions, and how was such a system sustained? At the outset of this discussion, it is important to see just how Assyria became and remained a dominant power in Middle Eastern affairs for almost exactly three hundred years.

Above all else Assyria was a state controlled by an absolute monarch, a person who regarded himself and was regarded by others as someone who acted on behalf of the gods for the benefit of the community. He alone was the personal instrument of Ashur. As it was expressed with characteristic immodesty, he was the 'Great king, mighty king, king of the Universe, king of the country of Assur'. But, for all that, he was – unlike the Egyptian pharaoh – only a man, the *ensi*, the *representative* of the gods. He was not elected to office – that would have opened up too many dynastic complications. Instead, he was chosen by his father, and this choice was 'confirmed' by the appropriate oracle.

Subordinate to the king was a hierarchy of state officials including an organized chain of governors, administrators, scribes and couriers. Not very much is known about the central administration. The highest officials appear to have functioned as advisers rather than ministers in our sense of the term. The three most important, the commander-in-chief, the royal cup-bearer and the palace superintendent were each appointed for thirty years – effectively, a lifetime – and had very broadly defined tasks. They held vast estates and lived in considerable state with their own courts and retinues of retainers. Next in the social scale were the professional men including the scribes and the artisans who were organized into guilds with their own apprenticeship schemes. Then came the free poor, a somewhat ill-defined class, and lastly the slaves who became increasingly numerous with the success of Assyrian arms. Their position was unenviable, but the evidence does suggest that they could own property, learn a profession, and even own slaves themselves.

Local jurisdiction was delegated to district and provincial governors. These were obliged to supply the king with detailed reports of exactly what was going on in their areas, especially of any subversive movements that might disturb the security of the empire. They were also responsible for collecting and forwarding the tribute paid by the vassal states to the central administration – in effect, the king. The Assyrians' almost continuous military activity was often directly or indirectly in support of the local officials, to help maintain their authority and ensure the payment of the tribute, which was often not in cash but in kind. The vassal states were required to provide Assyria with vast quantities of goods including both food and manufactured articles.

The economic system itself was really very uneven. Many necessities were imported while the state's own resources were largely diverted for military needs. Craftsmen too were gained by conquest, and we shall never know to what extent they contributed to Assyria's notable artistic achievements. Indeed, it may be that they and a large reservoir of slave labour did much of the work 'at home' while native Assyrians provided the sinews of the armed forces abroad.

Military officials commanded a network of garrisons in both Assyria and the occupied territories. These were manned by regular troops, although extra levies were often conscripted for particular campaigns. In the early days of the empire, governorships were mainly held by members of noble families, and these came to be regarded as hereditary fiefdoms. As the empire developed this was modified; provinces became more impersonally administered by government appointees who were themselves subject to regular visits from government inspectors. Obviously, this kind of scrutiny was thought necessary to obviate the possibility of corruption and the temptation of governors to try to set themselves up as semi-autonomous princes.

This inspectorate extended to every level of the bureaucracy, from the court which was especially concerned with matters of trade and foreign policy, to the directly governed provinces, and on to the vassal states which recognized the suzereignty of the Assyrian king. An intelligence system was also created to ensure that all was well, especially in the outlying areas. It was also used to glean information from rival neighbouring states as to any likely anti-Assyrian intentions. In the volatile vortex of Middle Eastern politics, any plots or conspiracies were possible; and in an atmosphere of repression and suspicion, any change of management might be thought desirable.

Generally speaking, if the vassal states paid up and did not murmur too loudly, they were left in peace. Local ruling families were often allowed to stay in place so long as they made their allotted contributions to Assyrian well-being. As Assyrian power increased, especially in the reign of Tiglath-Pileser (745–27 BC), so did the pressure on the vassal states. In fact, some which had been nominally independent (though, of course, subject to tribute) were later taken over as directly ruled provinces. The Israel–Judah situation is a case in point. Judah, the smaller, southern state recognized the overlordship of Assyria, and sometimes called on the king for assistance. In these circumstances relations remained good, and there was no question of annexation. On the other hand, the larger, northern state of Israel more than once resisted the king's advances for incorporation within the Assyrian Empire and eventually paid the price of complete destruction in 722–21 BC.

As a military nation, Assyria was capable of deploying huge forces, and it carried out numerous campaigns throughout the Middle East, controlling at its zenith territories as far afield as modern Turkey and Egypt to the West, and Iran in the East. The army had a large core of native Assyrians, but also recruited subject peoples who were allowed to retain a regimental identity. Its effectiveness is not to be judged in terms of mere numbers alone; it was its brutal efficiency and organization, and particularly its innovative use of siege-engines that made it such a formidable force. It had all manner of selected personnel including engineers, scribes and even ritual specialists; as we have already seen, confirmatory omens were always a welcome addition to the Assyrian armoury.

War was a source of great pride to the Assyrians – really their *raison d'être* – and it is profusely depicted on Assyrian sculptures and reliefs. Their steles recount the campaigns in all their graphic detail, though – one suspects – minimizing the failures and inconclusive encounters. These are the records of one of the most proudly militaristic societies known to history (see Luckenbill: 1926–7). It is estimated that the Assyrians fought thirty-four major campaigns during the period of their ascendancy, and that many of these involved long and terrible sieges in which the Assyrians could be both persistent and ruthless.

In ancient warfare where the walled city often proved to be such an insuperable obstacle, the Assyrians developed techniques which were probably not bettered until the advent of the Macedonians and particularly the Romans. It has been suggested (Humble 1980: 31) that the Assyrians adopted a basic pattern for a siege which involved four main objectives: (i) isolation – cutting the enemy off from any hope of relief, and shutting off their water and food supplies, (ii) preparation – including the building of any necessary ramps, bridges or causeways, and levelling the ground ready for their siege-engines, (iii) penetration – which involved mining and breaching the walls, and (iv) suppression – subjecting the defenders to maximum fire-power in order to reduce their capacity to hamper other siege operations.

In the face of such might, the fate of the rebellious and the reluctant could be dire indeed. Undoubtedly, as some authorities claim (see Saggs 1984: 248–50) the excessive use of force had a clear psychological value. It was often used to inspire terror in would-be recalcitrants so that they would not even think of questioning Assyrian authority again. And yet, oddly, this is what did happen, time and time again. Their hold on some territories seemed to be, at best, precarious. Despite the awesome sanctions at their disposal, the Assyrians found that some of their vassals were prepared to do all they could to throw off the Assyrian yoke. Among the quite detailed laudatory annals left by the Assyrian kings, we find the same peoples appearing and reappearing among the names of the vanquished foes.

Obviously, Assyrian brutality had generated not simply fear but hatred. The more the oppression, the more some peoples were determined to resist. For example, when the Assyrians faced a coalition of Israelite and Syrian states at Qarqar on the Orontes in 853 BC, Ahab, the king of Israel, fielded 2,000 chariots and 10,000 infantry – a huge armoured force for the time. Little wonder that despite Assyrian claims, the battle was actually indecisive. And when the Assyrian king, Shalmaneser, later moved against Damascus (842 BC), he had to abandon the siege – though he may have been promised – and certainly later received – a huge tribute.

But it has to be admitted that this was not the normal course of events, and the consequences of unsuccessful rebellion were terrible in the extreme; burning, tortures, mutilations and massacres. The scenario was frightening – and familiar. What began as expeditions for a booty of treasure and slaves became an institutionalized system of extortion on a massive sacle. Virtually every spring, the Assyrian army embarked on a new offensive. There was always someone to punish, some king to bring into line, some state or another to intimidate. The Assyrian king needed no pretext. His will was sufficient. So when one of the most famous monarchs, Ashurnasirpal II (d. 859 BC), decided on a punitive expedition against some rebel subjects, he records that he marched his army two hundred miles at the height of summer, and when he drew near their stronghold

> the terror of the splendour of Ashur, my lord, overwhelmed them ... [their] chief ... to save their lives came forth into my presence and embraced my feet, saying, 'If it is thy pleasure slay, if it is thy pleasure, let live' so with [courage and fury] I seized ... [them].
>
> (Roux 1966: 261–2)

It is interesting to note the declared ideological inspiration here besides the self-extolling way in which the king recounts his deeds.

Assyrian rulers generally could be cruel in the extreme – their monuments often show them striking poses of detached indifference before hordes of cringing prisoners – but Ashurnasirpal liked to add his own exquisite refinements. He had no compunction; innocent and guilty, women and children, none was excluded, though rebel chiefs were his speciality.

> I built a pillar over against the city gate and I flayed all the chiefs who had revolted, and I covered the pillar with their skin. Some I impaled upon the pillar on stakes, and others I bound to stakes round the pillar .... And I cut the limbs off the officers ... who had rebelled. ... Many captives ... I burned with fire and many I took as living captives. From some I cut off their noses, their ears and their fingers, of many I put out their eyes. I made one pillar of the living and another of heads, and I bound their heads to tree trunks round about the city. Their young men and maidens I burned with fire. ... The rest of their warriors I consumed with thirst in the desert of the Euphrates.
>
> (Roux 1966: 263–4)

Predictably, the same man proclaimed his prowess as a hunter and marksman, but, paradoxically, he was also very interested in zoology and botany, was a great builder and patron of the arts, and – as has already been indicated – a great supporter of the state cults.

Ashurnasirpal was not alone by any means. One of his successors, Sennacherib (704–681 BC) described at length on the walls of his palace at Nineveh how he commenced a campaign (701 BC) which took him through Syria and down the Lebanese coast to the cities of Judah. He boasts that he captured forty-six cities, including Lachish, a Judean stronghold, where archaeologists have now found the jumbled remains of over 1,500 bodies, and on to Jerusalem where he claims that he shut up the king, Hezikiah, 'like a caged bird'. The city was only saved from total destruction by the payment of a huge ransom. Sennacherib also recounts another engagement with the Elamites on the Tigris in 691 BC whom he portrays as a numerous force, 'like locusts in spring'. He tells how he donned his armour, and prayed, and adds that

> at the command of the great god, Ashur, I rushed upon the enemy like the approach of a hurricane ... [putting] them to rout. ... I transfixed [their] troops with javelins and arrows ... [their] commander-in-chief and his nobles, I cut their throats like sheep. ... My prancing steeds ... plunged into their welling blood as into a river; the wheels of my battle chariot were bespattered with blood ... I filled the plain with the corpses of their warriors like herbage.
>
> (Saggs 1984: 258)

And so it goes on, like some archaic horror comic, gratuitously revelling in the gruesome details. It is not so much that they actually did these things; after all, war was never pretty at the best of times. What strikes many as so repellent is the self-gratifying way in which it is all recounted. At a distance one wonders why it has been found necessary to recount it at all.

And yet here again we have anomalies. Sennacherib was interested in engineering projects, made great improvements to his capital, Nineveh, by structural alterations and the creation of a new water supply. He imported cotton plants from India, and established the growing of cotton as a state-subsidized industry. Yet this same king attacked Babylon in 690 BC where a usurpation of power had taken place. The city fell after fifteen months of siege exacerbated by famine, and – presumably – disease. The Assyrians were nothing if not persistent. It is said that the magnificent squares were littered with the dead. As the inscriptions put it, 'Its inhabitants, young and old, I did not spare, and with their corpses I filled the streets of the city.' Sennacherib allowed his troops to wreck the city. The temples were looted and property destroyed, and the troops even dug canals across the city to destroy its foundations, all to 'quiet the heart of Ashur, my lord'. Perhaps it was a kind of poetic justice that just a few years later (681 BC) Sennacherib was murdered in Babylon – by two of his own sons.

Assyrian culture presents us with all kinds of contradictions. Kings furthered the cause of medicine and science – especially mathematics – and gave considerable endowments to the arts and to the religious institutions. In the arts, particularly sculpture, the Assyrians achieved a vigour unprecedented at the time and, in some ways, rarely equalled since. Their depiction of hunting and battle scenes, for example, are regarded as some of the finest in the world. Literature and learning were also very advanced. The vast library of Asurbanipal, the last of the great Assyrian kings (ruled 668–32 BC), of which some 10,000 texts have been discovered, testifies to the high premium that was put upon the acquisition of knowledge.

It must be conceded that Assyrian achievements were considerable in many fields, but, as in so many societies, ancient and modern, high culture does not preclude low morality, especially as far as the treatment of subject peoples is concerned. Their campaigns were accompanied by wholesale slaughter, needless atrocities, and the often inhumane treatment of prisoners. Palace art seems to rejoice in showing lines of naked people yoked together being dragged away into captivity. We know, for instance, that 50,000 prisoners provided the labour force for the building – and rebuilding – of the temples and palaces of Calah (Nimrud) and for work on the ziggurat (temple tower).

We can see Assyrian occupation policies even more graphically in the practice of deportation or population transfer. This has been a feature of many occupying powers throughout history. It has been known in modern times and in one form it was practised by the Nazis during the Second World War. The Assyrians – possibly the prototype for all aspiring predators – had it down to a fine art. We find that even in the earliest days of Assyrian power in the thirteenth century BC, conquered populations were dislodged from their own territories and relocated elsewhere, usually among alien ethnic groups. This may have been done partly for economic reasons. For instance, we find a century or so later that the prisoners taken after the repulsion of certain nomadic peoples were allowed to settle in the land they had invaded and were henceforth regarded as subjects of Assyria. By the ninth century, however, it had become an institutionalized feature of Assyrian expansionism and it may be that over time the numbers deported reached as many as half a million. The evidence suggests that families were allowed to stay together. But at first they did not integrate easily with the indigenes of the territories in which they were made to settle, possibly because they were permitted to retain their own identities. This included the retention of their languages and their religious practices, providing they recognized the supremacy of Assyrian culture and accepted the paramountcy of the Assyrian gods. It must have been something of a heterogeneous culture, though after a generation or two the descendants of these deportees probably became indistinguishable in customs and manners from native Assyrians.

The problem of nationalist revolts on the fringes of the empire is well illustrated by recounting one of a series of deportations that took place in the kingdom of Israel. As we have seen, Israel had already suffered from Assyrian invasions before her final destruction in 722 BC. Some years earlier Tiglath-Pileser had spared Israel on the payment of 1,000 talents of silver which the Israelite king, Menahem – who was not too squeamish himself – raised by an enforced tax (2 Kings 15). But Israel did not know when she was beaten. There was a further rebellion under another king, Pekah. Tiglath-Pileser launched another campaign (733 BC) and this time reduced Israel's territory to the capital and its immediate environs. Depopulation was employed, and we read of the inhabitants of various cities being led away captive to Assyria (2 Kgs 15: 29–30). Only a year later the same fate befell the city of Damascus. Subsequently, the Old Testament records that

> in the ninth year of Hoshea, the king of Assyria [Sargon II] captured Samaria and he carried the Israelites away to Assyria and placed them in Halah . . . and in the cities of the Medes [modern Iran]. And the king of Assyria brought people from Babylon [etc.] and placed them in the cities of Samaria instead of the people of Israel, and then took possession of Samaria and dwelt in its cities.
>
> (2 Kgs 17)

Corroboration comes from the annals of Sargon who records that he deported 27,280 people and resettled the land with new people whose leaders met with Assyrian approval. From then onwards the state of Israel ceased to exist until its reconstitution in modern times.

It has been argued that the policy and practice of deportation was not necessarily a punitive measure dreamed up by unscrupulous conquerors for its own sake, nor just to make things unpleasant for the defeated. It is maintained instead that it was done for quite discernible, rational reasons (Saggs 1984: 125; 128; 262). But this does sound a little like special pleading. Admittedly, there could be economic and demographic motives behind it. Some areas to which people were deported *were* underpopulated, but this was by no means always so, as we have just seen in the case of Israel. It is true that people were needed as cultivators and craftsmen in particular areas, and that the policy was not just a matter of accident or expediency. But one can surely safely discount Assyrian intimations as to how well they catered for the deportees *en route* to their new destinations. Basic care there had to be – even for slaves; they must survive to work. It was a practical consideration. The further suggestion that the Assyrians were possibly aiming at a more cosmopolitan society, and that they cherished avant-garde notions of racial integration seems to be even more specious. It is difficult to credit these avowedly cruel and warlike people with such humane and high-minded intentions. Population dispersal had other more mundane functions. It is much more likely that the Assyrians were primarily concerned with neutralizing the possibility of insurrection by cutting people off from their cultural roots, and with removing or destroying their leaders and intelligentsia. Resettlement of the ruling classes in distant parts of the empire effectively left the rest of their peoples without much hope of resurgence.

Deportation was usually a final expedient, only part of a very sophisticated programme of conquest. The Assyrians created various degrees of dependence, all of which deprived lesser states of full autonomy. At first they might content themselves with declarations of loyalty from native rulers. This created a vassal relationship which automatically involved the regular payment of tribute. But if this was not paid or the native leaders entertained ambitious ideas about rebellion, the second stage was introduced, namely the reduction of the state concerned to a province with a new leader/king appointed by Assyria. Only when a vassal of such a rump state rebelled was the third stage put into operation; the population was enslaved or deported and its leaders exterminated. Cruelty and frightfulness were calculated elements in the Assyrian military repertoire as their own records testify. One has only to look at the bas-reliefs of, say, Sennacherib's Chaldean campaign showing the methodical and grisly process of heaping and counting the severed heads to know that we are not dealing with the most sensitive of people.

Like so many expansionist states, the Assyrians sowed the seeds of their own eventual destruction. It seems endemic to such societies that they do not seem to know when the optimum point has been reached – the point of marginal administrative returns when it pays less and less to try to administer more and more. This was typically true in the case of Assyria. When the end came, it came quickly – from the provinces which had decided that they must break free from Assyrian domination. It began with quarrels about the succession; at Asurbanipal's death in 626 BC, the kingdom was in disorder. That same year a Chaldean prince, Nabopolassar, declared himself independent and established a new dynasty in Babylonia. The Assyrians were obviously too weak to do anything about it, despite the fact that they had received reinforcements from Egypt, and in 616 BC all southern Mesopotamia rallied to the prince's cause. Assyria's problems intensified when Nabopolassar made an alliance with the powerful Median Empire in the East and in 614 BC the Medes took and sacked the old capital, Ashur. Two years later it was the turn of Nineveh itself. The Babylonians and the Medes, united, and with Arabian and Persian allies, conquered the city after a three-year siege. With the advent of the neo-Babylonian Empire the whole sorry cycle began all over again. The Babylonians eventually fell out with the Medes who united with the Persians to overthrow the Babylonians in 539 BC. And then it was the turn of the Greeks. . . .

So thoroughly was Nineveh laid waste that the Greek, Xenophon, two hundred years later in his epic retreat from Persia (recorded in the Anabasis), marched over the site never realizing that here was located one of the greatest cities of the ancient world. Assyrian craftsmen had been carried off to Media and elsewhere, and the ravages were such that after surprisingly few years, the old empire had been largely forgotten. The remnants of the population had been so dispersed or assimilated with other peoples that even the language was no longer spoken. It was an empire that was unloved and unmourned. For its victims, the prophet Nahum was able to say 'all who hear the news of you clap their hands over you, for upon whom has not come your unceasing evil?' (Nahum 3).

11

Selective control: Nazi non-Eastern occupation policies

The Second World War opened with a lightening campaign (blitzkrieg – as an Italian journalist dubbed it) by Germany against Poland on 1 September 1939. It was all over in just over a month, and then the *Wehrmacht* made ready for its anticipated attack on the West. The intervening military operations against Norway and the occupation of Denmark were something of a cleverly executed *ad hoc* measure to frustrate an invasion by the British and to secure her vital steel supplies from Sweden. The onslaught on the West opened on 10 May 1940, and was overwhelming in its speed and efficiency. Even the Germans were surprised at how well things went. This campaign too was frighteningly brief; it was completed in just about six weeks. All was now set for the attack on the Soviet Union the following year, but again there was a hitch, in this case caused by Italy's plans to conquer Greece. Mussolini, in trying to emulate his Pact of Steel partner, had launched this attack but with dire results and now had to endure the added humiliation of being rescued by the Germans. Hitler's Balkan campaign – another very swift success – was therefore something of an emergency operation that delayed the Russian campaign for over a month. The delay proved fatal; not immediately, of course, the Germans had some brilliant victories in the first year or so of the war, but their failure to take Moscow that first winter (December 1941) did wonders for their opponents, and provided a shock from which the seemingly invincible *Wehrmacht* never quite recovered. From then on, despite some further temporary gains in the Crimea in 1942, it was all a lost cause. In addition, there was the loss of North Africa through the efforts of combined British and American forces, and the terrible saturation bombing of German cities from 1942 onwards. These, and the punishing haemorrhage of German manpower on the Russian front, brought the whole awful conflict to an end in May 1945.

For the people of occupied Europe, liberation couldn't come too quickly. Most of them had had to endure all manner of privations, especially after the infamous Night and Fog Order of December 1941 which decreed that the only effective deterrent for infringements of occupation regulations was death – a decree that was implemented by both the German military and the police forces of the occupied states themselves.

But here we must sound a cautionary note, for so much depended on which part of Europe was concerned. German occupation policies differed, so we must make quite a sharp distinction between the conquered territories in the West (France, Belgium, Luxembourg and the Netherlands), those in the East (Poland and Russia) where the most extreme measures were taken, those in the South (Yugoslavia, Albania and Greece) where the treatment varied, and those in the North (Denmark and Norway) which – for a while, at least – enjoyed the most lenient treatment of all. Because of its gravity, especially in relation to the Jewish question, the Eastern situation merits a chapter to itself (chapter 12). In this chapter, we will take a very cursory look at affairs in the Balkans, but concentrate – for contrast – on the situations in Northern and Western Europe, especially France.

It hardly needs to be stressed that occupation by an alien power generated a wide range of responses from the conquered population, anything, indeed, from unyielding resistance to craven collaboration. Most people, however, just tried to carry on with their normal everyday lives and keep out of trouble. But this was not always that simple. There were all sorts of shortages and restrictions, usually including a curfew. Worse still there was the constant threat of searches and the distinct possibility that a citizen and one or more of his family might be hauled away for compulsory labour service either in Germany or – later – on one of the many military projects such as the V1/V2 sites or the Atlantic Wall. Those who became members of resistance groups often became known to collaborating local police or to the Gestapo and therefore had to spend much of their time trying to evade arrest. For them the dangers were quite different from those of members of the armed forces, say, shot-down Allied aircrew or escaped prisoners who were on the run from the Germans. Admittedly, aircrew ran the risk of being seriously maltreated by the public, even lynched, if they were caught, and commandos and parachutists faced the possibility of immediate execution under the notorious Führer order of 14 October 1942 (Nuremberg document 498–PS, USA–501). But, generally speaking, being in uniform afforded some measure of protection – at least, theoretically – under the Geneva Convention. It also helped to have officer status because even the Gestapo, somewhat curiously, were apparently more reluctant to execute an officer (Foot 1978: 33), although this was by no means an invariable rule. The civilians, on the other hand, who helped such people and who often ran escape lines for them, were liable to the most dire punishments.

Most commonly they would be shot more or less immediately after they had been interrogated, or perhaps they would be deported to Germany from whence they were unlikely to return.

This kind of treatment could be expected no matter which part of occupied Europe was concerned, but *general conditions* definitely varied from region to region. In the Balkans, for example, Greece and Yugoslavia were both under the authority of military governors aided and abetted by compliant civilian staffs. The occupation forces were largely Italian and Bulgarian – often not quite trusted on the Russian front – with a leaven of German personnel to make sure that there were not too many irregularities. In Greece there was a puppet government in Athens, and in Yugoslavia control was exercised by another puppet government, this time in Belgrade, and a separatist Croat state under a fervent pro-German fascist Ante Pavelic who had long led a right-wing terrorist organization, the Ustase, which had been largely financed by the Italians.

In Albania, Greece (including Crete), and Yugoslavia there was widespread partisan activity which was complicated by the fact that many of these groups were fighting among themselves for eventual political gain. This guerrilla warfare generated extensive reprisals. Many attempts were made by the Germans to rid the countries of resistance fighters using several divisions of valuable troops including, in Yugoslavia, a mountain division and a Waffen SS division – all to limited avail. In April 1943, the commander of German troops in the Balkans, General Lohr gave instructions for a massive campaign against the partisans (Operation White) especially those in Yugoslavia led by Josip Broz (afterwards Marshal Tito). Later, in August, Lohr ordered the most severe measures against them including the shooting and hanging of hostages and the destruction of property. This ruthless policy created a moral dilemma for the partisans: they debated whether or not to commit particular outrages against the enemy knowing that it would almost certainly not be them who suffered but that revenge would be taken on less culpable civilians. In one 'cleansing operation' alone in Greece eighty partisans were caught and murdered as a reprisal for the death of one German soldier. It wasn't until 1947 that many of the leading perpetrators of these crimes were brought to book including General Wilhelm-Muller and Bruno Bauer, the former Governor of Crete.

On balance, the Balkan region, perhaps because of its non-quiescent nature, fared very little better than Poland and Russia. It is estimated that a million and a half Yugoslavs were killed during the German occupation, and in Greece some 50,000 resistance fighters were killed and another 70,000 or so civilians were murdered in reprisals. Perhaps, most pitiful of all, were the 60,000 Jews sent to their deaths and the quarter of a million people who died from privation and hunger (Gilbert, 1989: 746).

Scandinavia presents rather a different picture, although even here a real distinction must be made between Norway on the one hand, and Denmark which was much more generously treated. Ideally, Norway wished to remain neutral when the war began, and early in the war her government refused to co-operate in a scheme to allow British troops through her territory to hamper supplies of iron ore from reaching Germany. But her strategic position and the fact that her coastline provided a secure haven for naval craft which could threaten shipping meant that the violation of her neutrality could hardly be avoided. In the event the Germans cleverly anticipated the British attack by a successful invasion of their own, and occupied the country after a very brief operation in April 1940. Denmark was also occupied without a struggle simply because it was *en route*.

Norway was controlled by a Reich Commissioner who had the authority to review and modify existing laws, and who was answerable directly to the Führer. His task was to appoint deputies, and generally to oversee the work of the existing administration. There had long been a minority pro-Nazi element in Norway led by Vidkun Quisling who had originally wanted to bring the country within the German ambit but who ultimately had to acquiesce to a direct German takeover. This ensured that although he took power as prime minister, he was really just an instrument of German policy working in an unhappy conjunction with the Reich Commissioner Josef Terboven.

The scope of the Civil Service was enlarged, and the powers of officials were modified; those considered politically sound often had their authority enhanced. But everything was done under the watchful eye of the representatives of the occupying power who were 'injected' at various levels of the administrative machinery. The Germans wanted to remain as unobtrusive as they could while ensuring that the state made the necessary contributions to the war effort and to Germany's post-war plans. Hitler, in the first flush of success in his Russian campaign, even ordered large supplies of granite for his monumental building projects for Berlin. More importantly, Norway was a valuable base for German bombers, and later became notable as the centre for the production of heavy water which was intended for the development of an atomic bomb – a project that was fortunately foiled by a daring combined British–Norwegian special services operation in 1943 and followed up by American air attacks.

In their occupied territories, the Germans were keen to scrutinize educational institutions and legal arrangements and especially court decisions which impinged upon or reflected attitudes to the occupying power. This generated a surge of non-violent protests in Norway from bishops and also prompted the resignation of most of the high court judges. It also called forth declarations of non-co-operation from teachers, besides thousands of letters from ordinary people objecting to German repression. But their effectiveness was limited because in the background, in tandem with the state police force, was the presence of the SS, the *eminence noire* of German occupation policy. This presence became increasingly important as troubles mounted for the invaders with the gradual reversal of German fortunes in the war. Resistance movements began to obstruct the German war effort by a range of activities from factory strikes – a reasonably modest form of protest – to actual industrial sabotage. Escape and espionage networks were organized, and clandestine newspapers set up to propagate the ethic of liberation. This resistance was inevitably followed by repression – and, of course, reprisals out of all proportion to the crimes themselves. It was the usual story: houses burned, workers deported and hostages taken and killed. Overall, civilian casualties were small in relation to most other occupied territories but quite high in relation to Norway's own small population. These included nearly half of Norway's tiny (2,000) Jewish community.

Perhaps the greatest contribution made to the Allied cause was made by default. Hitler was obsessed by the idea that the Allies would land an invasion force in Norway as part of their Second Front strategy, and persisted in this idea until the end of the war. Consequently, he committed thirteen divisions to the area which might well have been better employed elsewhere. When the war ended, nearly half a million men surrendered without having taken any effective part in the last great battles.

Denmark was more leniently treated than any other occupied territory. From the German point of view the Danes were fellow Aryans, so it was hoped that they would naturally be absorbed into the Greater German Reich. Unsurprisingly, the Danes did not share this quasi-mystical view of their racial affinities, and – by and large – therefore did not welcome the German occupation even if it was more the result of a takeover than an actual conquest. The Danish army itself, such as it was, was not disbanded, but was allowed only very limited functions. Because of their small numbers, the Danes were in no position to offer any kind of effective resistance, and for the best part of three years co-operated with the Germans in a reasonably amicable way.

Although technically 'neutral', Denmark aided Germany militarily by facilitating the use of bases for German planes, especially for the Battle of Britain in 1940. She also helped Germany economically by providing considerable food supplies from her extensive arable farming industry. Indeed, until 1943, relations between the two countries were conducted on a diplomatic basis. The Danish head of state, the king, was allowed to stay in office, as was the Danish cabinet. Furthermore, the educational institutions enjoyed more than usual freedom. Fortunately this freedom even extended to the universities where Neils Bohr, one of the great theoretical physicists who was engaged in atomic research, remained unmolested until his escape to Scotland where he put his gifts to use in the Allied cause.

Undoubtedly, the main contribution the Danes could make to Germany was in terms of goods and services. It was the German intention to gear the Danish economy to the needs of the Reich. It therefore paid to keep the Danes sweet – but all within limits. Their political forms were only untouched as long as they did not run counter to general National Socialist requirements. Oddly enough, little use was made of the small Danish pro-Nazi Party, a policy – or perhaps just a practice – that was pursued in a number of other occupied territories, though notably not so much in Holland or France.

All this changed dramatically in 1943. Germany's declining fortunes in the war brought out what may have been her true intentions towards Denmark. The occupation became more oppressive. Pressure was exerted to provide more and more men and materials for the war effort. This enforced conscription of labour was where Danes felt constrained to draw the line. They also saw only too clearly that Germany was a lost cause. So, as in other occupied zones, resistance movements began to form, small acts of sabotage took place, and – most public of all – there were open demonstrations against the occupation which sorely tested the patience of the overlords. In parallel with this were increasing German demands that the Danes should surrender their Jews to the SS for deportation – a policy which they resisted more vigorously and more successfully than probably any other occupied state. The SS effectively took over the country, and the usual programme of terror and intimidation replaced diplomacy and co-operation. One of the strongest features of all this was the fact that the Reich's representative in Norway, Dr Werner Best, may have actually connived to impede the full implementation of the SS programme.

Until 1943, Denmark had a rather uncertain reputation as far as the Allies were concerned. They were not too sure how much the Danes could be trusted. Many Danes seem to have entertained genuine anti-Nazi sentiments, and this is evidenced by the fact that some 90 per cent of their shipping outside Danish ports went over to the Allied side at the capitulation. But it takes a lot to compensate for three years of co-operative neutrality. However, it must be said that in the later days of the war – partly out of self-interest and partly out of a genuine feeling for the welfare of her Jewish citizens – Denmark did a great deal to make up for her earlier associations with a seemingly impregnable Reich.

In some ways, Western Europe presents us with a most ambiguous situation which even at this distance is still difficult to interpret. To a greater or lesser degree all the states we have considered both collaborated with the conqueror *and* offered resistance during the occupation; it was the same in Holland, Belgium and France, only more so. What makes their experience so perplexing is that they all had long democratic traditions which, in theory, should not have been conducive to a collaborative mentality. Yet in certain respects, they displayed features which were uncharacteristic of their cultures, in one sense recalling Plato who had noted how frequently authoritarian rule takes over when disillusionment accompanies the breakdown of democracy.

When the Germans attacked the West, the small kingdoms of Holland and Belgium had been unable to offer any appreciable resistance to the panzers. Their forces were weak and had no chance of stemming the German advance for more than a few days. There had also been a certain amount of political bungling and military incompetence on the part of the Allies. Co-ordination was lacking between the various forces, and the precipitate capitulation of Belgium had opened up a dangerous gap in the defences and created a crisis with which neither the French nor the British were able to cope. The subsequent failure of the French, in particular, who had one of the largest armies in Europe, is still being debated. There seems to be ample evidence that the real problem was one of political will and moral integrity as much as anything else.

Holland is a good case in point. An estimated 240,000 civilians died as a result of the occupation, a very high proportion of her population when compared with other occupied territories. Yet it should also be recorded that the Dutch had a small but fairly healthy Nazi Party under the leadership of Anton Mussert, and that 17,000 men joined the Waffen SS when it was frantically looking for suitable recruits outside Germany. It must also be borne in mind that some 12,000 took up security and police work under German auspices, and that this necessarily entailed duties which brought them into direct conflict with those who were doing their best to make life uncomfortable for the occupying forces.

Like Norway, Holland was ruled by a Reich Commissioner, in this case Artur Seyss-Inquart who had already had some experience as a controller in Vienna. He appointed his own officials and deputies, although these included few members of the Dutch Nazi Party. Potentially dangerous institutions such as press and radio were brought strictly under the control of the regime. Within two years of the occupation several hundred prominent Dutch people had been arrested and many of them executed, and when Dutch strikes were organized in protest against deportations for compulsory labour, the strike leaders were promptly arrested and shot. The pogroms against the Jews were particularly fierce. As usual, they began with petty restrictions, such as not being allowed to ride a bicycle, to more far-reaching prohibitions especially in the field of education. Soon there came the deportations to the East from which few returned; of Holland's 140,000 Jewish population only about a quarter survived.

Resistance intensified in the face of persecution. A flourishing underground press developed, and there were some notable SOE successes. But Holland was also the scene of one of the most significant failures of the intelligence services when the German *Abwehr* (Intelligence Service) ran Operation Northpole, a counter-espionage scheme which netted numerous Allied agents. The situation could have been much worse but for a bombing raid on the Gestapo offices in The Hague in April 1944 when most of their files were destroyed. Large numbers in the resistance networks were undoubtedly saved from arrest and probably death by this operation which, though both necessary and successful, highlighted one of the great problems of trying to aid those under occupation. The raid killed over sixty Dutch officials who could not possibly have been warned in advance. Similar tragedies occurred throughout the occupied territories as a result of Allied bombing tactics. It was one of the inevitable penalties that had to be paid to further a long-term strategy.

Our last examples, Belgium and France which, for convenience, we will consider together, illustrate another of the difficulties that vitiated occupation situations, both for the conquerors and the liberators. This was the problem of divided political allegiances. It was not peculiar to Belgium and France, but it was particularly acute there, and undoubtedly contributed to the task the Germans had of holding down the population, and the problems the Allies encountered in trying to free the people from German oppression.

It was here – and notably in France – that one can see the stark contrast between collaboration and resistance. The more conservative elements among the people often found they had certain, perhaps unsuspected, affinities with Nazi ideology. The emphasis upon discipline and order and upon national pride and military might undoubtedly had an appeal for some people, especially those who had become impatient with the debilitating disenchantment which appeared to be rife after the First World War. Both Belgium and France had their Nazi-type parties, and both were eventually to provide volunteers for German police and military formations, including the SS.

In contrast, both societies – especially France – had strong left-wing factions including communists, socialists and anarchists, besides those that treated politics with unstudied indifference. It was the socialists and communists that were better organized. Their main problem was that they often found it difficult to agree among themselves. But whatever their organizational divisions, their general disillusionment with commercial materialism, and the heady mixture of egalitarianism and anti-imperialism had a considerable attraction for a cerebral minority, especially among the young and idealistic. The communists were the most thoroughly politicized, and it did not seem to matter to the adherents that the general policies of the party were dictated by Moscow. They were thus the most difficult section of the population to control, and proved to be perhaps the best recruiting ground for those who wanted to develop an active resistance to the conqueror. After the German invasion of Russia in 1941 they could feel more confident that, despite class divisions, all were – at least temporarily – fighting on the same side.

Belgium and occupied France (which was the whole of France after November 1942) were under military government, and were, therefore, subject to the demands and directions of the Reich. There was an administrative change after the Allied invasion in 1944 when Belgium and north-eastern France were transferred to the authority of a civilian Reich Commissioner. In Belgium, there was a Flemish national party which, presumably in the hope of securing general recognition, welcomed the German occupation. So apparently did the Rexists, a non-Flemish fascist party led by Leon Degrelle. Flemish Belgium provided 3,500 recruits for the Waffen SS, and about the same number served with various auxiliary units. But the proportion of active support for the Germans was only about 1 per cent of the population. The resistance did far better than this. It was sadly ironic that Belgium suffered as much from the process of liberation as that of occupation, especially during the final weeks of the war when the Germans were in full retreat. In the forlorn hope of halting the Allies the Germans launched V2 rocket attacks which killed about 4,500 Belgian people.

Between 1940 and 1942, when France enjoyed the 'privilege' of being an unoccupied zone, there was relatively little interference with the collaborationist government of Vichy led by the one-time military hero, Marshal Pétain, which, in its own way, was as repressive and reactionary as that of the Reich. Pressure was, however, brought to bear on matters that affected Germany's conduct of the war, even to the point of trying to get the French to enter the fray on the German side – something which they consistently refused to do. Press and broadcasting were indirectly controlled by Germany and, in a relatively unobtrusive way, the German counter-espionage services and security police operated to ensure that resistance was kept to a minimum.

In the occupied zone covering the north and west coasts, conditions were more rigorous and control more direct. Movement was restricted and the military presence much more obvious. It was in the Reich's interests that life should continue with a semblance of normality, and that the economy should remain viable if only to meet the demanding German occupation costs. The lower echelons of civil administration, including the deployment of labour, education, the courts and the running of the public utilities were carried on much as before except that the whole system was infiltrated by German officials and subject to German influence.

In both Belgium and France, vast numbers of Jews were deported to the extermination camps in the East. The programme was well under way by the summer of 1942. Its instigators, the SS, do not seem to have been obstructed in their nefarious tasks by the military authorities, nor, apparently, were there any serious objections from the Foreign Office, according to the Reich's special representative in these matters, Adolf Eichmann, who was pleased to report this to his superiors in Berlin. Neither were there insurmountable problems with the subordinate governments; the French police actively collaborated in rounding up Jews for deportation.

France sent a brigade, the Légion des Volontaires Français (LVF), about 3,000 strong, to join Hitler's 'crusade' in the East. Later, in July 1943, about the same number volunteered for the Waffen SS, and they were eventually merged to form the SS Charlemagne Division. Their culpability in this is still a matter of controversy. The French sociologist Raymond Aron has written of the LVF,

> If they were not traitors, who is a traitor? If they were traitors, why are the Frenchmen who collaborated with the Americans and the British not traitors? . . . On the day on which each party has chosen its ideology, there is no longer a national entity. . . . There are just clusters of foreign parties accusing each other of treachery.
> (quoted in Boveri 1961: 64)

Whatever can be said in mitigation of the motivations or actions of the LVF, little can be advanced to excuse the activities of the 25,000 strong Milice Française which was formed early in 1942 under the leadership of Joseph Darnand. They were involved in seeking out Jews who had eluded the vigilant eyes of the German security police and were particularly active in the Lyon area, where in April 1944 they helped the Germans to search for Jewish children that had hitherto evaded capture thanks to the sympathy of French peasants. They were also directly responsible for arresting and actually executing fellow Frenchmen such as the ex-Minister Georges Mandel (for which the head of the Milice in northern France, Max Knipping, was later executed) and for carrying out purges of resistance 'areas' which included the mass killing of suspects as late as August 1944. By this time it was quite obvious that the war was lost, but this only seemed to increase their desperation.

As the war progressed, the Vichy government began to lose its grip on things. In the early days before the total occupation of France, it had not been that difficult to recruit ideologically sound people as officials and administrators, but with the German takeover, and the increasing likelihood of an Allied victory, the government gradually came to have less and less credibility. There were still ivory-tower theorists who were prepared to attend lectures such as those given by Werner Daitz on Franco–German solidarity and published in his magazine *Collaboration* (Herzstein 1982: 122). These propounded the European ideal; the view that Germany and France were in the vanguard of a new and innovatory movement towards European and, implicitly, anti-communist unity. Such ideologues were barely known to the general public, and were in much the same mould as the self-styled experts in the Reich such as Alfred Rosenberg, who commanded small departments and were not greatly heeded by those in charge of practical affairs. The conception was one thing, operationalization was another. The theories often had a kind of plausible potency because they were a pernicious mixture of idealism and cultural arrogance, and, as such, commanded some attention among the appropriate intellectual elite. As the prospects of a German victory dwindled, the Milice inverse-ratio phenomenon could be seen here as well: more and more ideological debate and planning with less and less chance of its actual realization.

Most people in the occupied territories were neither ferocious resistants nor opportunistic collaborators. Most went about their daily lives as normally as possible, hoping not to become involved in anything dramatic and trusting that one day things would change for the better. Most were neither particularly courageous nor especially cowardly, but it was often the case that those who were frightened could be unusually brave when suddenly confronted with a different kind of situation, and the seemingly brave could sometimes display unaccountable failures of nerve. Both war and occupation situations are fraught with perplexing contradictions which have to be 'solved' – in so far as they can be solved – on a greatest-happiness utilitarian basis.

It is extremely difficult for conqueror and resistant alike to temper national interest with mercy. It has been argued that even amid the inhumanity of war there can be an incongruous humaneness, a surprising observance of implicit rules of conduct regardless of the horror of things (Best 1980). But it is an argument that has to be necessarily suspect. It is very doubtful whether warfare can really be made more humane by rules. Of course, the *wish* to make rules is humane – but the decision to break them is all too human. There is just too much evidence against it (see chapter 13). However, there is no doubt that war can generate welcome – and even unsuspected – *acts* of humaneness; human nature is not totally depraved. This was true of those who were active resistants and partisans, but more particularly of those who were relatively 'immobilized' by military occupation but risked their lives by helping others.

12

Extermination: Nazi policies and practices in the 'East'

The discussion on military occupation so far has taken us into some rather unsavoury areas of policy and practice. But these pale into relative insignificance beside the calculated programme of terror and genocide instituted by the Germans during their campaigns in Poland and Russia during the Second World War. It has been noted elsewhere (Carlton 1990: 174) that the practice of extermination normally falls into three main categories:

   i) *accidental*, in that certain infectious diseases may be introduced which kill entire populations, as happened during the colonization of the Americas and Polynesia.
  ii) *incidental*, as part of larger policy of repression, as with the Spanish in South America.
or iii) – as in the case of the Nazis – *methodical*, a systematic attempt to liquidate whole populations.

Extermination – though not always clearly spelled out as a policy – was implicit in the Nazi programme from the beginning. This stemmed from the philosophy, derived from Social Darwinism, that healthy and 'proper' regulation of social development can only be achieved through natural selection. It was a very short step from this to the view that cruelty and annihilation could be justified in order to reduce or even obliterate the weaker or inferior species. By extension, this was taken to mean that the stronger races or cultures had the right – even a mission – to dominate others, and that the whole idea of innate human rights was alien to nature and was the enemy of human progress. Hitler, in a speech in June 1944, maintained that

Nature [teaches] us . . . that she is governed by the principle of selection: that victory is to the strong and the weak must go to the wall. . . . Nature . . . knows nothing of humanitarianism. . . . War is therefore the unalterable law of the whole of life. . . . What

seems cruel to us is from Nature's point of view entirely obvious.
(Krausnick and Broszat 1968: 29–30)

This all seems appositely ironic in view of Germany's impending defeat at this time as the obviously 'weaker nation'.

It should strike no one, therefore, as so unusual that Hitler decided on war in 1939. He had achieved some remarkable political successes in Austria and Czechoslovakia by a combination of guile and intimidation, and could possibly have wrung even greater concessions from Britain and France who were bent on conciliation at all costs. Conflict was too frightful to contemplate – so they were prepared for virtually any face-saving deal that would work. But Hitler did not want a deal; he was determined to have his war. This was made plain to his chiefs of staff when they were called together on 22 August 1939 to hear his momentous decision to attack Poland, knowing – though perhaps not quite believing – that this time Britain and France would honour their treaty obligations and support their ally against German aggression. To his surprise they came to the aid of Poland – though much too ineffectually and much too late. In that speech to his generals Hitler made it clear that this was going to be a campaign which ignored the usual rules of combat, it was going to be war without quarter, 'Close your hearts to pity. Act brutally, [Germans] must have what is their right' (Hohne 1969: 238). The blitzkrieg that was unleashed on Poland lasted less than a month. The Poles were hopelessly outclassed, and the savagery of the quite unnecessary bombing of Warsaw – virtually an 'open city' – did much to weaken Polish resistance. The cynical invasion from the east by the Russians, which had been implicitly agreed in a secret protocol in the Russo–German treaty only days before the outbreak of hostilities, made the Polish situation quite impossible. They had no choice but to capitulate.

With surrender came the terror which began with the planned elimination of a substantial proportion of the Polish intelligentsia, the nobility, clergy etc. – a task which was known to the army high command, but a task that they gladly left to the 'civil administration' which was quickly set up in the conquered territory. This, of course, meant the SS. In tandem with these operations was the rounding up of the Jews and their confinement in ghettos preparatory to the intended programme of mass slaughter.

'Special Units' (Einsatzgruppen) were formed which effectively became extermination squads. At first they were largely subordinate to the army, but later their 'special instructions' gave them a kind of administrative autonomy which meant that they were answerable to no one but the Reichsführer SS himself. Securing the occupied territories was a very wide brief, and in reality meant dealing with those categories of persons regarded as either undesirable or positively harmful by the Reich. These included intellectuals and other potentially dissident elements, as we have seen, as well as vagrants and gypsies. Pre-eminently, of course, it meant the Jews. Thus the mass shootings and the deportations began.

Germany had taken possession of roughly half of Poland – Russia had the rest. In German territory, the frontier areas which contained large numbers of ethnic Germans, and which were ostensibly the original cause of the dispute, were incorporated into the Reich. The remainder – a kind of 'rump' Poland – was designated the General Government, and was put in the charge of Hans Frank, a one-time member of the German Bar Association. This became a form of reservation for the unwanted and the potentially proscribed who were forced to leave their homes and livelihoods, and were transported to the General Government territory while their place was taken by ethnic Germans. Himmler, the head of the SS, was later to recount to fellow officers that many of these 'resettlements' took place in temperatures as low as 40 degrees below zero,

> we had to drag away . . . hundreds of thousands; we had to have toughness – you must listen to this and then forget it immediately – to shoot thousands of leading Poles . . . otherwise revenge would have been taken on us later . . . it is much easier to go to battle . . . than it is to suppress an obstructive population of low cultural level.
>
> (Graber 1980: 149)

Resettlement had its practical as well as its moral problems. The SS actually found it more congenial to carry out the distasteful task of 'population exchanges' to the General Government including the gratuitous killing of racial undesirables, than to settle the ethnic Germans on Polish lands. In fact, many of them never did settle, and simply lived in makeshift camps for much of the war. The General Government area became terribly overcrowded and extremely difficult to administer satisfactorily. Jews were compelled to live in certain urban areas where they could be 'contained' prior to the organization of the ghettos. The Nazi bureaucracies generated to cope with this proliferated. The General Government was peopled by its own officials, the security services and – quite separately – the army staff who were not supposed to interfere with these special operations. All sorts of key figures wanted a say in the running of the newly acquired territories, including the great high priest of race ideology, Alfred Rosenberg, who – like so many in the Nazi hierarchy – tried to fashion a little administrative empire for himself. This multiplication of offices and officials, functions and services hardly lent itself to increased efficiency. In fact, it simply led to squabbles and petty jealousies which militated against the smooth running of the system.

After crushing Poland, there were the lightning campaigns in Norway, Denmark, the Low Countries and France. Hitler then turned his attention to his next long-contemplated project, Operation Barbarossa, the invasion of Russia. This was originally planned for May 1941, but, as we have seen, was delayed by a necessary 'diversion' in the Balkans to rescue the ailing forces of his militarily incompetent ally, Mussolini. The attack was finally launched some six weeks later – a delay which eventually proved to be a serious miscalculation. At first, the invasion was very successful, and it looked as though the whole campaign would be over by the autumn. But, after a disastrous start, the Russians fought a series of cunning rear-guard battles until the arrival of their most valuable ally – the winter. The German armies were halted at the very outskirts of Leningrad and Moscow. They withstood serious and unexpected counter attacks, dug in and waited for the spring when their panzers would be on the move once again. By this time, the Germans had lost about a third of their army, some in battle, but very many in the severe weather conditions for which they were quite unprepared.

In the spring of 1942 they renewed their offensive and were particularly successful in the Ukraine and the Crimea, two very important agricultural areas, which the Russians ruthlessly but shrewdly abandoned as part of their 'scorched earth' policy. During that summer things also went reasonably well for the Germans elsewhere. The battle of the Atlantic favoured the U-boats; the submarine wolf-packs were having their best year yet at the expense of Allied shipping. The Canadians mounted a large-scale raid on Dieppe which was absolutely decimated by the occupying German forces – not a good omen for an early Second Front. And in Cyrenaica, Rommel's Afrika Korps which had been beaten back late the previous year, launched an offensive which resulted in the capture of Tobruk in June, and which then threatened Egypt itself.

But it was not to last. By the late autumn of 1942, the situation had changed dramatically both in Europe and in the Middle East. The turning point in Russia was undoubtedly the siege of Stalingrad in the winter of 1942–3. Again Hitler made a fatal misjudgement; he thought the battle was as good as won, and sent part of his forces to assist in the Caucasus where they were not really needed. The German 6th Army was then surrounded and virtually annihilated because of his insane insistence that they should stand and fight and not withdraw to a more strategically advantageous position. It was a loss from which the *Wehrmacht* never really recovered. Things now went from bad to worse. The Axis forces weathered increasing counter-attacks from the Russians who, apart from having seemingly inexhaustible reserves of men, were also employing superior weaponry. They failed to break the Russians at the battle of Kursk in 1943 – possibly the greatest tank battle in history, and despite the hurried mobilization of further armies, especially from their Balkan allies, they were never really able to mount any further offensives which brought lasting success. The war was now really lost; final defeat was just a matter of time.

While the German armies had been desperately trying to carve out this new empire in the East, the tentacles of the SS and its various subsidiary organizations had been assiduous in their allotted task of securing the civilian population. In Russia their first move was to deprive the people of their local party officials. Hitler ordered that all political commissars were to be liquidated, and instructions went out to the 'special units', who acted independently of the army, that some were to be decapitated and their heads brought back to Berlin for further study. The SS were obviously intrigued with the cranial characteristics of those who were classed as *untermenschen*, a species of Slavic sub-humanity. But this was only the preliminary stage – a mere curtain-raiser to what was to come. This barbaric treatment of prisoners of war became a byword even among some Germans themselves. The *Wehrmacht* was sometimes involved, but almost invariably these tasks were left to the not so tender mercies of the special units. A report of the Soviet Chief-of-Staff at Sebastopol in December 1941 gives us some idea of the situation: he states

> as a rule troop formations exterminate prisoners without interrogation ... the shooting of prisoners at the place of capture or at the front line, which is practised most extensively, acts as a deterrent to soldiers of the enemy wanting to desert to us.
>
> (Hohne 1969: 432)

The special units usually comprised Security Service (SD) personnel plus contingents of the Armed (Waffen) SS who were normally engaged on straightforward military duties, assisted by local militia. Some idea of the more general involvement of the military SS can be seen from a few random instances. Only two weeks after the opening of the Russian campaign, the 'Viking' Division shot 600 Jews in Galicia as a reprisal for 'Soviet crimes'. On some occasions entire villages were destroyed as a form of reprisal, and this kind of 'action' was by no means confined to the East. Lidice in Czechoslovakia was destroyed in 1942 in retaliation for the assassination of the Reich-Protector Heydrich. The 'Prinz Eugen' Division liquidated the inhabitants of Kosutica in 1943; and in 1944 came the destruction of Klissura in northern Greece. The year 1944 also witnessed the notorious murder of the inhabitants of Oradour-sur-Glane in France by the 'Das Reich' Division, and the killing of Canadian and British prisoners of war by members of the 'Hitlerjugend' Panzer Division during the battles in Normandy.

The worst of the atrocities were carried out by the re-formed Einsatzgruppen. There were four such units each comprising about 1,000 men, including support personnel such as wireless operators, drivers etc., and detachments from the Waffen SS and the police. Their instructions were couched – quite deliberately – in extremely vague terms. They were to act on their own responsibility to take 'executive measures against the civilian population' (quoted in Krausnick and Broszat 1970: 78). The implicit intention of shooting Jews is not stated overtly, and it is not clear to what extent the army itself was always aware of these plans, although the chiefs may well have guessed what was going to happen. According to the evidence of Otto Ohlendorf, the commander of one such Einsatzgruppe, when the groups were being formed in May 1941 in preparation for the invasion of Russia, they were told of the secret decree of 'putting to death all racially and politically undesirable elements where these might be thought to represent a threat to security' (Krausnick and Broszat 1970: 79). During the Nuremberg trials after the war, it transpired that at the time this was understood to include communist officials, second-class Asiatics, gypsies and Jews. Despite the care taken in disguising their intentions, members of the Nazi hierarchy were sometimes quite explicit in their planning on occupation policy. At one conference held in July 1941, the officials were told 'we are taking all necessary measures – shootings, deportations and so on ... [the area] must be pacified as soon as possible, and the best way to do that is to shoot anyone who so much as looks like giving trouble' (Krausnick and Broszat 1970: 82). It does not take much imagination to realize that almost any measures, no matter how ruthless and bestial, could be justified in the name of security even where the victims – especially women and children – could be shown to pose no real threat to security at all.

There is very little evidence as to what actually took place during one of these 'actions'. For example there is no documentary material for the events leading up to the destruction of the small town of Tuczyn in eastern Poland, although a vivid picture has been 're-created' by eight of the survivors – who gave their testimonies at different times in different places. There were only fifteen survivors in all out of a population of 3,500, and the stories that were told apparently have an amazing degree of consistency. For economic reasons Tuczyn was not destroyed at the same time as many of the surrounding Jewish settlements, so when the time came – as the inhabitants knew it must – they were 'prepared'. The head of the Jewish Council organized the people for resistance, but they had no weapons, only petrol, matches and bars. When the Germans came in the summer of 1942, the Jews set light to their own wooden houses, and the old and sick – led by the rabbi – jumped into the fire. Others tried to break out of the trap, and a thousand or so fled into the nearby Ukrainian forest. Only fifteen survived because of the actions of Ukrainian peasants who either killed them or handed them over to the Germans. Those who were saved were helped by the Baptist minority among the Ukrainians (Bauer 1976).

The actual executions were carried out on a massive scale by the members of the Einsatzgruppen, often with the active co-operation of local 'partisans' as, for example in Lithuania and the Ukraine. Thanks to the meticulous records kept by some of those involved, we often have complete breakdowns and statistics of their programme of mass murder. By 25 November 1941, Einsatzgruppe A had already executed 229,052 Jews; Einsatzgruppe B had killed 45,467 by 14 November 1941; Einsatzgruppe C 95,000 by the beginning of December of that year; and Einsatzgruppe D 92,000 by 8 April 1942. The speed at which these executions took place was frightening. For instance, in Kiev alone in two days in September 1941, reports showed that 33,771 persons were executed, mainly Jews. In fact, it is probable that by the end of 1942, as many as a million Jews had been killed. And this was just the beginning. The whole grisly process was about to be rationalized with the introduction of the gas chambers. Five extermination camps were set up for this specific purpose, as distinct from the other concentration camps which often functioned as labour industries for some eminent German firms.

It is not certain exactly when the 'final solution' of the Jewish problem was first mooted or the plan decided upon. After the defeat of France in 1940 the Nazi hierarchy had revived the pre-war and rather novel idea of sending all European Jews to the island colony of Madagascar. The scheme was abandoned because of anticipated transport difficulties, and also because of an increasing preoccupation with the Russian venture. It was at this point that plans for a 'final solution' of the Jewish solution began finally to take shape. There is some evidence that the term was being employed as early as 1939 before the outbreak of the war. Certainly, plans were afoot prior to the Russian campaign, and in its ultimate rationalized form from the beginning of 1942 when it was discussed at the notorious Wannsee Conference which took place under the auspices of Heydrich, the chief of the Security Service (SD). It was here that the general blueprint was decided upon. It is noteworthy that this was not only attended by SS officials and members of the party chancellery, but also by representatives of the Reich Ministry for the Eastern territories, the Foreign Ministry and – of all things – the Reich Ministry of Justice. By this time it was realized that the conquest of Russia would take more time than had been anticipated. Long-term plans for the occupied territories would therefore have to be brought forward. The *Wehrmacht* and especially the SS appreciated that in these circumstances too many prisoners and undesirables were going to be a considerable inconvenience. Extermination, therefore seemed to be the obvious 'answer'.

As in Poland, administrative areas were created which were governed by duly appointed Reich Commissioners. They controlled a vast army of lesser officials, whose task was to govern the territories with the help of indigenous personnel at the very lowest levels. These networks were under sole German authority, although considerable latitude was exercised by the rulers of these newly created 'kingdoms'. Part of their task was to facilitate the 'final solution' by co-operating with the Security Services, the police and – often – locally recruited militia, in the herding of Jews into ghettos so that 'selection' became that much easier. In order to facilitate a higher rate in the execution programme, gas trucks were used experimentally while the mass shootings were still going on. There was some hesitation about this because some Jews, especially more skilled males, were required to service the SS and *Wehrmacht* ordinance establishments. But eventually the ideology had to be realized, and the instruction went out to the effect that regardless of sex, age or usefulness to the economy, all Jews were to be liquidated. The machinery of destruction was thus refined, and gas chambers were built to order at Auschwitz, Treblinka, etc. which could 'process' several thousands of people per day. This was to be the basis of the German New Order.

For four years, the Germans thus dominated a population in occupied Europe several times the size of their own. They set out with something approximating to the ideal of a new Europe. Some of those involved took a pre-eminently pragmatic approach to this grand design – they were there for what they could get. Just how *much* they intended to get was unspecified; the plan changed somewhat as they went along. Others, especially those concerned with the racial aspects of conquest, and the settlement of the East by a superior racial stock, were – like Alfred Rosenberg – the visionaries who supplied the philosophical justification for the programme.

How then were these schemes to be realized? Only, it transpired, with considerable difficulty. The fundamental problems of policy, administrative jurisdiction – especially with so many interested agencies, and rival personnel, were never really solved. At its greatest extent, the *Grossraum*, or Greater Germanic State, stretched from the Atlantic to the Urals, and, almost inevitably this meant different treatment for different peoples, even within the East itself. In theory, the *Grossraum* was to consist of four main categories of people: the Germans themselves; other Nordic peoples such as the Scandinavians who were akin to the Germans but certainly inferior in terms of economic and political rights; and the *untermenschen* who fell into two main categories. First, the sub-human racial elements (Slavs and the like), whom Hitler insisted should 'know just enough to read the road signs so as not to get themselves run over' (Calvocoressi and Wint 1972: 212). They were to be a leaderless labour force, uneducated, unenfranchised and unrepresented (in fact in 1940 Himmler envisaged that within ten years the General Government in Poland would be reduced to such a remnant of sub-standard beings). The second category comprised those who were not fit to survive at all, but who might be kept alive on a temporary basis in so far as they could be of service to the state, mainly the Jews.

Other nations and cultures had ill-defined places in Nazi race theory, and particularly race practice. Negroes, for example, were *untermenschen* – but then the Nazis had had very little to do with them. Presumably they would have met a predictable fate had the Germans won the war and taken over the former African colonies. The Latin peoples were a very uncertain commodity. The Germans wooed the Spanish because they needed them, had scant respect for the French, and even their Axis partners, the Italians, were only accepted because of Hitler's irrational regard for Mussolini. As for the Mongoloid peoples of the East, one wonders what long-term prospects the master race had for them; the eventual fate of Germany's other main allies, the Japanese, is anybody's guess.

It was assumed that the projected Germanic Europe would be a self-supporting and self-sufficient economic entity. It was also envisaged that it would be a highly centralized system with Germany producing goods to supply wider markets in her more peripheral 'colonies'. They, in turn, would supply materials and goods for Germany. People could be moved or removed at will; industry and agriculture could draw on an international labour force – but all essentially in the service of the central German State which would direct all these multifarious activities. But herein lay the anomalies. As one text has put it,

> Its scope was international but its purpose was national. Long-range planning, long-term agreements, guaranteed markets, fixed exchange rates . . . could not conceal the fact that the basis of the New Order was German power and German requirements and not a European cooperative. The benefits to everyone else would be the crumbs from the rich man's table.
>
> (Calvocoressi and Wint 1972: 214)

The original plans drawn up by Alfred Rosenberg and his staff for the administration of the conquered territories were greatly modified by the alternative 'necessities' of the Security Police and the crises occasioned by a fluctuating military situation. In 1942, the SS produced a rather sketchy Eastern Plan for the next 25 years which was revised and re-issued again in 1943. This blueprint foresaw a system of permanent and temporary settlements or strongpoints throughout the territories. Its main feature was the heavy concentration of settlements on the border areas – rather like the forts on the Scottish and Welsh borders in medieval times – which would act as buffer zones in case of hostile incursions. Germans outside the heartland (*Volksdeutsche*) would be encouraged to take up privileged positions as community leaders and landowners – a policy that was only partly implemented during the war, and which could hardly be called successful. Settlements and re-settlements were taking place throughout the war – all to little avail. Plans were made, changed and then cancelled. Indeed, many *Volksdeutsche* either ended up as refugees or were lost altogether – presumably through exo-Germanic assimilation.

Between the Polish and the Russian campaigns, a new agency (which was really a revitalized version of an established, but minor, department of the Reich) was set up to examine the future of the Eastern territories. It was a pseudo-academic affair headed by Alfred Rosenberg and its brief was to research the issues and then formulate policies which might be implemented when the conquest was complete. It expanded to become the Ministry for the East, employing a vast staff whose chief war-time task seems to have been to milk the occupied territories of their art treasures. It hardly needs to be emphasized that such an agency cut across the jurisdiction of the Foreign Office and especially the SS. But then it seems to have been part of Hitler's domestic policy to set organizations against one another in this apparently inefficient way as part of the divide and rule principle.

Rosenberg's plans were for a fragmentation of the territories remaining to Germany after other satellite states, namely Finland and Romania, had been given a few territorial titbits as a reward for their services. In the vast German-controlled areas certain key cities – Warsaw, Leningrad and Moscow – were to be razed (according to Hitler's instructions). The territories themselves were to be divided into four, each under the auspices of a German Commissioner whose function was not only to ensure that order was maintained, but also to institute a programme of re-education and indoctrination on a selective basis. Despite the exigencies of wartime, these plans were partly put into effect, particularly in the Ukraine where, at first at least, there were some promising signs of indigenous response. But, again, none of these plans had any real success. Eventually, the organizations degenerated into agencies of extraction which specialized in a rapacious bleeding of the territories accompanied, of course, by the usual callous round of killings and deportations.

There is little doubt that if the Nazis had played their cards right many of the Eastern peoples could have been won over to the German cause. As it was, they were able to mobilize some into their forces, notably a modest contingent of Ukrainians under the leadership of an ex-Soviet general, Andrei Vlassov – a move that made nonsense of their *untermenschen* theories. The bulk of the people, however, were completely disillusioned by the savagery of the German occupation and the obvious intentions of the conquerors. Such practices merely seemed to increase their determination to resist the enemy, and ultimately this gave rise to a proliferation of partisan groups which greatly harrassed the Germans, particularly in the later stages of the war.

The general approach of the Nazi regime to the question of occupation can be seen from some of the statements of its principals. These make it clear that the Eastern territories were there simply to be plundered. The welfare of the conquered was not even a minor consideration. Early in the Russian campaign when victory had seemed certain Reichsmarschall Goering told the Italian Foreign Minister, Count Ciano, that it was appropriate that in the current year about 20–30 million Russians would die of starvation, and that any attempt to avert this would be prohibited. In an infamous speech at Posen in October 1943, when the tide of war had already turned against Germany, Reichsführer SS Himmler told a conference of SS officers

> whether nations live in prosperity or starve to death . . . interests me only in so far as we need them as slaves to our Kultur. . . . Whether 10,000 Russian females fall down from exhaustion while digging an anti-tank ditch interests me only in so far as the anti-tank ditch for Germany is finished.
>
> (Shirer 1960: 1150)

In the same address, Himmler – who had virtually fainted at the sight of an execution of eastern Jews put on for his personal delectation – referred to the 'extermination of the Jewish race' as a 'page of glory in our history' (quoted in Shirer 1960: 1117. The evidence makes clear that such a programme was designed not just in the interests of demographic or economic expediency but was the outcome of a master race ideology. A little earlier in the same year, Reich Commissioner for the Ukraine, Koch, during a conference in Kiev stated, 'we are a master race . . . the lowliest German worker is racially and biologically a thousand times more valuable than the population here' (Shirer 1960: 1118).

The actual plunder from the occupied territories can never be properly assessed. Gold reserves were taken from the various national banks, art treasures were confiscated (Goering alone – the plunderer *par excellence* – appropriated treasures worth an estimated DM 50 million), and goods – mainly foodstuffs – and services were commandered.

'Occupation costs' were fixed by the overlords in the respective areas which in all have been estimated at about DM 60 million, of which approximately half came from France. Altogether the total figure extracted as tribute may be as high as DM 104 billion; the less rich Eastern territories' contributions were mainly in goods, in addition to the many estates – primarily in Poland – that were taken over for the use of German settlers.

But as William Shirer eloquently argues, spoilation was the mildest aspect of the New Order; the real plunder was that of human lives. It was here that 'Nazi degradation sank to a level seldom experienced by man in all his time on earth . . . [an] incredible story of horror [that] would be unbelievable were it not fully documented by the perpetrators themselves' (Shirer 1960: 1126). By the autumn of 1944, when the Second Front had opened up in Europe and the war was as good as lost as far as Germany was concerned, some seven and a half million foreign slaves were working for the Reich, almost all of them as forced labour. In addition, two million prisoners of war were 'conscripted' for work in the Nazi munitions industries such as Krupps. The work was often degrading and the conditions in which they were made to work appalling. Many died for lack of food or from the punishments which, in many places, were part of the everyday routine. One of the most notorious instances of the Nazis' forced labour system can be seen in the case of Nordhausen. After the successful interruption of the German V-weapons (rocket) programme by Allied bombing raids at Peenemunde in 1943, virtually the whole operation was transferred to the old ammonia mine at Nordhausen in the Harz mountains. In September of that year the first batch of 60,000 inmates was sent there from Buchenwald concentration camp to transform the mine into a warren of forty-six 220-yard tunnels, 14 yards wide and up to 30 yards high. They, and those that joined them, worked without power drills or mechanized excavators. Food and medical supplies were short, and beatings and hangings were frequent. In these awful conditions life expectancy was about six months, but further supplies of labour could always be ordered from the SS at other concentration camps by those (including the star of the later United States missile programme, Werner von Braun) who were struggling to complete the project on time. In all, some 20,000 are believed to have died in this feverish but futile attempt to save the Reich from destruction (see Bower 1987: 125–6).

Forced labour was common practice, especially in the last desperate days. Those not designated for imminent death were given the 'privilege' of working for an illusory German victory. As one SS officer reported, 'underground workshops [were] organised on a massive scale. Orders were given to kill immediately only those unable to work as unskilled labourers' (quoted in Mandel 1986: 191).

The decision to invade Poland had been based on sheer aggrandizement and the subsequent – perhaps consequent – decision to expand further into Russia was, in Tallyrand's famous aphorism, more than a crime – it was a blunder. There is no clear evidence that it came about through fear of the Soviet Union, nor was it entirely based on a desire to destroy bolshevism, though this was certainly an important ingredient. Alexander Dallin's argument is also disputable that 'it was not ... reached by rational analysis, but [was] a rather foolhardy gamble that made no provision for failure' (Dallin 1981: 660). In its own way, it had its own peculiar rationality. Strategically, it made a certain kind of sense. Rather, it appears to have been born of a strange fusion of colonial expansionism and a misty idyllicism about German destiny in the East. Colonialism was justified in terms of living-space and economic considerations such as the need to secure Germany's future grain supply. The attraction of Russia's fertile plains, not to mention her incalculable mineral resources, were a constant lure to a burgeoning state, and their confiscation was easily wedded to the appropriate images of a utopian Thousand-Year Reich. Whatever the immediate aims, no one in the Nazi hierarchy doubted that they were there to stay: 'It was a common conviction not subject to discussion' (Otto Schiller in Karl Brandt et al. 1953: 67).

When the invasion did not succeed according to the allotted – and over-confident – timescale, and Germany urgently needed to replenish her depleted supplies, the policies governing the occupation had to be modified, and stringent measures intensified. It was here that the glaring contradictions in German policy and practice began to show; the original plan to create a subject state had to be re-cast in the light of the military emergency. There was a pressing need to enlist the aid of certain sections of Russian society as Germany's situation deteriorated. This division in German thinking was reflected in the bitter personal feuds that took place among the Nazi hierarchy itself, especially between Rosenberg and his staff, who had long-term plans for the germanization of the East, and those contemptuous atheoretical colleagues who advocated a more pragmatic approach to the problem.

By and large, the help that Germany now so desperately needed was not willingly given. So the screw had to be turned. And as intimidation increased so did the polarization between the occupiers and the occupied. By this time, German military setbacks were such that they could no longer supply the manpower to make the repression really effective. Partisan activity grew more threatening, sabotage and assassinations were rife. Again the Germans responded in inconsistent ways, and terrorization was actually eased on a selective basis where it was thought that it might pay small yet useful dividends. But this instrumental relaxation of practice did not really signal any real change of policy. The claims of the various competing agencies, the SD, the military, and German industry which was even hungrier for more slave labour, highlighted the conflicting aims and 'solutions' that were advanced, rejected, and sometimes partly implemented. It was all very *ad hoc*, and often hastily improvised, and only seems to confirm Trevor-Roper's insistence that totalitarianism – contrary to much popular thought – is fundamentally inefficient (Trevor-Roper 1947). In his definitive study, Dallin says that 'when victory seemed certain Berlin rejected co-operation . . . [but when the Third Reich] badly needed help . . . most Soviet citizens refused to entrust their fates to the Germans. The [new] measures . . . were too half-hearted, belated, sporadic and hypocritical to reverse the tide' (Dallin 1981: 664). Any amelioration was seen for what it was – a matter of temporary expediency.

For the main victims of German terror, the Jews, and other proscribed people, the measures made no difference at all – indeed, if anything, their situation became even more precarious. There was no let-up in the extermination programme. Yet more ideological fodder was found, especially in Hungary, even when the war was effectively lost. Untold numbers of passive executive agents, employees, clerks, minor officials, etc., were indirectly involved in the carnage besides the executioners themselves. It is interesting to note that one of the directors of the railway system, later to be chief of a transport board in post-war Germany, once received a congratulatory telegram from Karl Wolff, Himmler's personal adjutant, in which he noted with 'special joy' the huge consignments of the 'chosen race to Treblinka and so forth' (quoted in Mandel 1986: 186).

German occupation policies really defy description – and comprehension. True, they varied from state to state depending largely on Nazi ideological categorization, but for the East there was to be no future to speak of. The plan here was even worse than ancient Spartan helotage. At least in Sparta – while there was some discrimination – there was no virulent racism, as such. Certainly the indigenous slave population was not normally subject to systematic massacre and deportation. In the New Order it was not just the policies but the implementation of the policies which compounded the horror of the situation. In all, some six million Jews were killed besides an equal number of non-Jewish Russians and Poles, perhaps a third of whom were children. Possibly as many as two million Russian prisoners of war were also beaten and starved to death, and all this takes no account of the mass executions of hostages, gypsies and other undesirables that took place elsewhere in Europe where conditions were generally less repressive.

It has been argued that rather than the Holocaust being the acme of human irrationality it was a 'suicidal combination of "perfect" local rationality and extreme global irrationality' (Mandel 1986: 90), although the same writer goes on to add – less plausibly – that these are the typical characteristics of international capitalism. This marxist critique sees the Holocaust as the outcome of a fusion of capitalism and its natural child, colonialist imperialism, which is inextricably bound up with racist attitudes. Others have seen it as a 'rational' product of modernity. Thus Robert Rubenstein writes that 'it bears witness to the *advance of civilization*' (Rubenstein 1978: 91, my emphasis; *see also* 195), and Zygmunt Bauman endorses this by pointing out that it was in the 'final solution' that we see industrial potential and technological know-how employed in an unsuspected capacity, that of mass murder.

> Modern civilization ... was a necessary condition [of the Holocaust], without it, the Holocaust [was] unthinkable. The Nazi mass murder of European Jewry was not only the technological achievement of an industrial society but also the organizational achievement of a bureaucratic society.
>
> (Bauman 1989: 9; *see also* 13)

On the other hand, it could be argued that the mechanization of extermination which took place with the gas chambers was merely an extension of the work of the Einsatzgruppen which, in turn, was a rationalization of the anti-semitic pogroms of the 1930s and before. This mechanization of murder obviously is a product of modernity, but the impetus had little to do with technological society – technological society simply made it possible. Wasn't it the late President Kennedy who once hypothesized that perhaps other planets were extinct because their scientists were more advanced than ours. The seeds of the Holocaust are really to be found in the value-systems that underlie it.

There has never been a regime like that of Nazi Germany for methodical, mechanized murder. Death became an industry – perhaps as many as 150,000 people were engaged in the 'final solution' programme alone. All this was organized and perpetrated in the pursuit of an ill-defined racial idea which has never had, and never can have, any relation to reality. It was all done in the interests of a New Order which only endured for an awful historical moment, but in that moment its ideology found a strange and evil resonance in the irrational soul of mankind.

The story of Nazi Germany reads like a nihilistic tragedy. The New Order according to some Nazi idealists was to be a bulwark against the threat of an insurgent communism. It was the dream of Party ideologists like Alfred Rosenberg. In the winter of 1942–3, amid the disasters of Stalingrad and the increasing Allied air offensive, there was a great enthusiasm for the European idea, and a committee was set up by the Foreign Office and chaired by Professor Friedrich Berber to examine the historical, geographical and other statistical materials from other European countries. This idea also accorded with the aspirations of those Nazi sympathizers who were to be found in some of the conquered and allied states who were looking for a New Europe, although there was some difference in perception about the exact nature of this rather chimerical entity. It was all very unclear, even to the master race itself. Vidkun Quisling in Norway looked for a united Europe which would eradicate 'Jewish bolshevism'; in Holland, Anton Mussert suggested to Hitler that they form a 'League of Germanic Peoples'; the Hungarian leader, Ferenc Szalasi even spoke of a new federal arrangement for Europe organized on a tribal basis (Herzstein 1982: 6–7). But none of these ideas was ever taken that seriously by the Germans. If such a superstate had ever materialized, all the evidence suggests that it would have been a Europe organized as a German hegemony. Incongruously, as late as 1945, the ideologues were still ranting about the defence of Europe and Western culture which they had now successfully destroyed.

13

Excursus: The Holocaust and the SS intelligentsia

It does not require a very close look at the Holocaust literature to realize that the perpetrators of such atrocities were not all crude, semi-literate thugs and criminals. This was true of many of the actual torturers and executioners, but not of those who planned and promoted the extermination programmes. The question that is begged therefore is, what made them do it? Actually, there are two problems here. There is the fundamental problem as to why certain intellectuals were attracted to the Nazi ideology in general and the SS in particular and, by extension, the more 'practical' problem of how it came about that they were prepared to operationalize that ideology in lethal terms.

Hannah Arendt (1958) has insisted that totalitarianism in its particular manifestations, nazism and fascism, was essentially irrational. For her, the appeal of such movements stems from the isolation and alienation of those who have lost their sense of identity, and who therefore seek psychological security in those organizations which make monolithic claims. This obviously has some cogency, but it has been criticized by those who feel that much more emphasis should be placed on the loss of *class* identity, upon class fears and the struggle of class interests (e.g. Weiss 1967).

This question of rationality or irrationality is certainly a key issue, and has been subject to a great deal of debate. If we compare the broader nature of fascism with that of the narrower and more extreme phenomenon of nazism, we find that the irrational racial elements are secondary, and the general concerns of ultraconservatism are its primary *raisons d'être*. On this analysis, fascism can be seen to have its own peculiar rationality in that it acts – or purports to act – as a bulwark against the dual threats of liberalism and communism. If, on the other hand, we accept that rationality expresses a relationship between means and ends, nazism could also be given credit for a kind of rationality in that it was an ill-conceived attempt to unify an ill-defined entity – the German *Volk*. Indeed, it is doubtful whether, nazism could have appealed to so many Germans had it not contained these rational elements.

The question of rationality itself subsumes the further problem of *belief* – often intellectualized as ideology – which must be distinguished from actual *practice*. The nature of the system must be separated, in theory at least, from its actual implementation. And in thinking of the Holocaust it is the matter of implementation that concerns us most – after all, there were other ways of 'solving' the Jewish problem – if such it can be called – other than by genocide.

By its very nature, genocide is more organized and selective than traditional massacre, though the reasons and objectives may be much the same for both. Massacre may not take place as a matter of policy or premeditation, but this is hardly true of genocide which, by definition, is the methodical liquidation of an entire people or culture. This is almost invariably associated with – or actually precipitated by – a particular ideology. It is ideology which constitutes the distinguishing feature of genocide in so far as it gives it direction and focus, and above all 'meaning'.

The necessity – indeed, compulsion – to give meaning and coherence to behaviour has affinities with the traditional functions of religion. And there is no doubt that nazism did have many of the characteristics of a religious belief system. Yehuda Bauer, one of the most influential writers on the Holocaust, has maintained that the adoption of pseudo-religious forms and rituals by nazism was a purely political ploy based on an irrational foundation. Such rituals would give identifiable religious symbolization to an instrumentally manipulative regime. (Bauer 1976). This implies that the Nazis cynically created a religious type system and simply adapted it to their political requirements.

There is little doubt that this did happen, although there is also evidence to suggest that for some – particularly those absorbed in the more mystical aspects of Aryan research – there was a reality behind the symbols. In both its theory and presentation, the religious 'likeness' of nazism is obvious. One has only to think of its specific features to see the correspondence between both kinds of system:

i) *the charismatic leader* who possesses the ability to attract followers to his cause. Charisma can be seen as a non-moral quality which is both transient and unstable, but which nevertheless has system-forming potential. For some, Hitler had almost mesmeric capabilities, although looking back at some of the early films of his speeches, it is difficult to see how the crowds were so swayed by this slightly ridiculous, ranting figure. And yet observers have testified that at the Nuremberg trials, when film of some of the old rallies were shown, they could see these men in the dock – who were arraigned on capital charges – falling under the spell all over again. This is not to suggest that nazism succeeded by a kind of mass hypnosis, but the evidence does point to the presence of a forceful personality who had the power to recruit supporters and make an impression on world events.

ii) *the 'revelation'* is a typical feature of those with messianic pretensions. This may purport to be either a new truth or a pertinent reminder of an old truth which has been sadly forgotten or ignored – in this case, the Aryan superiority myth. The heuristic 'message' is that blood is the key to history; that the world can only be understood in terms of race, and that superiority is inherently the endowment of the German people.

iii) *the mandate*, which gives authority to those so specially endowed to claim their inheritance. It also commits them to the task of cleansing the world of racial and ideological impurities, of creating a New Order, and making the world safe for the future of the master race. This necessitated dealing with the Jewish 'problem'. The Jews were not to be the scapegoats of society, but – in the religious tradition – a form of sacrifice *for* society.

iv) *the call to action*, which summons the people to achieve their true potential. To mobilize, to fashion the state that the mandate requires, and to embark upon a programme of expansion in order to realize their destiny.

v) *ritual and cult*, which are symbolized and rehearsed in the appropriate ceremonies. These act as both reminders and reinforcers of the mandate. The stage-managed rallies, the flags, the fanfares, the serried ranks, the speeches, etc., all have an evocative appeal to the would-be believer. They anaesthetize the critical senses, and generate a willingness for total commitment.

vi) *the promise of a millennial future*: no religious system would be complete without a convincing eschatology – in this case, a *realizable* eschatology. The Nazis were about to create, in their own estimation, the Thousand Year Reich. Until well into the war, Hitler and his protégé, Albert Speer, were still planning the architectural splendours of the new Berlin. Dreams are often confused with ambitions, and Hitler the visionary never quite came to terms with Hitler the pragmatist. He obviously believed in its feasibility until almost the very end – and it certainly helped to sustain the people. Images of a dazzling future can often compensate for the rigours of a transitory present.

A study of the literature, then, indicates not only the powerful ideological dimension of nazism, but also that for many, particularly the SS, it was not just a cynical device which had been contrived to mollify the masses, but a believed 'truth' that was totalizing in its demands. Yet, according to good sociological theory, this should not have been the case. Ideology and ideological thinking are supposed – on a marxian intepretation, at least – to be about distortion. Ideology is used to mystify and mislead the masses by encouraging a false awareness of the historical process and their whole place in the overall scheme of things. It is illusion, yet, hopefully a vulnerable illusion in that it may ultimately succumb to the practical realities of actual situations.

This is where we come to the central theoretical problem of this discussion. The task of the intellectual is to try to take a detached view of the social process, it is his duty to apply rigorous standards of objectivity to the 'presence' of ideology and to question the whole issue of power relations in society. The social scientist, Karl Mannheim, actually insisted that it was the intellectual, *par excellence*, who had the ability to transcend the limitations of distorted thinking, and see situations for what they were. For Mannheim, himself an 'intellectual refugee' from nazism, the intelligentsia could remain aloof from distortion; they were the carriers of the 'truth', the bearers of tradition, the agents for the transmission of the 'real' culture. They alone were capable of exercising a certain academic detachment, and were, therefore, the least likely to be deceived by the obfuscations of ideology. And yet many – perhaps most – in the SS obviously were. Even its intellectuals were not untouched by much of the mumbo-jumbo of the more ardent devotees, and where they were able to a limited extent, to stand outside the system, as it were, almost without exception they were still willing to go along with its worst excesses.

The SS recruited some intellectuals directly into its ranks, and others – often academics – were given honorary positions within the SS. This was really something of a PR exercise in that it enhanced the image of the SS to have certain notables on the books. It is instructive to look at a cross-section of these men who came from various disciplines and professions. There was the lawyer, Lieut.-General Hans Frank, who became the Reich Commissar for the General Government in Poland, whose speeches betray a ruthless – one might almost say, diseased – lust for power and whose actions resulted in the deaths of innumerable 'subjects' in his state-within-a-state, crimes for which he was executed in 1946. There was a host of medical practitioners associated with the SS, such as the consultant for the SS Racial Commission, Professor Bruno Schultz, among others, including the infamous and superficially charming Josef Mengele, who were found guilty of carrying out some notoriously inhuman experiments in the concentration camps. Mengele, a highly intelligent SS officer who held two doctorates, became known as the 'angel of death' for his activities at the Auschwitz extermination camp. He was hunted for years after the war, but justice never caught up with him. He eventually died a natural death, unlike his fellow academics, such as Lieut.-General Joachim Mugrowski, professor of bacteriology and head of the SS Health Department, who was hanged for his crimes in 1948, and Lieut.-General Leonardo Conti who was also a 'health leader', and who committed suicide while in internment in 1945.

Another intellectual with intimate associations with Auschwitz was SS Lieut.-General Dr Heinz Kammler. He had come from the *Luftwaffe*, and eventually returned to take charge of the prestigious jet-fighter and V-weapons programmes. But not before he had helped to obliterate part of Warsaw after an uprising in which over 56,000 Jews had been captured or killed, and not before he had built the gas chambers at Auschwitz for the rationalization of the extermination programme.

The SS liked to recruit bright young men, and two of the very brightest were Walter Schellenberg and Franz Six. Both men had joined the SS in the relatively early days, and both rose to important positions within the organization. Walter Schellenberg was qualified in both law and political science, and had done some work for the Security Service (SD) while still at university. Before he was 30 he was already Deputy Chief of Amt. VI, the foreign intelligence section of the SD (1939–42), and from 1942 to 1944 he was chief of the section. In 1944, there came a showdown between the *Abwehr* (Military Intelligence Dept) and the SS, after which the two were amalgamated under the auspices of the SS. Schellenberg was so well thought of that he was put in charge of the whole operation, i.e. he became head of the united SS and *Wehrmacht* military intelligence with the rank of Lieut.-General, and personal adviser on intelligence matters to the Reichsführer SS himself. He was obviously trusted by his superiors but viewed with some suspicion by his colleagues who were perhaps jealous of his rapid rise to power. The evidence – though confused – suggests that from late 1941 onwards Schellenberg was playing a double game. Though still dutiful to his masters, he was no longer convinced that the war could be won, and was instrumental in making tentative overtures through his intelligence contacts with Allied sources about some kind of *rapprochement* which proved unsuccessful.

It was never proved that Schellenberg was ever directly linked with the 'final solution', though it is extremely difficult to believe, given his close contact with Reichsführer Himmler, that he was unaware of such a programme. A fellow SS intellectual, Otto Ohlendorf, gave it as his opinion that Schellenberg would have been quite willing to command one of the Einsatzgruppen ('action' commandos – extermination units) in Poland or Russia if he thought that it would please Himmler. But then, unlike Ohlendorf who was given such a command – possibly as a test or a punishment, he seems never to have been required to do so. It was probably the callous 'Commissar Order' that damned Schellenberg as far as the Allies were concerned. His plea that he was simply associated with an 'information service' and not involved with Hitler's directive that Soviet commissars were to be liquidated sounded rather hollow when it was discovered that the directive was 'handled' by some of his subordinates (Reitlinger 1956: 180). He was also convicted of complicity in the murder of other Russian prisoners of war in relation to the subversive Operation Zeppelin in 1942. Nevertheless, his sentence was lenient, a mere six years imprisonment, to date from 1945. But owing to severe ill-health he was released a year early, in 1950, and died only two years later at the age of 42.

Dr Franz Six was a year older than Schellenberg. He left his post as a professor of political science and Dean of the Economic Faculty of the University of Berlin to join the Security Service (SD). He specialized in 'ideological matters' which really means that at least part of his task was to determine the degree of loyalty within the regime and to ensure its ideological purity. William Shirer refers to him as one of those 'peculiar intellectual gangsters who [were] ... somehow attracted to Himmler's secret police' (Shirer 1960: 937), and it is interesting that as a colonel in the SS he was allotted the task of rounding up ideological undesirables in Britain after the half-heartedly planned invasion in 1940 which never materialized. He proved his worth in similar work by commanding one of the Einsatzgruppen after the invasion of Russia the following year, though he did contrive to leave his post – as did some others such as another SS high-flyer, Heinz Jost – and was eventually transferred to the Cultural Division of the Foreign Office. Much as these men may have demurred at the margins, they were still willing to go on serving a regime that could perpetrate such outrages.

Six became the co-ordinator of Nazi cultural propaganda abroad, and was a major literary popularizer of the vaunted European New Order. He made much of the anti-bolshevik theme, and as Head of the German Foreign Policy Institute emphasized the need to preserve European cultural continuity. To this end he 'mustered all his sanctimonious phrases to prove that German occupation policy was concerned solely with the welfare of European peoples' (Herzstein 1982: 42–3). As an expert in journalism and foreign policy, he had what was considered to be a brilliant SS career and rose to the rank of Brigadier-General. After the war, his interrogators found him to be a self-righteous and unconvincing 'lamb of innocence'. He was sentenced to twenty years' imprisonment as a war criminal at the Nuremberg Trials in 1948, but – given the nature of his crimes – was inexplicably released in 1952.

A comparable case of an intellectual who also made something of a switch in mid-career is that of Dr Werner Best, the son of a post office official who became a high-ranking member of the SS. Best studied law at Geisen, Freiberg and Frankfurt Universities, entered the legal profession and became a District Judge. He was an enthusiastic nationalist and an ardent advocate of authoritarianism, about which he once wrote, 'the more complete its predominance, the more perfect the State' (quoted in Hohne, 1969: 165). He gravitated towards the Nazis before they came to power, and through his judicious use of contacts became Police President of Hesse in 1931 at the age of only 28. After the Nazi seizure of power in 1933, he rose in the hierarchy to become legal expert of the SS and Deputy to Reinhard Heydrich, Head of the Security Service, and has been described as 'a man adept at surrounding inverted logic with legal smokescreens' (Graber 1980: 78).

Some idea of Best's mentality can be gleaned from his writings. For example, in defending the 1936 law that 'the orders and affairs of the Secret State Police are not liable to investigation by administrative tribunals', he is really maintaining the independent authority of the police, and arguing that the state's judgements are above question. In another article, he goes on to say that

> the establishment of the National Socialist Führer State [means that] Germany has a system of government [which has] the right to resist, with all the coercive means at [its] disposal, any attack on [its] present form [or] its leadership. . . . Any attempt to gain recognition for or even to uphold different political ideas will be ruthlessly dealt with, as the symptom of an illness which threatens the healthy unity of the indivisible national organism, regardless of the subjective wishes of its supporters.
>
> (quoted in Krausnick and Broszat 1970: 170–1)

There are hints of a participatory system here, but it is really a quasi-Hobbesian vision of a state where all authority is vested in the mystical power of the leader who both symbolizes and rules the people, and in their name – itself something of a fiction – can presumably do no wrong.

In his own way, however, Best was something of an independent thinker. With the fall of France, he became head of the military administration there, but gradually fell foul of his superiors, particularly Heydrich, who considered that he was too moderate in his dealings with them. After Heydrich's death in 1942, Best gravitated towards the Foreign Office, and it was from here that Hitler personally chose him to take over as Plenipotentiary in Denmark. This tiny but agriculturally important state was regarded as ideologically acceptable because of its Nordic racial composition, and therefore enjoyed a special status as a 'lightly' occupied territory. But some Danes had proved to be somewhat obstreperous, and Best was instructed to rule them 'with an iron hand'. However, it appears that he tried to pursue a reasonably lenient line in an effort to ensure that there was a continuous flow of goods and products to the Reich. In 1943, Best even allowed a general election to take place, and although the Danish Nazis did not do very well in the polls, there is no doubt that generally speaking, in the earlier days of the occupation, Denmark could be considered to be quietly collaborationist. Certainly there was no organized resistance to speak of until 1943. Best's reports to his masters spoke of Danish co-operation and friendship but he omitted to mention the increasing incidence of sabotage and the growing proliferation of resistance groups. It was obvious that the policy of 'moderation' was breaking down, and eventually matters became so bad that a state of emergency was declared and military rule imposed.

For Best, this was bad enough, but his real problems began when the Security Service started agitating for action against the Jews. At first, Best resisted. It was not that he was particularly kind-hearted towards the Jews or sympathetic to their cause, but he tried to calm an already inflamed situation by suggesting alternative measures such as token arrests and the removal of Jews from official positions. It worked temporarily, though not to Hitler's satisfaction, or that of Adolf Eichmann, his head of the 'Jewish resettlement' (i.e. extermination) programme. By this time, Best was not only in trouble with his superiors, but also at loggerheads with the military administration in Denmark. He prevaricated and temporized until his position became so untenable that he actually proposed details for an 'action' against the Jews in order to retrieve his reputation. Yet even here he may have been playing a double-game. There is some evidence that warning was given to the Jews in advance, so that when the 'action' came in October 1943, relatively few Jews were actually taken into custody because most had escaped, many to Sweden. There is no doubt that Denmark has the most impressive record in saving its Jewish population – very much a minority – compared with other occupied territories (Petrow 1975).

Posterity has treated Werner Best with some ambivalence. This was reflected in the obvious factors which mitigated his crimes, yet he was still condemned to death in 1946. His sentence was later commuted and he actually only spent five years in gaol, possibly in recognition of his 'services' in Denmark, and afterwards he took up a post in the Bonn government.

In some ways the last case in this representative sample of culpable intellectuals is the most interesting of all. Again the person concerned, Otto Ohlendorf, was an extremely able academic who studied at Leipzig and Göttingen Universities and held degrees in both law and economics and for a while was a professor for applied economic science. He was introduced to the Security Service by another intellectual, Professor Reinhard Hohn, who needed an economic adviser, and he was soon given a department of his own which was mainly concerned with analysing the economic health of the Reich. Ohlendorf was often sharply critical of Reich policy, for example, the rearmament programme, and later extended the scope of his activities to include critical analyses of German science, education, law and administration, and even the Party itself.

At first, these reports were largely ignored, but as they became more abrasive in tone Ohlendorf was severely reprimanded by his superiors in the SD, and from then onwards took a rather more cautious line in his work with the Reich Commerce Group. There is no substantial evidence, however, that he ever took a stand on the Reich's treatment of minorities, especially Jews; nor that he had any reservations about the Reich's programme of expansion or its calculated policy of ruthlessness towards conquered peoples. Instead he went on producing his 'spheres of life' reports and continued lecturing to wealthy and influential industrialists and administrators where he earned the reputation of being a rather austere and brilliant realist.

All this changed – at least for a while – with the invasion of Russia. Ohlendorf was put in charge of one of the Einsatzgruppen which operated behind the lines to 'capture' and execute partisans, and to initiate the much more sinister scheme for the extermination of 'undesirable elements', notably the Jews. There is some mystery as to why a person in his position should have been given this task. It may have been a proving operation; or it may have been part of a policy of ingratiation given his previously poor relations with his superiors. Whatever the reason, he seems to have accepted it without complaint, and afterwards at his trial maintained that he had performed this unpleasant work with the maximum humanity and efficiency. He claimed that the mass executions were carried out in such a way that there was no direct contact between executioner and victim – several men would fire at once, rather like a firing squad, so that no one would know if he personally had killed the person concerned. As he testified dispassionately '[This was done] because both for the victims and those who carried out the executions, it was, psychologically, an immense burden to bear' (quoted in Shirer 1960: 1142).

Ohlendorf discharged his duties with unfaltering conscientiousness. On one or two occasions he paused for more exact instructions from HQ, once, for example, when he was unsure whether a Crimean sect, the Krimchaks, might have some Jewish blood in their veins. When told that this was a 'possibility', he unhesitatingly had them exterminated. And so it went on – when in doubt, kill. Everything was precisely detailed and clinically recounted. He frankly admitted that between 1941 and 1942 his Einsatzgruppe had executed 92,000 people.

After this tour of duty, Ohlendorf was transferred back to a more comfortable position at the Department of Overseas Trade. There he carried out his routine work as *alter ego* of the Party, as if nothing had happened. When questioned later, he gave the impression that the Russian episode was one of those wearisome labours that one has to get on with – a hiccup in the otherwise smooth running of the regime.

At his trial in 1947, he tried to present a carefully framed defence of his actions and those of others engaged in similar tasks. He claimed (i) that he was a non-participant and that his duties were purely administrative, (ii) that the killings were reprisals only, (iii) that he was honour-bound to carry out the orders of his superiors, and (iv) that in total war such extremes may be necessary. Some of his underlings testified on his behalf – mainly to the effect that the killings were conducted in the most 'humane and military manner because otherwise it would have been a strain too great for the execution squad' (Lieut. Heinz Schubert quoted in Infield 1988: 66). Needless to say, the prosecution was not overly impressed by these rationalizations and evasions, and Ohlendorf was finally condemned and executed at Landsberg in June 1951.

It is really difficult to know just what to make of this sinister breed of intellectuals. Mannheim's point about intellectuals being the carriers of tradition can be interpreted in two different ways. It could apply to those (in the minority?) who did not succumb to the new thinking in Germany during the Nazi period. Or, in a quite different sense, it could be applied to the Nazis themselves. It is possible to take the position that it was the Nazis who were the true bearers of tradition if one interprets tradition in terms not of Beethoven and Goethe but of Frederick, Kaiser Wilhelm and Prussian imperialism.

Heinz Hohne sees these men as

> hard-boiled SS technocrats ... social engineers who provided
> the Führer dictatorship with the necessary veneer of legality and
> organisation ... astute realists with no ideology other than that
> of power ... spiritually rootless and uninhibited by any of the
> generally accepted norms of conduct.

(Hohne 1969: 124)

This is surely a perceptive comment, but is Hohne correct in under-
stating the ideological dimension? Were they cynical and dispassionate
or had they surrendered to a particular ideology which demanded
unquestioning obedience? Was there not a genuine commitment to a
system symbolized by – indeed, encapsulated in – the person of the
leader who could do no wrong? Someone who could speak *ex cathedra*
for the Volk, and who was therefore above reproach?

And yet, in a strange way, the SS held themselves above normal
obligations – indeed, above ordinary morality. In their own way,
they represented Nietzsche's supermen whose morality was 'heroic',
self-chosen and therefore not circumscribed or conditioned by normal moral requirements. Admittedly in everyday social intercourse
they maintained the usual standards of middle-class morality. As
Reichsführer SS Himmler stated in his 'consolatory' speech to SS
officers at Posen in 1943, the SS had remained 'decent fellows',
despite the fact that most of them knew what it was like to have
as many as a thousand corpses lying side by side. But – as Yehuda
Bauer has pointed out – outside their families, communities, and the
German state generally, they were prepared to turn these moral rules
upside down. 'Lies became truth, murder became a moral imperative
[and] slavery was termed freedom' (Bauer 1976: *see* 333–43).

How could this come about? Much surely turns on the Nazi perception of 'the enemy' (see Carlton: 1990). This must condition the
actions of one individual to another. Jews were not only 'partisans',
'troublemakers', 'communists', they were also seen as non-people,
human-like vermin who did not deserve to exist. And yet, on the basis
of any test, they were so patently human, and had to be – even to their
executioners. There was no convincing evidence of their capacity for
'contamination' or corruption despite the exegetical manipulations of
the ideologues. How could they come to experience such a denial of
reality? Jews looked human, acted like humans, how therefore could
they not *be* humans unless this is what their persecutors actually *wanted
to believe*? And wanted to believe because such a belief had essential
self-affirming functions. Perhaps they of all people should have seen
through the ideology, but for them it had an 'elective affinity' –

something which accorded with their own evaluation of themselves as superior beings.

No one kind of analysis can possibly explain what to most of us is still inexplicable. There can be no adequate justification for mass murder, especially when it is not – as in the Allied bombing raids – conducted in the prosecution of war. It would be an error to adopt a reductionist stance and try to attribute such acts to any single cause. But, having said this, it seems undeniable that ideology played a critical role in the whole unspeakable Holocaust programme which arguably is the greatest single crime in history.

14

Afterthoughts on models and morality

This whole discussion has been permeated by one persistent question, why conquest? Why do societies embark upon programmes of calculated military activity which wreak such havoc on so many people? Obviously, there are a number of reasons for war: economic advantage, revenge, anticipation of an enemy attack, even believed ritual imperatives. But none of these quite accounts for that gratuitous, unnecessary aggression which we associate with history's would-be expansionists – the Alexanders, Caesars, Genghis Khans and Hitlers of this world. Indeed, it is said that Alexander wept because he had no more worlds to conquer. Presumably the reasons were locked in the now unfathomable psyches of the individuals concerned. But such urges and ambitions could not have been put into effect without the conducive combinations of circumstances which attended their expression, nor the rationalizations (ideologies) which facilitated their operation.

Where a conqueror's intention was simply for short-term gain as with, say, the Mongols and the Tartars, there could be no lasting political pay-off. But where the plan was for a slow bleeding of the territories for long-term calculated rewards – as with many of the societies in our study – some kind of *rapprochement* was usually necessary. And there was no better way of effecting an accommodation of this kind than through the medium of ideology. This might involve the straight imposition of one religious culture upon another as occurred in certain colonial situations; it might take the form of a fusion of beliefs – in effect, a kind of syncretism; or it might simply entail the tolerant recognition of the conquered people's gods, as in the case of Alexander who did obeisance to Egyptian deities in order to please his subject people, an unnecessary but prudent act, while also taking out a little celestial insurance. This example of Alexander is particularly interesting as it points up one of the pitfalls of conquest; the possibility – even the tendency – for the conquerors to be absorbed by the conquered: a situation which does little for the pride of

174

the autocrat himself. In this case, the Persians had a considerable influence on the Greeks and Macedonians – especially on the king who affected Persian dress and manners, and who insisted that even his companions acknowledge his newly acquired divinity. A similar situation obtained with one of Alexander's successors, Ptolemy, who 'inherited' Egypt as a kind of legacy after the king's death, and who was so won over by Egyptian culture that he took on all the trappings of pharaonic power and regal display. In such instances, we might well ask who has conquered whom?

Some conquerors are anxious to demonstrate their liberality and flexibility because they know it will have long-term benefits. But they often make a bad start, and then try to compensate for it afterwards, as with, say, Caesar in Gaul or Augustus in the Roman provinces whose initial depredations did not exactly endear them to the indigenes. In other instances, conquerors have been known to make a good start, and then either by necessity or default find that they have to resort to more repressive measures because they are just not getting the co-operation they desire. In various ways, the Assyrians, Babylonians and especially the Persians come into this category; expansionist nations that could turn very nasty when their subjects proved resistant to their demands.

There is a theory in the social sciences which maintains that new political and religious movements must be socioculturally compatible with those of the 'host' society if they are going to have any hope of success. This sounds like common sense, and is particularly pertinent to conquest situations. But, in fact, it often does not work like this. There are occasions in the sorry saga of war and conquest when the respective combatants are so *close* in ideological terms that an understanding is never reached. The histories of so many conflicts sound more like family feuds. The Jews versus the Christians, the Christians versus the Muslims – yet all sharing a common religious base. And the Jews versus the Muslims, both from Semitic racial stock, and each having so much in common. Paradoxically, it is almost as though their ideologies are *too* alike for reconciliation.

The motto theme of our study has concerned the incalculable and penetrative influence of ideology. The strength of ideology can probably be most clearly seen in the situations where there is no intention of assimilation or accommodation; where the dominant ideology is so powerful and inflexible that it takes no account of the feelings or wishes of the conquered, as with the Italian New Empire, the Japanese Imperial Empire, and pre-eminently – the Nazi New Order. Here we have seen that if the ideology so demands there can be a complete disregard for the feelings, susceptibilities, property, and even the lives of the subjects. Other factors play a part, of course, not least of all economic aggrandizement, status and power, but it is the *belief* in the validity of the objectives of the dominant culture, and the conviction of its inherent superiority that ultimately determine the fate of the subject peoples.

Social control is never easy – either for the controllers or the controlled. But without it there can be no order in society. It is a necessary pre-requisite for social stability. Control is underpinned by an implicit system of values which, in turn, is expressed as ideology. It may, therefore, be an index of social consciousness – indeed a condition of social emancipation – that both controllers and controlled are critically aware of the implications of ideology. For where people are not prepared to study and question the thought processes of the system, they may well contribute to their own unfreedom.

It is with this question of control in mind, therefore, that we can summarize our findings on the exercise of power in occupation settings. Having looked at the operationalization of control in various contexts we might compare these with those occupation policies and practices which characterize the model subject states. Models cannot, of course, be entirely abstract conceptions; all constructs have to be based upon what we know of the real world, as they reflect rather than represent reality. The ideal-type model, though subject to all sorts of qualifications (Bendix 1960) is helpful in that it provides us with a limiting case with which empirical phenomena can be contrasted. Ideal-types are simply analytical devices; they enable us to order reality, as it were, by isolating certain factors and forming them into a coherent system – according to the bias of our interests – then comparing them with actual cases and identifying the differentiae. They lack the elegance of models used in the physical sciences, but they are still a convenient conceptual aid when applied with refinement and discretion (Carlton 1977: 5–7).

Different models of social order are, therefore, possible (see, for example, Klapp 1973) but what concerns us here are those features which characterize the subject state. Obviously, subject states can be thought of as 'objective probabilities' i.e. actual states that have existed, but they can also be seen as 'subjective possibilities' i.e. yet-to-be possible events in future societies (Lasswell 1968). These 'events' may accord with past experience, but they may take different forms in as-yet unknown situations where techniques of control have reached more sophisticated levels. In this text, we have assumed that the ultimate in control is complete repression attended by the threat or actuality of selective extermination. One assumes that future dominant societies will abjure such crudities, and introduce refinements of conditioning which will be far more potent than the old well-tried methods. It is here that ideology, correctly and subtly inculcated, can be a useful adjunct,

176

as it is certainly the most effective and least expensive means of mass control, as we can see in parts of, say, the Muslim world today.

It is arguable whether anything other than modern societies has the means of total control because only they have the advanced technology to make this possible. This is why it is maintained by some theorists that particular pre-industrial societies such as, say, ancient Egypt, can be characterized as autocracies but not as totalitarian systems because they are just not 'total' enough in their means of control (Friedrich and Brzezinski 1965). Important as this observation is, it tends to minimize the scale factor in control. In certain small-scale traditional societies there was considerable *intensity* of control. In Zulu society at its zenith early in the nineteenth century, nothing much could happen anywhere in the kingdom without the king knowing about it, and infringements – or even suspected infringements – could meet with the most lethal consequences (Morris 1968). It is all a question of extent and degree. *Extent* of control, that is to say control over a large state can actually mean a rather tenuous grip on affairs, especially in the outer reaches of the empire. But small, compact societies can often exercise a much greater *degree* of control over their subjects.

The subject state, then, is at the mercy of a dominant power with the technological means at its disposal for ensuring complete compliance in its occupied territories. This includes such obvious features as superior military hardware, and a highly organized bureaucratic machinery to administer the territories in question. This necessitates a monopoly of all effective means of control; arsenals are under the strict authority of the occupying power (this is why modern rebellious 'popular front' movements have to be supplied by outside powers – a situation little known in the pre-industrial world).

A key element in the subject state is the control of education. Teachers are vetted; there is careful scrutiny of teaching materials in order to ensure complete congruance with the state's ideals. The inculcation of the correct attitudes in the young is a prime requisite in so far as compliance can only serve the long-term plans of the regime. There may even be a selection system whereby suitable candidates can be promoted from serf-like status to that of minor official or the like in the service of the ruling power. This indirectly reinforces public awareness of the nature of the stratification system and encourages competitive divisions among the rank and file. Active collaboration, from officials down to the cell-block trusty, can only be to the advantage of the system. There may even be an extension of the franchise to favoured entities resulting in wider recruitment to specialized organizations or echelons of the regime. This is reminiscent of the Nazi attempts to incorporate certain non-German subjects into the SS, and must be regarded as something of a war-time exigency, which played havoc

177

with their racial policies. It is atypical of an occupying power to grant privileged status to its subjects, although it was practised with some success by the Romans.

The administration of the subject state is also geared to the economic requirements of the occupying power to enrich its own population and possibly contribute to further expansionist programmes. The subject people is encouraged by necessary inducements to work for the 'greater good' of the regime. Recruitment of labour is both intensive and extensive; industry and agriculture are both rationalized in such a way that the main benefits accrue to the dominant power. It is not exactly a slave state – that has built-in disadvantages – but the organization of production and rewards resembles a form of highly systematized serfdom. Work for the state is a duty. For those who cannot or will not comply the consequences are ominous. The state has no place for those who are unfit or deliberately recalcitrant. Compulsion is, therefore, a potent instrument for internal control. But in tandem with this, the regime will try to ensure conformity by the inculcation of a plausible ideology and the manufacture of the appropriate symbols and rituals. It is all part of the ceremonialization of repression. This may be introduced quite cynically, as an opiate for the masses, or it may actually be believed by those who manipulate opinion. This was, of course, the case with the Nazi ideologues who actually ruined their chances with the conquered by their refusal to be flexible and abandon, or at least modify, their particular forms of racist repression.

As a necessary back-up to the ideology there must be a system of terroristic police control which utilizes the technical, biochemical and psychological techniques available to modern science. Coercion is exercised where necessary and without compunction against demonstrable enemies of the state, and even – where 'appropriate' – against arbitrarily selected sections or classes of the population. The operations of the security police are given legitimacy by the courts which act as mere instruments of the state, and there is little – if any – appeal from their judgements.

Political freedom does not exist in the subject state, therefore political activity is minimal. There are no rival political parties, although there may be a notional consultative body to assure some token representation for the subject people and to consider their 'interests'. All relevant information is mediated through official channels, so subjects are quite incapable of making valid judgements or informed decisions. Thus petitions take the place of plebiscites. Above all else, the people are never given the opportunity to change their own status, their lives are committed to permanent servitude, somewhat like the helots of ancient Sparta.

As with political parties, so all independent associations have disappeared. All social activity is governmentalized and strictly supervised, so as to ensure that there are no temptations towards unwelcome heterodoxy. The main problem for the occupying power is what to do about religious assemblies. If they are banned altogether, as has been the case for many years in modern Albania, or restricted to assembly but no propagation of ideas, as in most Eastern-bloc countries until recent times, it may generate more disaffection than it is worth. Much depends on the religious system concerned. It may be induced to serve the regime, and act as a necessary soporific for the people. On the other hand, it may take the form of a dangerous counter-ideology, and the assemblies may become breeding grounds for dissension and even subversion, and generate their own popular leaders.

No *actual* subject state has been quite like that depicted here, but there have been many which approximated to it in a number of respects. And these actual states have been long-lived or transitory for quite identifiable reasons. The Spartans, for example, maintained a subject state for several hundred years, largely because of their military supremacy and because their institutions – bizarre as they may appear to us – were recognized and even admired by others. Whereas in the case of Nazi Germany, her ideology of race and her expansionist ambitions brought her into mortal conflict with most of the world. In theory, there is no reason why a dominant power should not be able to maintain a subject state if it is as shrewd as it is repressive. Everything really depends upon the nature and the implementation of that repression, and – pre-eminently – on the continuing military ascendency of the state in question, in which case, she can make her own rules.

We have already seen how some theorists have felt it important to emphasize the more positively humane aspects of war. They have stressed how all societies formulate rules and observe certain conventions which, to some extent, condition the conduct of war (e.g. Best 1980) and are then extended to cover the situations attending conquest and even subjugation. For example, there have been general improvements in the way that prisoners of war are treated (a category largely unknown in the ancient world). But even this – as we have noted – can be extremely selective, and subject to the most 'flexible' rules, depending on the circumstances. Starvation, deprivation, torture and execution may not be on the official agenda, but they have been very widespread. Whether society in general is making any progress in this respect is still a matter of debate. The formulation of rules to govern such situations is obviously very laudable and utilitarian in intent. But how predictable is it? It is all very well concocting codes aimed at bringing the least pain to the greatest number, but it involves a conceptual confusion between the formulation of the law and the application of the law which in some ways is analogous to the Roman *jus ad bellum*, the law governing going to war, and *jus in bellos*, what you do when you get there: in short, the conflict between theory and practice. Few would dispute that the rules, in this case about warfare, are drawn up by legislators with the very best motives, but the reason why they are then applied by military authorities or observed by military personnel may have little or nothing to do with utilitarian morality, but everything to do with military expediency. No one is suggesting that there should be no attempt to make such rules, but these may well prove to be worthless in situations where they can be changed, rationalized or simply ignored.

It is similar with occupation policy and practice. The policy of the dominant power in relation to a subject state may be reasonably humanitarian, as, for example, with the Allied occupation of Germany after the Second World War. Or it may intend to be humane but fail in practice, as in certain colonial situations. Alternatively, there are instances where the policies have been oppressive, but where practice slowly improved; Roman Britain would be one such example. And of course, there are the tragic situations where the policies were ruthless to begin with and virtually genocidal in practice, as in Cambodia in the 1970s. The truth of the matter is that despite the urgings of others – even the international community – conquerors, if they are powerful enough, do what they like. And where their intentions do not accord with the 'rules', then the rules can always be redefined to suit the circumstances, as, for instance, when massacred civilians are re-designated as 'terrorists', as the SS did in the Ardennes towards the end of the Second World War.

In the ancient world, the conquered belonged, by right, to the conquerors to do with as they pleased. There were few, if any, clamorous voices raised in denial of this prerogative. So what the Assyrians did to subject peoples, Alexander decided to do with plotters and rebels, or Caesar did to the barbarians was up to each of them. Protest was not an option. And so it continued, regardless of the earnest debates of the medieval Schoolmen. It is only in relatively modern times that there have been any really serious attempts to make rules which would limit the freedom of nations to make war, and to impose certain restraints on their rights to treat the defeated as they wished. But how far has it got us? We have had open defiance of international rule-making bodies such as the League of Nations; in fact, arrogant dictators such as Mussolini exposed the weaknesses of such bodies. We have also had the deliberate flouting of generally agreed conventions regarding such horrors as saturation bombing, the use of poisonous gas, and mass atrocities. In short, we have experienced the worst wars in history and in the cases of Japan, Germany and the Khmer Rouge, a treatment of the conquered which beggars description. The numbers of those massacred this century in tribal, colonial and national conflicts – and particularly in the aftermath – defies any meaningful assessment. Formulating rules to stop or restrict such things is fine, but who is going to enforce them?

There is still a prevailing view that the world is actually getting better; that for every two steps backward, humanity is taking three steps forward. This idea is linked with optimistic notions about moral progress and the ultimate goodness of human nature. But where is the evidence? Few people deny that there has been considerable scientific progress, of actual and potential control of the environment, but what about *moral* progress? This implies the clarification of moral ideas and the removal of moral inconsistencies; a clearer understanding of human needs and purposes, and – presumably – an enlargement of the areas of moral application. The problem is not only to know whether moral development is ascertainable, it is also to discern whether differences in moral attitudes are due to ethical values, *per se*, or to certain *external* factors as with, say, the virtual abolition of institutionalized slavery which was largely the result of technological change. It is true that society is becoming more and more sensitive on a number of issues with a moral dimension: health, security, education, etc., but on the question of violence and aggression there does not seem to have been any appreciable change for the better. Indeed, if anything, crime figures and the widespread incidence of terrorism, and – perhaps most significant of all – the preparedness to use the most unthinkable weapons of mass destruction, all seem to indicate the reverse.

Moral progress must be one of the most persistent myths of our time. It assumes that human nature is rather better than its performance to date, and that all it needs is a little re-orientation and encouragement. Yet history gives us no reason to suppose that humans are dauntlessly advancing towards perfection. No one doubts our competence and rationality, but experience teaches us that these may well be directed to most unworthy ends. Fifty million dead in two world wars cannot give us that much room for optimism. Of course we must go on trying, on the assumption that there is nothing in human nature that must admit of ultimate defeat. But technological hubris could still be our undoing. Wasn't it Aldous Huxley who perceptively suggested that it was the fruits of progress that helped us to retrogress more efficiently?

Postscript: The Iraqi occupation of Kuwait

The Iraqi invasion of Kuwait was hardly unexpected. Not only was it not surprising that a large, burgeoning state such as Iraq should have expansionist designs on its diminutive neighbour, it is readily comprehensible – if morally reprehensible – that she should covet the wealth of an oil-rich state with one of the highest per capita incomes in the world. It is a well-known feature of totalitarian dictatorships that they need 'incidents', preferably triumphs of some kind, to sustain their credibility. Iraq's autocratic President, Saddam Hussein, having failed in his abortive and extremely costly campaign against Iran, badly needed a conquest to restore his pride and to bolster his reputation as the aspiring leader of the Arab world. The eight-year war with Iran had brought him precisely nothing. It had looked to be something of a pushover, given that Iran was still shuddering from the tremors of its biggest political upheaval in recent history. But it cost several hundred thousand men and achieved nothing but seriously disputed territorial claims. Small wonder that Saddam, who had now become *persona non grata* in the West, should contemplate easier and richer pickings elsewhere.

Kuwait ('little fort'), at the head of the Persian Gulf, was a barren wasteland until the influx of its oil revenues. Its inhabitants are predominantly Arab, although about 70 per cent of its population are foreigners, particularly Palestinians. It was originally settled in the early eighteenth century by Arab nomads who established a sheikdom in 1756. At the end of the last century, in order to counter German and Ottoman encroachments, Kuwait handed over control of its external affairs to Britain, and became a British protectorate in 1914. Its borders were fixed in 1922–3 including a 'neutral zone' which it shared with Saudi Arabia. It was a poor area with almost no natural resources until oil was discovered in quantity in 1938. This entirely transformed the economy after the Second World War.

Kuwait gained her independence in 1961, but this much-prized political autonomy was always somewhat precarious. She managed to survive by a combination of shrewd diplomacy and strict neutrality. Such a small state, of barely two million people, had no really effective defence forces of her own, so after independence she requested troops from Britain so as to avert, even then, the threatened annexation of her territory by Iraq. Until this invasion materialized in August 1990, she was one of the largest oil producers in the world, with oil revenues generating half the GNP, and oil-related services accounting for most of the rest. Her phenomenal prosperity meant that she was able to import technological know-how to develop some industries, and commence a very ambitious building programme, particularly in Kuwait City itself, including a university (1962) and some very impressive modern facilities – especially in the areas of health and education.

The ruling al-Sabbah family was directly descended from original Arab stock, and until the petro-dollars started flowing in, appears to have exercised control in a reasonably relaxed way; members of the family could even be seen shopping from time to time in the local market. Things changed with the almost unimaginable wealth from oil. They became billionaires and the state generally flourished so that its wealth became a byword among Westerners. But not everybody benefited. Political representation was still restricted. The population was divided into first- and second-class citizens; very few had the vote, and women were not enfranchised. The emir was something of an autocrat, even Parliament itself was dissolved when it became too critical of rumoured ruling-house corruption. Perhaps as many as 60 per cent of the population got only a very modest share of Kuwait's luxurious living standards (Geraldine Brooks, *The Sunday Times*, 12 August 1990). Real riches were largely the preserve of a fairly well-defined elite which comprised only about 4 per cent of the population. But all this was changed completely by the invasion. The leading members of the al-Sabbah family fled to Bahrain and Saudi Arabia where they were still not exactly penniless – there was too much money invested abroad for that – but, in exile, there had to be much greater financial stringency.

The distress of the al-Sabbahs and their 'court' was of little concern to the Iraqis. They took the view that both Kuwait and Iraq had once been part of the old Ottoman Empire, and that they had been 'swindled' out of the territory following the British–Ottoman agreement of 1913 and the British occupation of Iraq in 1914. The Iraqis therefore argued that they had justifiable claims to the land. They maintained that from August 1990 they were not occupying Kuwait but merely repossessing what was already rightfully theirs. The Iraqi Press Office also insisted that the invasion was precipitated by the American–UAE 'conspiracy' to flood the international market with cheap oil, in contravention of OPEC resolutions, and thus seriously jeopardize Iraq's economy.

President Saddam Hussein stated that a 'one dollar decrease would result in Iraq losing one billion dollars yearly'. The Iraqis said that their representations to Kuwait and the UAE generally were more or less ignored, and that they had little choice but to respond to 'the Kuwait uprise [sic] on the 2nd August . . . [and] offer all brotherly help . . . to put an end to the conspiracy and corruption of the Al-A'Sabbah [gang] who were commissioned . . . to protect [British] oil interests'. The Iraqis thus resorted to force, or, as they put it in their official pronouncements, 'responded to the . . . historical request . . . of the temporarily free government of Kuwait'.

Saddam Hussein regarded the al-Sabbahs as a pseudo-monarchy of doubtful legitimacy which was established by the British for their own purposes. He described them as the parasites of the Arab world – indolent and undeservedly rich oil emirs. And he cunningly manipulated the prejudices of the Arab world against all those desert sheiks who have become fabulously wealthy just because they happened – quite fortuitously – to be sitting on what is perhaps the richest source of oil in the world. His argument was that ordinary Arabs went barefoot while these would-be monarchs controlled near-feudal states to their own advantage, and that these injustices were supported by the West in its own economic interests. He even suggested that all the oil-rich states should donate two dollars to the non-oil-rich states for every barrel they produce. This may have been a mere propaganda ploy, but it had a definite resonance among the Arab poor, especially in Jordan and Egypt. The Americans, on the other hand, insisted that the al-Sabbahs have ruled wisely and invested the riches for the good of the state. Sympathizers pointed to the example of Oxford-educated Hussa-al Sabbah who, with her husband, used much of her fortune to create the much-admired Islamic Museum in Kuwait.

The Iraqi claims of legitimate suzereignty over Kuwait do not accord with what actually happened there during its 'liberation'. Kuwait was not treated as part of Iraq but rather as a subject state, and if we apply our model of a subject state to occupied Kuwait, we can see that this has to be qualified in a number of significant ways.

As was to be expected, the scale factor entirely favoured the occupying power. Kuwait is such a small, discrete and manageable state that it provides few problems for a determined conqueror. Furthermore, the terrain is such that it does not provide cover for partisan activity, although we know that certain resistance groups did operate in the area. The Iraqis were able to exercise control in both degree and extent, with their vastly superior forces, and virtually complete command of military hardware. But the fact that both sides had a common culture and language meant that clandestine operations were – in theory – that much simpler in both directions.

The media and communications agencies were taken over immediately; this is now accepted as the first rule of conquest. And in collaboration with certain sympathetic elements in the subject population – particularly Palestinians – the Iraqis were able to infiltrate the Kuwaiti administrative bureaucracy and take control of the principal state institutions. But, unusually, there were few signs of the organized exploitation of the economy and the re-orientation of education that one would expect in the subject state. Rather there was a process of systematic looting and confiscation, especially by the military, though more in the nature of opportunistic rapacity than the slow squeezing of the system that one associates with those who have come to stay. In a way, this was symbolized by the devastation of 'Entertainment City', the Kuwaiti equivalent (imitation?) of Disneyland. This government-funded £120 million leisure complex was stripped of most of its principal assets, even to the point where certain novelties were dismantled and transported to Baghdad. Everything was regarded as legitimate war booty. This kind of hasty dismemberment of a state can be particularly advantageous in a situation where the economy is undiversified, and the conquerors want to take what they can get, and then concentrate all their energies on exploiting a single, rich resource, namely oil, a vital product whereby they can 'regulate' external markets.

After the invasion, the actions of the Iraqis seemed to bear little relation to their claims that Kuwait was really part of their country. American experts and Kuwaiti exiles described how the land was depopulated and the society dehumanized by the Iraqis who instituted a system of calculated repression. Amnesty International reported that the military and secret police carried out widespread arrests, interrogations under torture, summary executions and mass extrajudicial killings in order to counter actual and threatened Kuwaiti resistance. Initially, the Kuwaiti partisans, aided by covert Saudi and American personnel, had some success, but soon most dissident activity was curtailed on instruction from the exiled Kuwaiti rulers for fear of further reprisals.

At first, the West's response to all this was greatly influenced by the danger to the foreign hostages in Kuwait who had been trapped by the invasion. But although this was of great concern to the West it was not as serious as what was happening to the native population. There were mass deportations, women and children were arrested, and reports were received of gratuitously inhumane acts such as removing life-support incubators and leaving babies to die, besides confiscating essential X-ray and radiotherapy machines, and various items of surgical equipment. Dr Mohsin Yousef, professor of medicine and cardiology at Kuwait Hospital, described how he had to work under Iraqi military authority with grossly depleted resources (John Cassidy, *The Sunday Times*, 7 October 1990).

Factories and offices were at a virtual standstill, and the only things working in Kuwait City were the electricity and water plants and, of course, for a while, the oil wells – many of which were later vindictively destroyed. Private and public institutions were dismembered. Newspapers were closed and stripped of their presses and technological hardware. Local radio and television stations were similarly plundered. Schools and research institutions as well as the hospitals were all affected. In fact, Amnesty International insists that the university became the HQ of the Iraqi secret police, and that the campus was actually used as an execution area for those suspected of anti-Iraqi subversion. Kuwaiti currency was declared to be no longer legal tender, and identity cards, car licences and licence plates were all cancelled in the anticipation that all Kuwaitis would re-register as Iraqi citizens. These privations affected less than 50 per cent of the state's original inhabitants, the remainder, both citizens and foreign residents, fled the country for safety.

The Iraqi depredations were so thorough that it soon became apparent that the invasion was not just for plunder but for a wholesale experiment in social engineering which conceivably included a policy of repopulation. This is not as far-fetched as it sounds because the Kuwaiti situation was already seriously exacerbated by the presence of so many Palestinians who were sympathetic to the Iraqi cause and who seemed poised to take over the country. In many ways, the Kuwaitis were responsible for encouraging the growth of this politically restless element among the population in the first place. It was in Kuwait that Yasser Arafat founded the Fatah movement and was soon joined in the 1960s by members of expatraiate Palestinians. It did not take long for the Kuwaitis to realize the possible political dangers posed by the Palestinian community – a problem that they shared with both the Lebanese and the Jordanians.

At the time of the invasion, Palestinians may have comprised as much as 25 per cent of the total population. They were never regarded as full citizens – a fact that may well account for their growing disaffection. This does not mean that all of them were actual or even potential collaborators; many of them were doing reasonably well in commercial terms, and had effectively made Kuwait their home. But the evidence suggests that many more were prepared to take full advantage of the Kuwaitis' plight. Reports suggest that some took over abandoned Kuwaiti houses and even their shops and businesses; certainly it was the Palestinians who kept things going during the initial period of the occupation – presumably with implicit Iraqi approval. Rather more sinister were reports that Palestinians were recruited into a special militia to help police the occupied territories, and that some actively co-operated with the occupying forces even to the point of denouncing prominent Kuwaiti citizens and identifying police officials, some of whom were subsequently shot.

This has all had serious economic and political repercussions on the Palestinian community generally. Sympathetic Arab states are known to make generous contributions to the Palestinian cause. Kuwait – through its Palestinian community – was no exception, and Palestinians working for the Kuwaiti government were contributing 5 per cent of their income to Palestinians abroad. In fact, it is estimated that in the year 1989–90 alone, Kuwait sent some £45 million to the PLO and various kindred groups (John Swain, *The Sunday Times*, 23 September 1990). These recipient Palestinians, though generally supportive of the Iraqi position, were somewhat divided in their loyalties. The community in Abu Dhabi, for example, – no doubt fearful of annoying their hosts – repudiated the entire Iraqi venture.

In many ways, occupied Kuwait approximated to our model of the subject state, but there were significant differences. First of all, the hostage situation was initially a complicating factor not normally found in subject state situations. It is, of course, commonplace for occupying forces to take hostages as an insurance against partisan activity, but it was *foreign* hostages that were held in the Iraqi invasion and this inevitably both aggravated world opinion and, at the same time, influenced the gravity and unanimity of its response. Furthermore, there was the Palestinian factor – a huge potentially collaborative and, in some cases, actively hostile community within the state. The Palestinians, though culturally similar to the Kuwaitis, had a different history and considerably different nationalist aspirations. This state-within-a-state presents us with a situation quite unlike any others that we have encountered in our studies. It may well be that they and the Iraqis had very different perceptions of the situation. Sympathetic as the Iraqis were to the Palestinian cause, it is highly doubtful whether they ever envisaged Kuwait as a possible Palestinian homeland. They were naturally only too glad of Palestinian co-operation, despite the fact that they must have been very aware of the problems that Palestinians have caused in other Arab states. The truth is that they were a useful pawn in the game; Hussein needed them to provide an ongoing *casus belli* in relation to Israel. It is intriguing to speculate on what the future status of the Palestinians in Kuwait would have been under Iraqi sovereignty. Would they have exchanged one form of citizenship for something even less desirable?

Finally, there was the ideological factor, or – in this case – the *lack* of an ideological factor. In the typical subject state situation the ideology of the dominant power is either imposed on the conquered, as in the colonizing of the Americas, or it constitutes a limiting factor in as much as it is held to differentiate the superior from the inferior race or culture, as with the Nazis in Eastern Europe. The Iraq–Kuwait situation is especially interesting because both countries have a common religious ideology, the same language and a very similar culture. In certain sectarian forms, and in particular social contexts, Islam is an all-powerful ideology. But not so here. Elsewhere, for example in Iran, all other considerations would pale into insignificance beside its overarching ethical and ritual demands. But in this instance, it has been shown to be a diluted and dependent variable. In Iraq, its imperatives were re-interpreted in military terms – something which recalls the early days of Muslim expansionism. There was no need of a pretence at propagating the Muslim faith, the Iraqis had attacked fellow Muslims, and were quite indifferent to the religious affinities or moral susceptibilities of the Kuwaitis. Military conquest was what mattered. In this case, the faith had become subordinated to naked political ambition.

Bibliography

Almond, G. and O. Powell, (1966), *Comparative Politics: A Developmental Approach*, New York, Little Brown.

Arendt, H. (1958), *The Origins of Totalitarianism*, New York, Meridian.

Arnold-Foster, M. (1983), *The World at War*, London, Thames Methuen.

Ashton, S. L. (1988), *Colonialism in India*, London, British Library.

Auguet, R. (1972), *Cruelty and Civilization: The Roman Games*, London, Allen & Unwin.

Baer, G. W. (1967), *The Coming of the Italo–Ethiopian War*, Cambridge, Mass., Harvard University Press.

Barry, W. Theodore de (1958), *Sources of Indian Tradition*, New York, Columbia University Press.

Bauer, Y. (1976), 'Contemporary history: some methodological problems', *History*, 61(203): 333–43.

Bauman, Z. (1989), *Modernity and the Holocause*, Cambridge, Cambridge University Press.

Bendix, R. (1960), *Max Weber: an Intellectual Portrait*, London, Heinemann.

Best, G. (1980), *Humanity in Warfare*, London, Weidenfeld & Nicolson.

Blanksten, G. (1962), 'Fidel Castro & Latin America', in M. Kaplan (ed.), *The Revolution in World Politics*, New York, Wiley.

Boak, A. and Sinnigen, W. (1972), *A History of Rome to A.D. 565*, London Collier-Macmillan.

Bosworth, A. B. (1988), *Conquest and Empire*, Cambridge, Cambridge University Press.

Boveri, M. (1961), *Treason in the Twentieth Century*, London, Macdonald.

Bower, T. (1987), *The Paperclip Conspiracy*, London, Paladin.

Brandon, W. (1969), *Book of Indians*, New York, Dell (fourth edn).

Brandt, K. *et al.* (1953), *Management of Agriculture and Food in German-Occupied and other areas of Fortress Europe*, Stanford, Stanford University Press.

Brown, D. (1970), *Bury my Heart at Wounded Knee: An Indian History of the American West*, London, Barrie & Jenkins.

Burland, C. (1976), *Peoples of the Sun*, London, Weidenfeld & Nicolson.

Burn , A. R. (1973), *Alexander the Great and the Middle East*, Harmondsworth, Pelican.

Bushnell, G. (1967), *Peru*, London, Thames & Hudson.

Calvocoressi, P. and Wint, G. (1972), *Total War*, London, Allen Lane.

Carew, T. (1960), *The Fall of Singapore*, London, Anthony Blond.

Carlton, E. (1977), *Ideology and Social Order*, London, Routledge & Kegan Paul.

189

Carlton, E. (1990), *War and Ideology*, London, Routledge.
Cassels, A. (1969), *Fascist Italy*, London, Routledge & Kegan Paul.
Cecil, R. (1972), *The Myth of the Master Race*, New York, Dodd.
Chambers, M. (ed.) (1970), *The Fall of Rome*, New York, Holt, Rinehart & Winston.
Chapman, B. (1971), *Police State*, London, Macmillan.
Clark, A. (1965), *Barbarossa: the Russo–German Conflict 1941–45* New York, Morrow.
Collier, J. (1956), *Indians of the Americas*, New York, Mentor.
Collier, R. (1978), *Duce*, Glasgow, Fontana.
Contenau, G. (1969), *Everyday Life in Babylon and Assyria*, London, Edward Arnold.
Crawford, M. (1978), *The Roman Republic*, Glasgow, Fontana.
Dallin, A. (1981), *German Rule in Russia 1941–45*, London, Macmillan.
Dank, M. (1978), *The French against the French*, London, Cassell.
Deakin, F. W. (1966), *The Brutal Friendship*, Harmondsworth, Pelican.
Delzell, C. (1961), *Mussolini's Enemies: the Anti-Fascist Resistance*, London, Oxford University Press.
Dombrowski, R. (1956), *Mussolini: Twilight and Fall*, London, Heinemann.
Driver, H. (ed.) (1964), *The Americas on the Eve of Discovery*, Englewood Cliffs, NJ, Prentice-Hall.
Edwardes, M. (1975), *Red Year: the Indian Rebellion of 1857*, London, Cardinal.
Fein, H. (1979), *Accounting for Genocide*, New York, Free Press.
Fest, J. (1970), *The Face of the Third Reich*, Harmondsworth, Pelican.
Fine, J. (1983), *The Ancient Greeks*, Harvard, Belknap.
Foot, M. R. D. (1978), *Resistance*, London, Granada/Paladin.
Fox, R. L. (1975), *Alexander the Great*, London, Futura.
Friedrich, C. (ed.) (1954), *Totalitarianism*, Harvard, Harvard University Press.
Friedrich, C. and Brzezinski, Z. (1965), *Totalitarian Dictatorship and Autocracy*, New York, Praeger.
Galbraith, K. (1984), *The Anatomy of Power*, New York, Hamilton.
Gallagher, M. (1963), *The Soviet History of World War II*, New York, Praeger.
Gellner, E. (1963), *Thought and Change*, London, Weidenfeld & Nicolson.
Gilbert, M. (1989), *Second World War*, London, Weidenfeld & Nicolson.
Gordon, G. (1962), *The Rise and Fall of the Japanese Empire*, Connecticut, Monarch Books.
Graber, G. (1980), *History of the SS*, London, Macmillan.
Grant, M. (1982), *From Alexander to Cleopatra*, London, Weidenfeld & Nicolson.
Green, P. (1973), *Alexander the Great*, London, Weidenfeld & Nicolson.
Harmon, G. (1941), *Sixty Years of Indian Affairs*, Chapel Hill, University of North Carolina Press.
Hassell, L. von (1948), *Von Hassell Diaries*, London, Hamish Hamilton.
Haywood, R. (1971), *The Ancient World*, New York, McKay.
Hemming, J. (1974), *The Conquest of the Incas*, London, Macmillan (first edn 1970).
Herzstein, R. (1982), *When Nazi Dreams Come True*, London, Abacus.
Hess, R. (1966), *Italian Colonialism in Somalia*, Chicago, Chicago University Press.
Hibbert, C. (1965), *Benito Mussolini*, Harmondsworth, Penguin.
Hilton, S. (1981), *Hitler's Secret War in South America*, New York, Ballantine.
Hinz, W. (1972), *The Lost World of Elam*, London, Sidgwick & Jackson.
Hobbes, T. (1963), *Leviathan*, introduction by J. Plamenatz, London, Fontana.

Hohne, H. (1969), *The Order of the Death's Head*, London, Pan.

Hopkins, K. (1978), *Conquerors and Slaves*, Cambridge, Cambridge University Press.

Hoyt, E. (1987), *Japan's War*, London, Hutchinson.

Hultkrantz, A. K. E. (1979), *The Religions of the American Indians*, London, University of California Press.

Humble, R. (1980), *Warfare in the Ancient World*, London, Cassell.

Hunt, G. (1940), *The Wars of the Iroquois*, Madison, Wis., University of Wisconsin Press.

Ienaga, S. (1980), *The Pacific War*, New York, Parthenon.

Infield, G. (1988), *Secrets of the SS*, New York, Military Heritage Press.

Innes, H. (1970), *The Conquistadores*, London, Thames & Hudson.

Iriye, A. (1987), *The Origins of the Second World War in Asia and the Pacific*, London, Longman.

Johnson, P. (1983), *A History of the Modern World 1917–1980's*, London, Weidenfeld & Nicolson.

Jones, F. (1954), *New Order in East Asia 1937–45*, London, Oxford University Press.

Jouvenel, B. de (1948), *Power: The Natural History of its Growth* (trans. J. Huntington), London, Hutchinson.

Kahn, D. (1978), *Hitler's Spies*, London, Hodder & Stoughton.

Kendall, A. (1973), *Everyday Life of the Incas*, London, Batsford.

Kirkpatrick, I. (1964), *Mussolini: Study of a Demagogue*, Englewood Cliffs, NJ, Prentice-Hall.

Klapp, O. (1973), *Models of Social Order*, Palo Alto, Mayfield.

Knox, MacGregor (1982), *Mussolini Unleashed 1939–41*, Cambridge, Cambridge University Press.

Krausnick, H. and Broszat M. (1970), *Anatomy of the SS State*, London, Paladin (first edn 1968).

Kren, G. and Rappoport, L. (1980), *The Holocaust and the Crisis of Human Behavior*, New York, Holmes & Meier.

Laqueur, W. (ed.) (1979), *Fascism*, Harmondsworth, Pelican.

Larousse (1963), *Encyclopaedia of Ancient-Medieval History*, London, Hamlyn.

Lasswell, H. (1968), 'The Garrison State', in L. Branson and G. Goethals (eds) *War*, New York, Basic Books.

Lee, S. (1987), *The European Dictatorships 1918–1945*, London, Routledge.

Lloyd, S. (1978), *The Archaeology of Mesopotamia*, London, Thames & Hudson.

Lowe, C. and Mazari J. (1975), *Italian Foreign Policy 1870–1940*, London, Routledge & Kegan Paul.

Luckenbill, D. (1926–7), *Ancient Records of Assyria and Babylonia (ARAB)*, Chicago, University of Chicago Press.

Lyons, G. (ed.) (1976), *The Russian Version of the Second World War*, London, Cooper.

—— (1981), *Mussolini*, London, Weidenfeld & Nicolson.

Mack Smith, D. (1979), *Mussolini's Roman Empire*, Harmondsworth, Peregrine.

Mandel, E. (1986), *The Meaning of the Second World War*, London, Verso.

Mason, J. Alden (1964), *The Ancient Civilizations of Peru*, Harmondsworth, Pelican.

Millar, F. (1967), *The Roman Empire and its Neighbours*, London, Weidenfeld & Nicolson.

Mills, C. Wright (1960), *Listen, Yankee*, New York, Ballantine.

Minear, R. (1971), *Victors' Justice, the Tokyo War Crimes Trials*, Princeton, Princeton University Press.

Morris, D. (1968), *The Washing of the Spears*, London, Sphere Books.
Mosca, G. (1939), *The Ruling Class*, Maidenhead, McGraw-Hill.
Myers, P. and R. (eds) (1984), *The Japanese Colonial Empire*, Princeton, Princeton University Press.
Nilsson, M. (1962), *Imperial Rome*, New York, Schocken.
Nova, F. (1986), *Alfred Rosenberg*, New York, Hippocrene Books.
Oates, D. and J. (1976), *The Rise of Civilization*, Oxford, Elsevier–Phaidon.
Olmstead, H. (1960), *History of Assyria*, Chicago, University of Chicago Press.
Oppenheim, A. L. (1972), *Ancient Mesopotamia*, Chicago, University of Chicago Press, fifth impression.
Pacific War Research Society (1972), *Japan's Longest Day*, New York, Ballantine.
Pareto, V. (1966), chapter (title not known), in S. Finer (ed.), *Sociological Writings*, London, Pall Mall.
Patch, R. (1960), 'Bolivia: US assistance in a revolutionary setting', in R. Adams (ed.) *Social Change in Latin America*, New York, Harper & Row.
Paxton, R. (1972), *Vichy France*, London, Braine & Larkins.
Payne, R. (1964), *The Roman Triumph*, London, Pan.
Petrow, R. (1975), *The Bitter Years*, London, Purnell.
Phillips, C. H. (ed.) (1962) *The Evolution of India and Pakistan 1858–1947*, London, Oxford University Press.
Plato (1981), *The Republic* (trans. G. Grube), London, Pan.
Reitlinger, G. (1956), *The SS: The Alibi of a Nation*, London, Heinemann.
Revill, J. (1962), *World History*, London, Longman.
Ribbens, G. (1979), *Patterns of Behaviour*, London, Edward Arnold.
Robert, C. (1982), *The Japanese Mind*, New York, Fawcett.
Roberts, R. (1946) 'The glory of Greece', in W. Weech (ed.), *History of the World*, London, Oldhams.
Robertson, E. (1977), *Mussolini as Empire-Builder*, London, Macmillan.
Rositzke, H. (1977), *CIA's Secret Operations*, New York, Crowell.
Roux, G. (1966), *Ancient Iraq*, Harmondsworth, Penguin (second edn 1969).
Rubenstein, R. (1978), *The Cunning of History*, New York, Harper.
Saggs, H. (1984), *The Might that was Assyria*, London, Sidgwick & Jackson.
Scott, J. (1979), *Corporations, Classes and Capitalism*, London, Hutchinson.
Shirer, W. (1960), *The Rise and Fall of the Third Reich*, London, Pan.
Sigmund, P. (1969), *The Ideologies of Developing Nations*, New York, Praeger.
Speer A. (1970), *Inside the Third Reich*, London, Macmillan.
Stefan, J. (1984), *Hawaii under the Rising Sun: Japan's plans for conquest after Pearl Harbor*, Honolulu, University of Honolulu Press.
Sunoo, H. (1975), *Japanese Militarism, Past and Present*, Chicago, Nelson Hall.
Swanson, E., Farrington, W. and Bray, W. (1976), *The New World*, Oxford, Elsevier.
Thorne, C. (1978), *Allies of a Kind: the War against Japan*, London, Hamish Hamilton.
—— (1985), *The Issue of War*, London, Hamish Hamilton.
Thucydides (1972), *The Peloponnesian War*, (trans. R. Warner), Harmondsworth, Penguin.
Tomasek, R. (ed.) (1970), *Latin American Politics*, New York, Anchor.
Toynbee, A. and V. (1954), *Hitler's Europe*, Oxford, Oxford University Press.
Trevor-Roper, H. (1947), *The Last Days of Hitler*, London, Macmillan.
Tucker, R, (1960), *The Just War*, Baltimore, Md., Johns Hopkins University Press.
Turner, H. (ed.) (1975), *Reappraisals of Fascism*, New York, New Viewpoints.

BIBLIOGRAPHY

Underhill, R. (1971), *Red Man's America*, Chicago, University of Chicago Press.

Wakin, M. (ed.) (1979), *War, Morality and the Military Profession*, Boulder, Col., Westview Press.

Wallace, A. (1972), *The Death and Rebirth of the Senaca*, New York, Vintage Books.

Waterlow, C. (1969), *India*, London, Ginn.

Weech, W. (1945), *History of the World*, London, Odhams.

Weiss, J. (1967), *The Fascist Tradition*, New York, Harper & Row.

Wells, C. (1984), *The Roman Empire*, Glasgow, Fontana.

Wiskemann, E. (1966a), *Europe of the Dictators*, London, Fontana.

—— (1966b), *The Rome–Berlin Axis*, London, Collins.

Woodhouse, C. (1960), *European Resistance Movements 1939–45*, London, Maxwell.

INDEX

194